Branden Johnson

il: 1276 381

Due Date June 8

# NUCLEAR RISK ANALYSIS IN COMPARATIVE PERSPECTIVE

# List of contributors

**Gotthard Bechmann**  Division of Applied System Analysis, Nuclear Research Centre, Karlsruhe, Federal Republic of Germany

**James E. Dooley**  Faculty of Management, University of Toronto, 246 Bloor Street West, Toronto, Ontario, Canada M5S 1V4

**Gunter Frederichs**  Division of Applied System Analysis, Nuclear Research Centre, Karlsruhe, Federal Republic of Germany

**Frita Gloede**  Division of Applied System Analysis, Nuclear Research Centre, Karlsruhe, Federal Republic of Germany

**Bengt Hansson**  Docent, Department of Philosophy, University of Lund, Lund, Sweden

**Friedrich-Wilhelm Heuser**  Gesellschaft für Reaktorsicherheit, Cologne Agency for Nuclear Safety, Cologne, Federal Republic of Germany

**Helmut Hörtner**  Gesellschaft für Reaktorsicherheit, Cologne Agency for Nuclear Safety, Cologne, Federal Republic of Germany

**Roger E. Kasperson**  Hazard Assessment Group, Center for Technology, Environment, and Development (CENTED), Clark University, Worcester, Mass. 01610, USA

**Jeanne X. Kasperson**  Hazard Assessment Group, Center for Technology, Environment, and Development (CENTED), Clark University, Worcester, Mass. 01610, USA

**Timothy O'Riordan**  School of Environmental Studies, University of East Anglia, Norwich NR4 7TJ, England

**Herbert Paschen**  Division of Applied Systems Analysis, Nuclear Research Centre, Karlsruhe, Federal Republic of Germany

**John B. Robinson**  Department of Environmental Studies, University of Waterloo, Waterloo, Ontario, Canada N2L 361

# NUCLEAR RISK ANALYSIS IN COMPARATIVE PERSPECTIVE

## The impacts of large-scale risk assessment in five countries

Edited by

**Roger E. Kasperson & Jeanne X. Kasperson**

*Center for Technology, Environment, and Development,
Clark University, Worcester, Massachusetts*

A study by The Beijer Institute, the Royal
Swedish Academy of Science

Boston
ALLEN & UNWIN
London    Sydney    Wellington

**Allen & Unwin, Inc.,**
**8 Winchester Place, Winchester, Mass. 01890, USA**
the U.S. Company of
**Unwin Hyman Ltd**

PO Box 18, Park Lane, Hemel Hempstead, Herts HP2 4TE, UK
40 Museum Street, London WC1A 1LU, UK
37/39 Queen Elizabeth Street, London SE1 2QB, UK

Allen & Unwin (Australia) Ltd
8 Napier Street, North Sydney, NSW 2060, Australia

Allen & Unwin (New Zealand) Ltd in association with the Port
Nicholson Press Ltd,
60 Cambridge Terrace, Wellington, New Zealand

First published in 1987

ISSN 0261-0507

**British Library Cataloguing in Publication Data**

Nuclear risk analysis in comparative perspective: the impacts
of large-scale nuclear risk assessment in five countries.
— (The risks and hazards series, ISSN 0261–0507).
1. Nuclear industry—Safety measures
2. Risk
I. Kasperson, Roger E.   II. Kasperson, Jeanne X.
III. Series
363.1'79        TK9152
ISBN 0–04–301260–4

**Library of Congress Cataloging in Publication Data**

Nuclear risk analysis in comparative perspective.

(The risks and hazards series, ISSN 0261–0507; 4)
Includes bibliographies and index.
1. Nuclear power plants—Risk assessment.
I. Kasperson, Roger E.   II. Kasperson, Jeanne X.
III. Series: Risks & hazards series; 4.
TK9153.N857 1987        363.7'28        87–12588
ISBN 0–04–301260–4 (alk. paper)

Typeset in 10 on 12 point Times by Phoenix Photosetting
and printed in Great Britain by Biddles of Guildford

# Foreword

Energy supply issues worldwide have never been far from the news headlines after the fivefold jump in oil prices occurred at the end of 1973. The benefits and risks of switching away from expensive oil to other energy sources, especially coal and nuclear power, have been hotly argued about ever since. The vehemence of the public debate, particularly over the future role of nuclear energy in several countries, has been accompanied by the emergence of strongly expressed anxieties about the safety of atomic power among certain sectors of public opinion, and a similar concern has arisen among some in the scientific community. Official government reactions to this state of affairs have varied. Many administrations have re-affirmed their commitment to a nuclear future, often in the face of "grassroots" dissent of public opinion or by opposing political parties, making atomic power a contentious and socially divisive issue. Others have remained non-nuclear; some are re-investigating nuclear safety and the pros and cons of a nuclear policy, or have introduced legislation tying any further growth of nuclear energy and the export or import of reactor technology to a satisfactory solution of the problem of radioactive waste disposal.

Whatever the stance taken up by various governments, all have embarked upon some form of nuclear assessment. Many have publicly recognized that the nuclear question is extremely complicated, involving sensitive socio-economic, political and even cultural costs and benefits in addition to the highly technical engineering problems, all of them marked by a troublesome level of uncertainty. Additionally, although every country has its own special "style" of decision making, it was realized by many that a more publicly accountable dimension would have to be added to it to satisfy public opinion. In response, many countries embarked upon large, exhaustively detailed and very costly commissions of enquiry to analyse and assess all the benefits, risks and costs of the various energy options, atomic power in particular.

How useful have such highly complex analyses been in clarifying contentious issues, forming and settling opinions among technical specialists and the public, and in guiding government actions over energy policy, particularly in respect to nuclear power?

This volume is a discussion of these specific questions, drawing evidence from the situations prevailing in Sweden as compared with Canada, the Federal Republic of Germany, the United Kingdom and the United States of America. The work has emerged as part of a wider programme of energy risk assessment first embarked upon by the Beijer Institute (The International Institute of Energy, Resources and the Human Environment) in 1979, in response to a request from the Swedish Energy Research Commission.

It is a great pleasure to thank, most warmly, all the authors involved in the national studies and a privilege to acknowledge the skilful writing of Roger and Jeanne Kasperson who synthesized the main findings of these studies, resulting in the present volume. My special thanks also go to the Energy Research Commission of Sweden (formerly the Energy Research and Development Commission) for their generous financial support of this work.

GORDON T. GOODMAN
Executive Director,
The Beijer Institute

# Preface

In 1979, the Swedish Energy Research and Development Commission (now the Energy Research Commission) asked the International Institute for Energy and Human Ecology (the Beijer Institute of Stockholm, Sweden) to examine new research possibilities in the general area of energy development and associated health and environmental risks. After lengthy consultation with international experts in the field, the Beijer Institute compiled a report comprising a number of proposed research projects. A summary of the report appears in a proposed agenda for international risk research (Kasperson & Morrison 1982).

The Commission expressed interest in two of these, and the Beijer Institute agreed to conduct a research project entitled "Evaluation of major Swedish energy risk assessments in an international perspective," which contained the essential parts of the two proposals. The study was to focus on the influence of major risk studies of energy-generating systems in terms of their success in enlightening the specialists, informing public opinion, clarifying issues and choices for the politicians, and influencing the design and operation of existing and proposed nuclear power plants. As the study proceeded, research largely focused on nuclear energy risk assessment, except perhaps in Sweden where all major energy risk assessments undergo review.

As originally conceived the study involved both a Swedish and an international analysis. The latter consisted in turn of five national studies (Sweden, West Germany, Canada, the United Kingdom, and the United States) that aimed to evaluate how different countries approach the question of nuclear risk within their particular cultural "style" of decision making and in the context of their national energy policies. The role of nuclear energy in the national energy mix and the presence of major risk studies guided the choice of countries for research. The Beijer Institute then approached experts on risk management issues in each country to conduct the national studies. These researchers convened at the Beijer Institute to formulate common objectives and compatible research designs. The research entailed an examination of one or more existing risk studies and associated societal impacts.

Because each risk study so examined reflected the unique priorities in the respective country of origin and had emerged from widely varying political processes, no uniform approach was possible. The researchers did, however, address common questions and provide results that were generally comparable. The national studies, conducted during 1981–83, underwent updating in 1985. Comparative analyses and editing occurred during 1985 and 1986. This volume summarizes the major findings that emerged in the form of background and national settings (Chs. 1 & 2), detailed national studies (Chs. 3–7), and comparative results and the future of major risk assessment (Ch. 8).

## The concept of risk

The meaning of the word "risk," which plays such a central role in this study, is notorious for its ambiguity. A conceptual clarification of risk is not undertaken here, although some distinctions serve to clarify usage in this volume:

(a) *Hazard* is a circumstance with a potential for harm to life, limb, property, or social value.

(b) *Risk* is the possibility of the realization (occurrence) of a hazard of a particular type of character (level). Thus, risk includes both the consequence and the probability (or possibility) of an accident or release.

(c) *Individual risk* is the risk associated with that part of a hazard that relates to a given individual. Typical measures would be expected monetary loss or probability of death or injury from a given cause.

(d) *Societal risk* is the danger associated with a hazard which relates to society generally or to a sizable subpopulation, especially where this risk is treated collectively, and where individuals are usually unable to alter the risk circumstances in which they find themselves. A typical numerical measure would be expected number of deaths following an event, expressed in some probabilistic term.

In this volume, the central concept of a "risk study" relates primarily to societal risk as defined above, though inevitably such studies will contain very detailed descriptions and appraisals both of hazards as such and of individual risks.


## Objectives

The purpose of this comparative investigation is to evaluate the role and usefulness of nuclear risk studies in the formation of societal opinion and safety decision making, and not to judge their scientific accuracy, technical qualities, or intrinsic merits. The principal research objectives are:

(a) to examine the factors that led to the production of major energy risk studies in the context of the continuing debate over the role of nuclear power as part of a national energy strategy;

(b) to assess, where possible, the various ways by which safety designers, policy makers, the scientific community, the regulators, the principal environmental groups, the media, and the informed public interpreted and responded to the risk studies;

(c) to consider the extent to which such studies have helped to clarify the nature and extent of the risks that they set out to analyze;

(d) to evaluate the extent to which such studies have narrowed the scientific debate;

(e)   to assess the degree to which such studies have influenced safety measures and regulatory policy.

Chapter 1 presents an overview of the emergence of the large-scale risk study on the national and international scenes. In Chapter 2 we analyze the political situations and energy–policy settings in which the risk studies were commissioned. The analysis focuses on the manner of approaching the risk problem against a climate of public disquiet over nuclear power and in relation to a given political culture. Objectives b–d fall into the *public dimension* of nuclear risk studies – their effects on society at large, on the nuclear debate, and on public attitudes toward nuclear power. The relevant analyses appear in the five national studies (Chs. 3–7) and in the comparative findings (Ch. 8). The other key aspect of the risk studies (objectives c and e) is their *private* or *inward-looking dimension* – their effects on the conduct of safety and on the nuclear establishment itself. These objectives are also treated in the national studies and summarized in the comparative findings.

## Research strategy and methodology

Methodologically, the research aimed to examine major risk studies, prepared in the five countries, in order to review the similarities and differences in societal response. Researchers addressed in particular the managerial and political debate as well as the discussion in the media (primarily newspapers). The initial intent was to trace the pathways along which particular conclusions emerged from the original studies and made their way into subsequent analyses, actual safety measures, and specific regulations. In practice, however, differing national practices of confidentiality and secrecy all but precluded this. Each national study also sought to portray how key officials, politicians, and environmentalists viewed the value and impact of major risk studies, either through review of the documentary evidence in the public record (as in the United States and West Germany) or through extensive interviewing (as in Sweden and the United Kingdom).

As for the choice of countries, Sweden was, given the funding source, a mandatory inclusion. In addition, Sweden has been an international leader in major energy risk studies. Selection of the United States and the United Kingdom occurred because of their contrasting styles of government generally and regulatory practice in particular. The United States has an open, adversarial style of government where most arguments are fully documented and subject to extensive public scrutiny, debate, and judicial challenge. The British, by contrast, seek a far more consensual form of government based on limited publication of documents, strict confidentiality, and carefully conducted consultation. Whereas the Americans have a very precise regulatory style with specific rules and regulations emerging from exhaustive public debate and legal argument, the British display a far more flexible, if closed, approach, based on guidelines and targets that the regulated industry is expected to accommodate through reasoned discussion and self-imposed discipline. Since the Sizewell proceedings have recently exposed some of this process to public view, considerable additional insight into British regulatory attitudes and procedures has become available.

The choice of the United States and West Germany also reflects the enormous investment both countries have made in major nuclear risk studies, although the West German experience was also considered valuable because of the importance of judicial review, uncommon in most European countries, and the virulent public debate over nuclear power. Finally, a Canadian study was included because Canada operates its affairs in a way that incorporates features of both the British and the US approaches to government and safety regulation, together with its noteworthy use of a wide-ranging special commission of inquiry as an approach to risk assessment and public scrutiny.

R. E. KASPERSON AND J. X. KASPERSON

## Reference

Kasperson, R. E. and M. Morrison 1982. A proposal for international risk management research. In *Risk in the technological society*, C. Hohenemser and J. X. Kasperson (eds.), 303–31. AAAS Selected Symposium 65. Boulder, Colorado: Westview Press.

# Acknowledgements

We are grateful to the following individuals and organizations who have kindly given permission for the reproduction of copyright material (figure numbers in parentheses):

Atomic Energy of Canada Ltd., Ontario (2.5); Mr Gene Pokorny, President, Cambridge Reports Inc. (6.4); Table 7.2 reproduced from *U.K. energy* by Richard Bending & Richard Eden with the permission of Cambridge University Press.

# Contents

# List of tables

# 1 *The emergence of risk analysis on the international scene*

JAMES E. DOOLEY, BENGT HANSSON, JEANNE X. KASPERSON, ROGER E. KASPERSON, TIMOTHY O'RIORDAN, and HERBERT PASCHEN

Historically, societies have come to learn of the risks of technology by experiencing consequences. The prices have often been high; witness the attributed decline of the Roman empire from lead consumption, the accumulated air and water pollution impacts of the 20th century, the unfolding toll of asbestos exposure in the workplace, or the periodic technology-related disasters of transportation crashes, oil spills, or chemical releases. As technology has become more complex and pervasive and as societies have become more concerned about health and environment, pressure has mounted to assess the impacts of new technologies in advance of their large-scale deployment. So, beginning a scant several decades ago, modern risk analysis, as we have come to know it, has appeared as the scientific collection of concepts and methods to assure that potential dangers are identified and assessed in advance. From an initial concern with major accidents and performance failures (as in the space program), risk assessments have become wider in scope to cover such varied technologies as pharmaceuticals, consumer products, energy systems, and, more recently, genetic manipulation, large-scale use of computers, and electronics.

Although much of the growth of risk analysis has been incremental in the industries that fashion products and the public agencies responsible for assuring health and safety, a particularly noteworthy development has been the appearance of large-scale assessments designed to provide a comprehensive treatment of risks involved with a particular technology. Beginning with the introduction of nuclear power in the 1950s, augmented by the space program of the 1960s, and given added impetus by the environmental and consumer movements of the 1960s and 1970s, efforts at comprehensively analyzing the hazards of technology in major assessments designed to guide public policy and technology choice have increased dramatically through the 1970s and 1980s. In addition to emerging practice, a flood of major books dealing with risk has occurred since 1970 (Kates & Kasperson 1983) and has yet to peak.

The contributions of such major risk studies remain a matter more of conviction than of analysis. The *Reactor safety study* (us Nuclear Regulatory

Commission 1975) sparked intense controversy among its critics and relative neglect by the regulatory agencies, despite appreciation of its potential methodological contributions. The *German risk study for nuclear power plants* (GRS 1980) appears to have been more important for industry than in influencing public policy. Various scientific studies suggesting the limited societal risks involved in nuclear waste disposal have done little to assuage public concern and opposition. As some countries (e.g., the US) head pell-mell for widespread use of large-scale risk assessment, others (e.g., the United Kingdom) have carefully limited the growth and use of such analyses. What these large-scale investments have actually wrought in potential contributions to safety remains primarily a matter of conjecture and debate.

The authors of this volume inquire into the responses that have accompanied the intrusion of large-scale risk studies into public policy, social debate, and industry practice. This chapter provides the historical backdrop of the evolution of major risk studies in the context of nuclear power. An initial overview of the growth in the use of such studies gives way to an analysis of the context of public concern over this technology and the societal motivations for the studies. A detailed portrait of the emergence of nuclear risk assessment in the five countries treated in this volume rounds out the chapter.

## Evolution of the comprehensive nuclear risk study

The most important forerunner to the comprehensive nuclear risk studies of the 1970s and the growth of probabilistic risk analysis in the 1980s is the study commonly known as WASH-740 (US Atomic Energy Commission 1957), essentially a consequence assessment aimed at defining the upper limits of damage. The first study explicitly to advocate the abandonment of "maximum credible accident" and related concepts and to support the need for a numerical estimate of the probabilities for all types of accidents was the Swedish *Close-siting study* (Närförläggningsutredningen 1974), initiated in 1969. The results were presented in a series of two-dimensional diagrams, relating sizes of consequences to frequencies of accidents.

The *Reactor safety study* (US Nuclear Regulatory Commission 1975) was undoubtedly the most influential major nuclear risk study and has become the standard of comparison for all similar studies. The report drew fire from many camps, however, but the criticism was aimed less at the goals of the study and more toward the accuracy of the numerical values, the question of bias, and the accuracy of the executive summary. The widespread criticism resulted in the appointment of a special panel to conduct a peer review of the study. The report of the panel, the so-called Lewis report (US Risk Assessment Review Group 1978), accepted the principles upon which the *Reactor safety study* methodology rested but regarded these more as promising for future research than as something sufficiently developed to yield reliable numerical values.

The methodology of the *Reactor safety study* made its way into the first phase of the German counterpart (GRS 1980), a project comparable in scope to its American predecessor. The German study aimed to assess the societal risks associated with potential accidents in nuclear power plants of German make and under typical German site conditions. The report from the first phase of the German study was published in 1979. A second phase, aiming at improving the methodology at some crucial points, is still in progress in 1987.

The accident at Three Mile Island (TMI) naturally sparked a number of risk studies. Apart from detailed technical investigations, the so-called Kemeny report (US President's Commission on the Accident at Three Mile Island 1979) and Sweden's own study of reactor safety (Reaktorsäkerhetsutredningen 1979) are of interest. The former was a report from a Presidential commission set up to conduct an investigation of the accident, from both technical and institutional viewpoints. Numerous other post-mortems of the accident, many of which reached similar conclusions (see Ch. 6), accompanied the Kemeny report. The latter was the report of an expert group charged with the task of re-evaluating the work of all previous risk studies in the light of the lessons learned following the Three Mile Island accident (see Ch. 3).

Since 1980, the large-scale nuclear risk assessment has met a variable fate on the international scene. The United States has witnessed a remarkable growth in plant-specific probabilistic risk analyses, each involving hundreds of days of effort and millions of dollars in investment. By early 1987, some 15–20 large-scale assessments had been performed, and eventually most US nuclear power plants will undergo such studies. Meanwhile, the results, which enjoy continuous updating and use in design, operating, and maintenance decisions, occupy a more prominent (if still uncertain) niche in regulatory decision making. Canada had betrayed a general reluctance to commission another WASH-1400. Asserting the unlikelihood of resolving the numerical debate the Canadians thought that attention should focus on safety assurance rather than quantitative estimations of risk. A major risk study under way at the Ontario Hydro utility emphasizes the improvement of safety and the provision of requisite information for licensing (King & Vijay 1985). In the United Kingdom, probabilistic risk analysis has been more limited in scope, with less attention to whole plant studies. But the science of probabilistic risk analysis, applied to all aspects of hazardous technology, has reached a high point. The Federal Republic of Germany has continued its active follow-up on its risk research, but has not dramatically expanded its scale and efforts. Similarly, Sweden, perhaps because of the restrictions on the scale of its nuclear program, has not conducted nuclear risk studies at a rate parallel to the expansion of those in the United States.

*Related risk studies*

Reactor risks have not been the only area of interest for major assessments of the nuclear fuel cycle. Recently, nuclear waste has generated regulatory attention as well as public concern. The first comprehensive study of final storage of spent nuclear wastes is the Swedish Åka study (Åka 1976a, 1976b). The report of a government committee judged safe storage of spent fuels to be possible in principle, although it did not go into technical details. The most important effect of the Åka study was its role as a basis for a law, the so-called Stipulation Law, which required the owner of a nuclear reactor to show how and where "an absolutely safe final storage" of the waste could be found before loading any nuclear fuel into the reactor. To prove that the requirements of the law could be achieved, the Swedish industry set up the so-called KBS (short for *Kärn–Bränsle–Säkerhet* (Nuclear Fuel Safety)). The KBS project published two reports (KBS 1977, 1979), one dealing with waste from reprocessing, the other with direct disposal of spent fuel. The reports, which received broad international review, played a leading role in initiating research into accident scenarios and consequences of disposal.

Although not a risk study in the conventional sense of the word, the hearing held in 1979 by the state government of Lower Saxony into the proposed integrated nuclear reprocessing and waste disposal center in Gorleben, West Germany, merits attention in this context. The project had drawn fire, both within Germany and abroad, and a group of foreign experts, known as the "Gorleben International Review," prepared a bulky report that served as a basis for the public hearings. The hearings themselves involved a series of rounds, with an equal number of critics and "counter-critics" taking part in each. None of the published transcripts or summary reports received endorsements by both critics and counter-critics.

Although they have not produced the visible, large-scale assessments that characterize the nuclear reactor risk area, the radioactive waste disposal programs in the United States and Canada have enjoyed the support of a broad program of risk assessment. The US program has included the specification of a large number of accident scenarios, including human intrusion, for both aboveground and below-ground activities, and an attempt to estimate probabilities (although not for intentional human intrusion). The environmental standard that eventually emerged is stated in probabilistic terms (US Environmental Protection Agency 1985).

In Canada, the Nuclear Fuel Waste Management Program, established in 1978, is addressing the risks attendant on the disposal of high-level nuclear waste (Boulten 1978). A generic research program focuses on immobilization and subsequent disposal of nuclear waste deep in stable, crystalline rock within the Canadian Shield. This research, which is the responsibility of Atomic Energy of Canada Limited (AECL), includes an environmental and safety assessment. The Technical Advisory Committee, established in 1979 to review the Program, issues annual reports that offer constructive criticisms of the research.

Another Canadian study was conducted by the Cluff Lake Board of Inquiry, appointed on February 1, 1977 by Order-in-Council to the government of Saskatchewan with terms of reference to ". . . review all available information on the probable environmental, health, safety, social, and economic effects of the proposed uranium mine and mill at Cluff Lake . . ." (Cluff Lake Board of Inquiry 1978, p. 308). The terms of reference also asked for provision of information to the public, the implications of expanding the uranium industry, an assessment of the protection measures offered by the proponent, and a recommendation that a proposed project should proceed, not proceed, or proceed subject to specific conditions. The Lieutenant Governor in Council, acting upon the recommendation of Saskatchewan's Minister of the Environment, ordered the inquiry. The procedures adopted were dictated by ". . . the terms of reference, the provisions of the Public Inquiries Act, the nature of the relevant questions, the type of inquiry, common sense and the rules of common justice" (Cluff Lake Board of Inquiry 1978, p. 8).

A second type of related risk study is the assessment that compares risks from different kinds of energy systems. The comparison may address the risks associated with the different stages of the nuclear fuel cycle, or it may compare the risks attendant on different kinds of energy production. A number of countries have produced more or less ambitious studies of both types; this volume discusses those that fall into the latter group – namely, the Swedish *Energy, health, environment* (Ministry of Agriculture and Environment 1978), the report from a subgroup of the Swedish Energy Commission (EK-A 1978), and the report of the (Ontario) Royal Commission on Electric Power Planning (1980). Perhaps the most noteworthy, and controversial, study of this type is that of Inhaber (1982), which seeks to provide a comparative assessment of the full spectrum of risk, including the manufacture of materials and the disposal of wastes, presented by alternative fuel cycles. Inhaber examines both occupational and public risk, and his findings present a very favorable picture of nuclear power as compared with fossil fuels (except for natural gas). The report has received extensive criticism, especially by Holdren *et al.* (1979). The International Atomic Energy Agency in Vienna has continued this line of work (Fremlin 1985).

A third type of major risk study is oriented to major industrial complexes and facilities. The UK Health and Safety Executive's (1978, 1981) analyses of the risks of a petrochemical complex located at Canvey Island on the Essex coast are perhaps the best-known studies of this type. The reports estimate the risks associated with the refineries and other installations on, or adjacent to, the site, and recommend changes to lower the risks through cost-effective measures. A critique of the first study argues that the risk estimates may be overly pessimistic (Cremer & Warner Ltd. 1980). More recently, Cremer & Warner Ltd. participated in a risk analysis of six industrial installations located at Rijnmond, a huge chemical and petrochemical complex in the Rotterdam harbor. The report (Rijnmond Public Authority 1982) includes an analysis of various failure scenarios, their probabilities and consequences, and a lengthy discussion of methodological and calculation issues. Cohen & Pritchard (1980) have prepared a useful overview of the major energy risk studies through 1980.

As with the large assessments of reactor risks, critiques and analyses of these studies have been largely technical in nature. What can be said with some certainty is that the methodology of probabilistic risk analysis has advanced substantially from its inception in the late 1960s and its early development in the *Reactor safety study*. Internally, the industry has obviously benefited enormously from the major risk studies and their critiques. The extent to which these studies and critiques have shaped or altered public policy or public attitudes, on the other hand, remains unknown. Meanwhile, it is entirely clear that public anxiety has been a major stimulus for large nuclear studies and their reception.

## The public disquiet over nuclear power

The worldwide public disquiet over nuclear power has, along with the fall-off in rates of energy demand, inhibited the nuclear programs of most countries. In the United States, for instance, no nuclear plant has been ordered since 1979 and delays due to time-consuming regulatory processes have adversely affected the economics of nuclear electricity generation and the completion of nuclear plants planned or under construction. The building of nuclear power stations in the US now takes about 12 years, double the time in France and Japan. Meanwhile, the public disquiet has grown. Several states have voted to ban nuclear plant construction pending a demonstrated safe method of disposing of the radioactive waste; the citizens of the state of Washington voted to block further state authorization of the expensive five-reactor Washington Public Power Supply System; and widespread state restrictions have been placed on the transport of nuclear materials. The total cost of the Three Mile Island accident will exceed \$1 billion resulting from the reactor damage, clean-up costs, liability payments, and the purchase of alternative power, and all US operating utilities face extensive backfitting safety costs. The 1986 Chernobyl accident has again raised the vivid imagery of nuclear disaster and will certainly add to public anxiety in Europe and North America.

In West Germany, the expansion of nuclear power almost came to a standstill between 1977 and 1980. The year 1980 saw no nuclear plant commissioned, no license granted, and only one order placed. By early 1982, however, the Federal Minister of the Interior gave the green light for three new PWRs (with a capacity of 4,000 MWe) to be granted a first partial construction permit. A proposed integrated nuclear reprocessing and waste disposal center at Gorleben in Lower Saxony was stopped in 1979, on the grounds that the political preconditions for the construction of a reprocessing facility did not exist (given the public's views over the lack of necessity for the plant and its questionable safety). In 1985, however, the DWK (Deutsche Gesellschaft für Wiederaufarbeitung von kern-brennstoffen) decided to build a 350 tonne per year reprocessing plant in Wackersdorf (Bavaria) where the political conditions are viewed as more favorable. The first partial construction permit for this facility was issued in 1985 under the shadow of a nationally organized demonstration against the facility.

In Sweden, the nuclear issue split the political parties and forced a national referendum in March 1980 in which all the alternatives implied a halt to nuclear power in the foreseeable future and in which 39 percent of the Swedish people voted that they would like to see this accomplished by 1990. In the Canadian province of Ontario, where the main political parties favor nuclear development, opposition groups have actively raised safety issues. Strong doubts about the real need for nuclear power and its cost-effectiveness in the context of other energy supply possibilities and investments in energy conservation have clearly grown. Moreover, current estimates of the demand for electricity in Ontario indicate the need for additional supply by the year 2000, so the debate is about to re-open. (Current lead time for the planning, approval, and construction of a nuclear power plant is 14 years.) The nuclear issue strongly influenced both the West German 1980 (but *not* 1983) election and the Dutch general elections, although nuclear disarmament dominated the argument. In West Germany, the political dispute over civilian nuclear energy also extends to the state level and has recently contributed to a governing Social Democratic Party (SPD)–Green coalition in Hessen, with the Greens rewarded with a Minister for Environment and Energy.

Many countries have conducted public opinion polls on nuclear power. Such polls are notorious for their strong dependence on the precise wording of questions and the context in which questions are placed, so it is not useful to compare specific response figures from different countries. Some general trends, however, are obvious. Many polls in the United States and in Europe indicate that a majority or near majority opposes nuclear power, although the extent of opposition seems to diminish when nuclear power is discussed in relation to the benefits of electricity and to the risks of energy alternatives. Opposition is stronger to nuclear plants in unspoiled settings than in sites where nuclear plants already exist. In other countries, such as Brazil, Australia, Japan, and Korea, opposition is weaker but not insignificant. In the United Kingdom, West Germany, and the United States, the recent trend has favored a more antinuclear stance and polarization of opinion, though one should be wary of the political implications. In few countries does a major political party oppose further development of nuclear power, with the SPD of West Germany a prominent exception.

The promotion of nuclear power inevitably generates controversy, impassioned scientific and public debate, and political unease. We suggest six main reasons:

(a)  Opposition groups joined forces across international barriers by sharing scientific expertise and arguments. The publics were then confronted by serious scientific dispute regarding the need for, and the ultimate safety of, nuclear plants, shattering the illusion cultivated during the 1960s that nuclear power was cheap and undermining the argument that it is environmentally less damaging than fossil fuels.

(b)  Numerous accidents and near-accidents at nuclear plants are nourished by seeds of doubt sown by scientific controversies. Disclosure ("whistleblowing") by insiders revealed a frequent reaction by the nuclear industry to cover up. The dramatic incident at Three Mile Island confirmed in the minds of many people that nuclear power generation could not be made safe and that "establishment" risk analyses were not fool-proof; the impact of the Chernobyl accident, despite differences in technology and safety systems, seems likely to add to these concerns.

(c)   Few people seem to be prepared to tolerate either the transport of radioactive material or the disposal of radioactive waste near where they live. Important ingredients in this attitude are the inequity of risk concentration in one location and a distrust in assurances by the regulatory agencies of safety at the disposal site (Kasperson 1983). Although a technical consensus appears to exist among scientists that safe methods and sites exist for the final disposal of radioactive wastes, it remains a particularly contentious political issue in the continuing nuclear debate and affects the nuclear industry in all five nations studied in this report.

(d)   The linkage between the civil and military uses of nuclear power has always been unclear but apparently present. Curiously the nuclear disarmament movement has not always been active in antinuclear activity, although this is now more common, particularly in West Germany, France, and more recently in the UK and the US.

(e)   Militant groups of extreme political persuasions anxious to exploit unease with centralist and right-wing governments have sometimes infiltrated opposition groups. This has led on occasion to public disorder in protests against the construction of nuclear plants and the response by authority to exercise the tough use of police and military power. This, in turn, has led to adverse media publicity, some deaths, many injuries, and a symbolic association in some people's minds of a close relationship between nuclear power and authoritarian forces of oppression.

(f)   The mechanisms used to debate economic and safety aspects of nuclear power were normally the conventional devices of public inquiry, public hearings, and special commissions of investigation. In many instances, these procedures were ill-adapted to cope with the complexities of nuclear power technology and economics. They also had difficulty confronting the political commitments already built into the nuclear option as part of a national energy strategy. Since these public devices were flawed or limited, some people questioned the ability of long-established political institutions to deal adequately with the nuclear issue.

## Motivations for large-scale risk assessment

Why has so much money and effort been invested in these various studies of nuclear risk? A full answer to this question is beyond the scope of this volume, but some motivations are apparent. First, of course, is the distinction between officially stated reasons and the hidden hopes and ambitions of interested parties. Addressing for the moment "official" reasons, the most direct reason is that one needs to know something, such as "What is the probability of a major nuclear accident?" or "Is it better from an environmental point of view to have nuclear reactors or coal-fired plants?" At a deeper level, one could also answer by pointing out the necessity for an answer to precisely these questions. This chapter notes only the stated purposes and some of the most obvious political motivations. The relation between the emergence of major risk studies and factors such as political culture, structure of nuclear industry, and general energy policy will be taken up later in this chapter, again in the next chapter, and later in the individual country studies.

The driving force behind the early major American studies was a desire to further the use of nuclear energy by reducing the uncertainties of the utilities about their liabilities in case of reactor accidents. Thus, the posing of the relevant question, "How dangerous, in general terms, is nuclear power?" betrayed the clear intent of seeking an answer that would reassure insurers and the Congress. This question was also an important one subsequently for the Lewis panel. The *Reactor safety study*, facing the rising tide of environmentalism and growing public opposition, clearly had, as one motivation, settling once and for all the reactor safety question as an issue of public debate. To some extent the Kemeny Commission, which was charged with investigating the impact of the accident at Three Mile Island on public health and safety, also aimed at a generic assessment of safety. The Commission (as we shall see in Ch. 6) had other duties as well, such as analyzing the role of the managing utility, assessing the emergency preparedness of the Nuclear Regulatory Commission and other authorities, and deliberating on the perplexing question "How can we make nuclear power safer, or safe enough?" But even if such general questions underlay the major American nuclear risk studies, a particular policy mechanism – the passing and renewal of the Price–Anderson Act (which defines and limits liability for nuclear plant accidents) – was also needed to respond to them.

A similar triggering proposal lay behind the first Swedish risk study, the *Close-siting* study (Närförläggningsutredningen 1974). Plans to erect a nuclear power station very close to the center of Stockholm (not unlike the ill-conceived Ravenswood proposal to locate a nuclear plant in New York City) naturally raised questions as to whether such a siting would significantly increase the accident risk. The terms of reference for the Swedish Åka Committee (Åka 1976a, 1976b), by contrast, basically asked the question: "It is possible, isn't it?" The Committee was asked to analyze technical, economic, and safety related problems connected with reprocessing, treatment, storing, and transportation of radioactive wastes and to find suitable methods for the handling of radioactive wastes in Sweden.

In the case of the two Swedish comparative studies, *Energy, health, environment* (Swedish Governmental Committee on Energy and the Environment 1977, Ministry of Agriculture and Environment 1978), and the *Energy commission report* (EK-A 1978), the decision framework within which the studies were placed did not demand urgency. A decision about a national energy strategy was several years away. The charge of the two committees was a comparison of all feasible energy production alternatives in terms of health and environment (acknowledged to be the two most important aspects of energy production) within the limiting condition of reducing Sweden's excessive dependence on foreign oil. The perspective betrays less concern with nuclear power as such than with the question, "How can we balance the goals of safety, clean environment, low price, and a reasonable national self-sufficiency in relation to energy production?"

The basic question for the *German risk study for nuclear power plants* (GRS 1980) was "the *Reactor safety study* is all very well for the US, but does it apply to us?" The significant differences between the US nuclear power plants that served for reference in the *Reactor safety study* and those erected in West Germany and a population density in central Europe higher than that of the United States called for a separate German study which adapted the *Reactor safety study* to German conditions. The shift is thus toward more reliable knowledge in a circumscribed area, and not toward a widening of the policy scope by bringing in broader societal and institutional mechanisms – a trend that is discernible in some other countries.

In the case of the Ontario Royal Commission on Electric Power Planning in Canada (see Ch. 5), the terms of reference did not mention risk. The safety of nuclear power was not the stimulus for establishing the Commission, although the general terms of reference did not exclude risk. In this respect, the impetus for the study contrasts with the other cases in this volume. Yet, risk nonetheless emerged as a major issue during public hearings, and its scope stretched beyond the scientific treatment. This is a noteworthy example of the impact of the public and critics on the structure and objectives of a major risk study.

Apart from the specific political situations in which these studies were commissioned, it is important to note that their initiation and completion occurred in a societal context of growing public disillusionment over nuclear power, hushed-up accidents, regulatory failures, public concern over military–civil nuclear links, emerging technologies of conservation and alternative energy sources, internationalization of nuclear opposition, and differing political party perspectives on the role of nuclear power. These factors all varied in degree, of course, from country to country. Although it is obvious that the combination of these factors has significantly affected the emergence and development of the comprehensive nuclear risk study, it is not possible to link a specific factor or motivation with the genesis of a particular risk assessment.

The drive for a better technical understanding of nuclear power risks has obviously sparked the growing sophistication of probabilistic risk analysis (PRA). The application of PRA in many diverse fields of engineering, the contribution to regulatory activity (e.g., design considerations), quality control in manufacturing and operations, and maintenance and backfitting decisions has also been important. Clearly, the major risk study has transformed the technical assessments of safety, if not the public confidence in the industry performing them. This is ironic but a reality of nuclear politics.

Implicit political motivations have also contributed to the rapid increase in large-scale studies of nuclear risk during the 1970s and 1980s. Risk assessment inevitably narrows the universe of political discourse about technology by limiting the domain of risks and impacts to quantifiable health and safety issues. It thereby avoids such troublesome "soft" issues as social equity, civil liberties, and the welfare of future generations, but all the while raises the entry price of policy discussions to include substantial financial and technical resources. Addressing the question of why risk assessment made such a "big splash" in the nuclear industry in the 1970s, Allan Mazur (1984) argues that this mode of analysis has permitted the promoters of nuclear power – by equating catastrophic and routine risks, by downgrading the issue of uncertainties, and by translating socially complex problems into monetary tradeoffs – to make their strongest case. Perspectives other than risk assessment, he goes on, would tend to be advantageous to the critics of nuclear power.

Whatever the role of these implicit factors in the growth of risk assessment, the studies have generally achieved their official goals, namely to analyze, assess, or evaluate certain things. Simultaneously, it is unlikely that they also achieved the implicit political aims of those who commissioned them. The chapters that follow take up the uneven, and oft unintended, outcomes of these studies. First, however, a more detailed account of the emergence of major nuclear risk assessments in the five countries sets the context.

## Emergence of nuclear risk assessment in five countries

With the appearance of large-scale risk assessment, the issues posed by growing public concern, and the differing motivations involved in their genesis, it is appropriate to review in greater detail the evolution of risk assessment in each of the five countries studied in this volume.

### THE US EXPERIENCE

The history of nuclear risk assessment in the United States is closely linked with considerations of liability and financial indemnification for nuclear power plants and the role of the federal government in providing subsidies to the nuclear industry.

In 1957, three key events occurred: the first nuclear power plant in the US was located at Shippingport, Pennsylvania, the Atomic Energy Commission (AEC) completed the first formal reactor risk assessment (WASH-740), and Congress passed the Price–Anderson Act, which limited liability in the event of an accident and provided federal subsidies. These events were greatly interrelated, of course. In order for nuclear power plants to be built, questions of liability and insurance had to be settled. The motivation for

WASH-740 was to provide Congress with information functional to such a decision.

At the request of the Atomic Energy Commission, Brookhaven National Laboratory produced WASH-740, entitled *Theoretical possibilities and consequences of major accidents in large nuclear power plants* (US Atomic Energy Commission 1957). Using hypothetical accidents, the report reached two basic conclusions:

(a)   It could not be proven that fission products would not be released as a result of a major accident in a nuclear power plant although the probability of a large-scale release was believed to be extremely low.

(b)   If half of the fission products were released to the atmosphere, damages to the public would comprise lethal doses ranging from 0 to 3,400 persons and land contamination ranging from 19 to 150,000 square miles (49–388,500 sq. km). These wide ranges depend upon weather conditions prevailing at the time of release.

The report provided the basis for congressional approval in 1957 of the Price–Anderson Act which limited liability to $560 million in a nuclear accident and provided government subsidies of insurance premiums paid by utilities.

Anticipating that the Act would come up for extension in 1965, the Congressional Joint Committee on Atomic Energy requested that the Atomic Energy Commission arrange for an update of WASH-740. This new assessment was to consider whether experience since 1957 suggested any alteration in basic assumptions underlying the form of financial protection provided in the Price–Anderson Act. Specifically, the Joint Committee wanted to know if:

(a)   operating experience, safety research, and engineered safeguards altered estimates of the probability of a major accident;

(b)   there were any significant changes in the 1957 estimates of the theoretical consequences of a major reactor accident, assuming all safeguards such as emergency cooling, fission product retention devices, containment, etc. should fail to function.

The AEC once again commissioned Brookhaven National Laboratory to conduct the study. As work progressed, it became clear that the results would not be comforting to the nuclear industry or to the Joint Committee. Despite improvements in engineered safeguards (particularly containment), reactors were much larger than those envisioned in 1957, fuel cycles were longer and fission product inventories larger, and reactors were located closer to population centers. In the light of these facts, it is not surprising that the Brookhaven study group confronted predictable conclusions, namely that with the same kind of hypothetical accidents, the consequences would not be less and could be substantially larger than those estimated in 1957. Viewing these ominous results, the AEC suppressed the results, aborted the study, and chose not to release the working papers to Congress or the public. Only through persistent efforts by nuclear critics armed with the Freedom of Information Act did the study finally become available for public inspection some seven years later (in 1973). Nevertheless, the Price–Anderson Act was amended and extended in 1965 and 1966.

The next major milestone in nuclear risk assessment was linked both with this history and with the next chapter of the Price–Anderson Act. Although the Act did not require renewal until 1977, the Joint Committee on Atomic Energy had decided on an extension tendered in 1974 to avoid any disruption in the nuclear program. The nuclear industry, of course, was also facing the release of the long-suppressed update of WASH-740 at a time when the political climate for nuclear energy was less favorable and environmentalists were actively engaging nuclear issues. A new, ambitious risk assessment that would settle once and for all the issue of reactor safety had appeal.

In 1972, the Atomic Energy Commission asked Norman Rasmussen, professor of nuclear engineering at the Massachusetts Institute of Technology (MIT), to conduct a searching quantitative analysis of the safety of light-water reactors. The purpose of the study was to examine one typical pressurized-water reactor (PWR) and one typical boiling-water reactor (BWR) to determine the most significant sequences of events that could lead to an accident and to estimate both the probability and consequences of each sequence. The consequences were to include prompt fatalities, the induction of latent cancers, genetic damage, and property damage.

The monumental study commanded a 60-person staff, 4 years of effort, and $5 million in support. The final report was also imposing, comprising more than 2,400 double-columned pages. The study made extensive use of both fault-tree and event-tree analyses and, unlike earlier risk assessments, estimated the probabilities of major accidents. The overall probability of a sequence of events leading to a core melt, according to estimates in the report, is 1 chance in 20,000 reactor-years of operation. The Rasmussen group also estimated an average citizen's likelihood of being killed in a reactor accident as about the same as the chance of being killed by a falling meteorite.

If one aspiration of the study was that it would narrow the debate over reactor safety, the result was quite the reverse. The report immediately set off a storm of criticism, including highly critical reports from the Union of Concerned Scientists, the American Physical Society, and the US Environmental Protection Agency. The major objections to the report, as summarized by Lewis (US Risk Assessment Review Group 1980, p. 59), were:

(a)  the system is simply much too complex to quantify;
(b)  the data base on component-failure rates does not support such a calculation;
(c)  improper and incorrect statistical procedures were followed;
(d)  common-cause failures (in which several ostensibly independent components fail at once owing to a separate common cause such as an earthquake) were inadequately treated;

(e)   low-probability events are instrinsically impossible to quantify;
(f)   human behavior was inadequately treated;
(g)   the role of quality assurance and failures thereof were inadequately treated.

The report, and its criticisms, entered a changed institutional structure. Both the AEC and the Joint Committee on Atomic Energy were facing dissolution in 1974. Although the Nuclear Regulatory Commission (NRC) largely retained the personnel and practices of the AEC, congressional responsibilities passed to a number of more skeptical oversight committees. Meanwhile, a vigorous set of environmental organizations – Friends of the Earth, Union of Concerned Scientists, the Sierra Club, and Ralph Nader's Critical Mass Energy Project – had taken up the cudgels against nuclear energy. And public opinion polls revealed a substantial growth in public concern over nuclear energy (Kasperson et al. 1980).

Upon its publication, the *Reactor safety study* immediately entered the congressional debate over the Price–Anderson Act. Although extensive criticism had greeted the draft report, the final report was rushed to the Nuclear Regulatory Commission and Congress without the benefit of peer review. Endorsement by the Commission quickly followed, with Commission Chairman William Anders informing Congress that the report represented a "full objective and scientific analysis of risks" (Bradford 1980, p. 4). But many members of Congress were more skeptical. On November 26, 1974, Representative Udall asked for a deferral of congressional consideration of the Price–Anderson Act pending a full review of the final report in view of the fact that it constituted the central justification for the Price–Anderson scheme. The House of Representatives denied this request, however, and in December 1975, both houses approved the bill to extend the Price–Anderson Act and President Ford signed it into law. Continuing criticism in the scientific community and in Congress, however, eventually resulted in the appointment of a special prestigious and balanced panel (the Lewis Commission) to conduct a searching peer review of the *Reactor safety study*.

The years that followed the appearance of the study witnessed relatively little use of its conclusions. Those uses that did occur were primarily political rather than regulatory. Industry exerted considerable effort, largely unsuccessful, to convince the Nuclear Regulatory Commission that the results of the study justified a curtailing of the extent of regulatory review in many areas (Bradford 1980, p. 4). Both industry and the Commission widely cited results purporting to show that the risks of nuclear power plants were small. Yet the Commission consistently refused to use the results centrally in either regulatory or licensing procedures. Even in the area of reactor safety research, where the report carried important messages, few changes occurred in ongoing programs. Three specific areas of research need – transients, small breaks in loss-of-coolant accidents, and human errors – identified in the report were not pursued, and all subsequently figured as central features of the 1979 accident at Three Mile Island (Lewis 1980, p. 64).

The so-called Lewis report, presented to the Nuclear Regulatory Commission in 1978, reached a number of important conclusions concerning the *Reactor safety study*:

(a) the study was a "conscientious and honest effort" to apply the methods of fault-tree/event-tree analysis to an extremely complex system;
(b) numerous sources of both conservatism and nonconservatism in the probability calculations render it impossible to determine whether the overall probability of a core-melt calculated in the study is high or low;
(c) the error bands on the probabilities are understated;
(d) the study is "inscrutable" and the executive summary is a "poor description" of the contents of the study;
(e) the peer review process for the study was defective in many ways and the review was inadequate;
(f) the methodologies used constitute "an important advance" over earlier methodologies and should be developed and more widely used where appropriate. (us Risk Assessment Review Group 1978)

The Nuclear Regulatory Commission labored for several months to produce a balanced policy statement in response to these findings. In January of 1979, it issued such a statement endorsing the Lewis report and withdrawing any endorsement of the executive summary of the *Reactor safety study*. At the same time, it instructed its staff that quantitative risk assessment could be used in the licensing process and requested, by June 30, 1979, detailed procedures to ensure the proper and effective use of risk assessment theory, methods, data development, and statistical analysis. In short, whereas the Commission's review sustained a substantial part of the adverse criticism of the *Reactor safety study*, the use of formal risk assessment received a strong boost.

The response by the Commission's staff, of course, was interrupted by the accident at Three Mile Island. The various post-mortems on the accident (see Ch. 6), critical as they were of a wide range of aspects of nuclear safety management, strongly supported increased use of quantitative risk analysis as pioneered in the *Reactor safety study*. This was also the message of the us Reactor Safety Research Review Group, commissioned by the Nuclear Oversight Committee, which concluded in September, 1981, that the "use of probabilistic analysis is rapidly expanding. A significantly larger research program is needed to improve and standardize the methodology as much as possible" (us Reactor Safety Research Review Group 1981, p. v–4).

Since 1981, the United States has witnessed a dramatic expansion in formal risk assessment procedures. This use has ranged from estimating the reliability of specific plant systems to making complete integrated estimates, similar to those of the *Reactor safety study*, of overall plant systems. Some 15–20 utility-sponsored large-scale probabilistic risk studies have been completed or are under way for us nuclear plants and it is likely that most of the 125 nuclear plants to be operating by the end of the century will eventually undergo such major assessments. Meanwhile, probablistic risk analysis is increasingly enjoying application in other parts of the nuclear fuel cycle, particularly radioactive waste management. Chapter 8 takes up the achievements and implications of this rapid growth of probabilistic risk analysis in the United States and abroad.

THE SWEDISH EXPERIENCE

In 1968, the Electricity Supply Authority of Stockholm applied for permission to erect a nuclear combined power and district-heating plant at a site located only a few kilometers from the center of Stockholm. There was no precedent of such a siting, either in Sweden or internationally. When reviewing the project, the Swedish safety authorities decided that further theoretical and empirical studies were prerequisites for the acceptance of such a close siting. In 1969, they commenced a broad study involving collaboration between governmental authorities and the utilities concerned, of the problems involved in close siting. The task of the study was to analyze both the economic and environmental justifications for such a close siting and the safety problems connected with it. In early 1970, a governmental committee reorganized the study.

The Commission concluded that the distance factor is not excessively important, and at any rate less important than, for example, the release height and the amount of released iodine. If a restricted zone with a radius of 2 km were set up around the reactor, the worst possible accident would involve only a few tens of fatalities, even if the reactor were sited only 5 km from the center of the city. The risks could be very significantly reduced, however, if population centers were more than 40 km away. Better iodine containment (e.g., through filters) or a higher point of release for accidental discharges, or both, would have more safety relevance than more distant siting.

The second Swedish nuclear risk study related not to reactor safety but to the technical, economic, and safety aspects of waste handling in general and reprocessing in particular. The so-called "Åka study" (Åka 1976a, 1976b) was primarily a restatement and systematization of existing studies, with very little in the way of new quantitative assessments. Because the committee included parliamentarians, it was seen as an expression of political will and its lack of specificity discouraged public debate.

A comparative study, *Energy, health, environment* (Swedish Governmental Committee on Energy and the Environment 1977), of the risks associated with hydro, fossil fuel, and nuclear generating systems, appeared in 1977. Again it involved a parliamentary committee, again it comprised primarily a compilation of existing reports, and again it was largely qualitative in its mode of analysis. It also made no attempt to develop a methodology for integrating the total risk picture for each source of energy. Because yet another parliamentary study was initiated before the report was completed, this document received very little publicity.

1976 was a dramatic year for nuclear power in Sweden. In May the Åka Committee published its report, which recommended the erection of a reprocessing plant in Sweden and thereby supported the development of a nuclear industry. In the general election in September of the same year, the nuclear issue played a crucial role. The election resulted in the overthrow of the social democratic government. Under the new coalition government, the strongly antinuclear Center Party became the most influential participant in energy policy. So, for the first time, antinuclear forces played a dominant political role in a western democracy. The results are reflected in the so-called Stipulation Law, which requires the owner of a nuclear reactor to prove that ultimate disposal of used nuclear fuel and radioactive wastes can be made "absolutely safe".

In the response to this law, the nuclear industry formed a project group called KBS (*Kärn–Bränsle–Säkerhet*), charged with the task of proving it possible to satisfy the requirements of the Stipulation Law. KBS performed a large number of empirical studies that supplied some of the background data which the Åka study termed necessary for a detailed risk analysis. Not surprisingly, the KBS project concluded that the Stipulation Law requirement could be satisfied. The actual content of the KBS reports proved to be of rather little interest in the general debate, and attention focused on the political implications of the studies. The day the first KBS report was released, the nuclear industry made an application to start the Ringhals nuclear plant, thereby putting the government into the position of having to take a decision that would become a precedent for the whole nuclear program.

The new government which took office in October 1976 comprised three parties with diverging views on energy in general and nuclear energy in particular. To minimize political risks, the new government postponed consideration of the energy issue. The mechanism chosen for this was the appointment of a special commission, charged to prepare a major decision concerning Sweden's future energy policy. The commission was instructed to develop a number of major policy alternatives and to analyze the risks, environmental effects, effects on national security, and costs associated with each alternative. Five subcommittees of technical experts had responsibility for various aspects of the commission's task. It is the report from subcommittee A, on safety and environment, which is of interest here. As with all studies of this kind, the subcommittee was hard put to bound satisfactorily the energy production systems. Nevertheless, it strove to make a systematic comparison of different energy sources, initiating new studies where required. Despite its inevitable shortcomings, the report probably gives the most complete and the best integrated picture available at the time.

In the Energy Commission itself, opinions about the report were divided. The majority (10 out of 15 members) believed that the risks associated with nuclear power were acceptable compared to available alternatives and given the overall social benefit of the activity. A minority of five held that the report of the subcommittee did not sustain such a conclusion. The press coverage of the Energy Commission, like that in the US for the BEIR III report (National Research Council 1980) focused mainly on the antagonism within the Commission and again largely ignored the factual content.

After the Three Mile Island accident, the Swedish government established a new committee of highly qualified scientists to review again all the risks associated with nuclear power and to analyze what measures, if any, should be undertaken to improve safety in Swedish nuclear power plants. Although that committee accepted much of the previous nuclear risk work done by Swedish and foreign groups, it did have reservations regarding the low probabilities applied to very severe accidents. It also believed that safety measures should be tightened because such accidents were in fact credible. In particular, the committee explicitly rebuked the majority of the Energy Commission for its light-hearted treatment of the safety questions of nuclear power. The committee recommended substantially greater efforts, both by the industry and by the regulatory authorities, to improve nuclear safety. To reconcile this recommendation with another finding of the Swedish Reactor Safety Committee – that there was no reason to re-evaluate the factual content of earlier risk studies – it is apparent that relevant authorities, and (perhaps) responsible politicians, failed to observe properly much of what was demonstrated in these studies.

THE WEST GERMAN EXPERIENCE

The *German risk study for nuclear power plants* (GRS 1980), commissioned by the Federal Ministry for Research and Technology, comprised two phases. Phase A comprised the German equivalent of the *Reactor safety study*. Although it applied the analysis to a particular German pressurized-water reactor – Biblis B – it considered over all 19 sites and a total of 25 reactors. This was a critical study for the German nuclear industry, since a federal law stipulates that the most competent safety assessments possible must be carried out before a plant is licensed. The German study differed from the American *Reactor safety study* in that the German reference plant had different engineered safety features, and the study took into account the closer proximity of the population. The study sought not only to estimate societal risks associated with all known classes of potential accidents but also to examine the scope for further developments in risk assessment methodology and safety research. Phase B, still in progress, is looking in considerable detail at the problem areas uncovered in phase A.

The West German contribution to this volume (Ch. 4) compares the findings of phase A of the German study with the *Reactor safety study*. Whereas both studies viewed the overall probabilities of core melt as similar, the German assessments of loss-of-coolant accidents (even though different component parts and safety features were involved) were more cautious and calculated a greater contribution of small leaks to the core-melt frequency than did the American assessment. The West German study shows early-fatalities curves that are somewhat lower than those for the United States, but the reverse is the case for late fatalities. This is largely due to the application of linear dose–response curves (as recommended by the International Commission on Radiological Protection or ICRP) and to the higher population densities in central

Europe. Yet the German study paid only limited attention to common-mode failures and virtually ignored the influence of operator error. Nevertheless, the study was judged to be of great value as it identified (usually at the interface between different systems and where different technical disciplines had to coordinate, for example, engineering, metallurgy, ultrasonic inspection), weak points in design, how and why accident sequences could develop, and potential emergency protection measures.

Phase B of the *German risk study*, still in progress, involves a much more detailed treatment of the phase A analyses, encompassing about 20 projects covering accident analysis and systems analysis, core meltdown and the discharge of radioactivity, accident sequence models, and methods and techniques. The aim is to move beyond the rather conservative assumptions that phase A drew from the *Reactor safety study* to more exact analyses based upon "best estimate" conditions, improved understanding of system reliability, more specific reference to particular experience, and more careful incorporation of human error.

The second major nuclear related risk study in West Germany was the Gorleben hearings. Convened by the state government of Lower Saxony, this six-day symposium addressed a proposed integrated nuclear reprocessing and waste-disposal center. Its aim was not only to determine the acceptability of the risks associated with the projected scheme, but to establish public confidence in the public hearing as an exercise in technology assessment. The hearings took the form of a scientific "court," with an international panel of critics pitted against the advocate scientists. This panel, called the Gorleben International Review, produced a 2,200-page report, which largely formed the basis of the cross-examination. Although the original intent was that burden of proof should fall upon the advocates of the scheme to show that it could be made safe, the organizers believed that the tables were turned and that the burden was on the critics to show that the facility was unsafe. In general, the advocates of the scheme won the technical argument; that is, they made a convincing case that a reprocessing plant could be constructed and operated safely. But the politicians sensed that the public would not support such a move and decided against the reprocessing plant, and hence the whole scheme as originally proposed.

A Commission of Inquiry, established in 1979 by the German Parliament to inquire into a wide-ranging array of issues relating to a future nuclear policy, conducted a third West German risk study. The Commission inquired into:

(a)   recommendations of criteria against which to gauge the acceptability of nuclear power and its risks compared with those associated with other sources of energy;
(b)   demonstration of the potential necessity of alternative fuel cycles;
(c)   the merits or otherwise of breeder reactor technology;
(d)   the wider societal implications of a major investment in nuclear power; and
(e)   the implications of abandoning nuclear energy.

The Commission was composed of politicians and scientists, some of whom were avowedly antinuclear in sentiment. Though it met for 22 sessions over a period of 13 months, it did not complete its work. (The continuation of the first commission, charged only with recommending that parliament abandon its "reservation" regarding the fast breeder reactor of Kalkar, so recommended in July 1982.)

The first report consisted of three parts: criteria for the evaluation of energy systems, different energy paths to the year 2030, and conclusions on a number of problem topics. The Commission split on the issue of the future status of nuclear power in West Germany, with a majority counseling delay on any firm decision regarding a long-term commitment to nuclear power until at least 1990 (implying that no firm decision on a commercial breeder reactor should be made before then). But a minority viewed this judgment as too harsh and thought that determining a nuclear energy strategy on a plant-by-plant basis would be too unfair on the industry and would place unrealistic restrictions on future energy choices. With respect to the reactor safety issue, the Commission split 8–7, with the majority believing that existing safety requirements were satisfactory and the minority advocating further improvement (though admitting that existing reactors were rigorously regulated and apparently safe). A majority wanted further risk assessment panels to be more representative of the various viewpoints regarding energy futures, including, for example, representatives of the labor unions and antinuclear critics. This point was also directed at the composition of the commission that was undertaking phase B of the *German risk study*. It also recommended new risk-oriented analyses for the prototype breeder reactor, under construction at Kalkar (SNR 300), to show that it would be as safe as the Biblis B pressurized-water reactor, the reference design for the *German risk study*.

THE BRITISH EXPERIENCE

The Safety and Reliability Directorate of the UK Atomic Energy Authority (UKAEA) in Britain has, since the mid-1960s, continually developed risk methodologies. This work rests principally on probabilistic risk analyses that use fault-tree analyses and estimates of component reliability. The related attitude is that risk assessment is an evolving technique; that there is never an endpoint in such work, even when plants are commissioned. Thus, large-scale probabilistic risk analysis, although methodologically interesting and intellectually satisfying, is treated in part as a historical document as soon as it is published. It is also noteworthy that the major comprehensive risk studies have been devoted to light-water reactors (PWRs and BWRs) that, until recently, were not of interest to the UK nuclear industry, which, until the mid-1970s, devoted its efforts to gas-cooled reactors (magnox and the advanced gas-cooled reactors).

The first noteworthy public investigation of nuclear issues in Britain was the sixth report of the Royal Commission on Environmental Pollution (1976), the so-called Flowers Commission, which studied nuclear power and the environment. The Commission looked at the *Reactor safety study* calculations and accepted the UKAEA's conclusion that the societal risk as outlined by the American study was plausible. The Commission also noted that for common-mode failures, the British demand tougher standards, requiring at the very least two completely independent systems, and, for critical components, four separate systems. The Commission maintained that the nuclear industry can produce plants with an acceptably low societal risk, but many wider considerations must enter the equation prior to any large investment in nuclear power. Nevertheless, the Commission wanted to see greater use of probabilistic risk analysis by both the designers and the regulators and questioned the apparent bias in favor of analyzing particular accident sequences ("most credible accidents"), a bias which they felt might starve analyses of other possible accident sequences. The Commission was most controversial in its critique of the "plutonium economy" and its concern over the apparent lack of security in the handling of plutonium for reprocessing facilities. It was also not convinced that existing knowledge about safe high-level radioactive waste disposal was sufficient and recommended that any commitment to a large program of fission power should await demonstration beyond reasonable doubt of the feasibility of a safe method of disposal.

The report of the Royal Commission shocked the British nuclear establishment. Although the industry received a fairly clean bill of health on environmental grounds, it had not anticipated from a prestigious body such a chilling reaction regarding the possible drawbacks of an expanded nuclear program. The report of the Flowers Commission resulted in the initiation of a test-drilling program to identify rock formations that might be suitable for long-term storage of high-level wastes. All test-drilling sites save one, however, had to undergo local inquiry, due to objections from the local planning authorities. The public reaction at each of the three inquiries proved so hostile that the whole program was abandoned. It was officially stated that this was for scientific reason (namely, so that relevant experience could be gleaned from other countries), but it is widely believed that the decision was more a political one (two senior ministers directly involved represented constituencies where test drilling was proposed). Here is a case where needed experimentation in site investigation was not even allowed to proceed, making it very difficult to find a satisfactory long-term solution.

Despite its historical commitment to gas-cooled reactors, the British nuclear industry began to favor the PWR in the mid-1970s, on the grounds of cost, export potential, and substantial operating experience. Many scientists believed that it was possible to design and manufacture an operationally safe PWR. Taking the Trojan plant in Oregon as an initial reference design, the UK Nuclear Installations Inspectorate (NII) conducted a general safety study of the PWR in 1977. Broadly speaking, the Inspectorate (the government-appointed, but technically independent, nuclear licensing authority in the UK) concluded that a PWR could be "acceptably safe" so long as British safety principles and standards were applied. (This would require some modifications in design and component reliability.) The NII standards, laid down in a subsequent report as a series of guiding principles, gave a fair degree of maneuverability to the judgment of the regulatory official in discussion with clients and designers. For example, all likely dangers are to be reduced to levels as low or as remote "as reasonably practical" and to the point at which the particular NII inspector is satisfied that all reasonable calculations have been made. In any case, techniques using fault-tree or event-tree analysis are to be regarded only as "aids in the logical evaluation of the fault potential of any plant."

The true safety test for the first UK PWR lies both in the official licensing process and in the report of the public inquiry into a proposed plant at Sizewell in Suffolk (see Ch. 7). This plant is based on a second US PWR reference design, namely the Callaway Westinghouse/Bechtel plant at Fulton, Missouri. As a result of the NII review and with regard to British safety principles, however, the UK PWR incorporates important design changes. These include a larger number of independent systems for emergency core cooling, a borated-water injection system, heaters for the emergency cooling water, ring-forged steel welds for the pressure vessel and at all pipe joints, a second containment, and improved design of the central console and operations room.

Such important modifications are not the result of a particular generic risk study but the outcome of prolonged discussions among Westinghouse, Bechtel, the construction company (National Nuclear Corporation), and the client (the Central Electricity Generating Board), in consultation with the Nuclear Installations Inspectorate. All this work has made its way into the preconstruction safety report (published in May, 1982) for the Sizewell B reactor. The report consists of 12 volumes to which are added the 14-volume reference design and the extensive report by the CEGB in its Official Statement of Case. This is not all: there are also some 400 supporting documents plus the updated version of a special UKAEA task force on pressure vessel integrity. In addition, both the Nuclear Installations Inspectorate and the independent Advisory Committee on the Safety of Nuclear Installations (reporting to the Health and Safety Executive, the parent body of the NII) have published reports on the safety features of the proposed design. All these reports indicate that the Sizewell B plant is capable of meeting the British regulatory standards, and formal licensing of the design has occurred. Yet this is only one part of a four-stage licensing process, as described in the next chapter. In any case, the decision to go ahead with the plant awaits publication of the report of the independent inspector. Then, of course, there will have to be a parliamentary debate before a final political decision occurs. It is especially noteworthy in all this that safety assessment is in the hands of the proponents, but the decision to proceed depends upon many other considerations.

THE CANADIAN EXPERIENCE

The Canadians, like the British but unlike the Americans, Swedes, and Germans, have conducted no formal comprehensive nuclear risk study that was available for close public scrutiny and careful appraisal by informed critics. As indicated earlier, this is partly a matter of a governmental "style" that prefers a more flexible consultative approach to societal risk analysis and partly because, until recently, the issue of societal risk has not been sufficiently unsettling as to require a more formal and public analysis.

The key study, reported on in Chapter 5, is the work of the Royal Commission on Electric Power Planning (1978) under the chairmanship of A. Porter. The so-called Porter Commission was not established primarily to examine societal risks arising out of nuclear power but rather to consider the various implications of Ontario's future energy program and planning methods. Paralleling the work of the Porter Commission was an investigation by the Select Committee of the Ontario legislature of the financial affairs of Ontario Hydro, the publicly owned provincial electricity utility. Since Ontario Hydro was a monopolistic supplier of electricity, the legislature was keen to evaluate the utility's pricing of the electricity that the utility produced.

Within two years of its operation, however, extended terms of reference charged the Porter Commission with looking more closely at nuclear power, including risk. The results appear in an interim report (Royal Commission on Electric Power Planning 1978). This action was taken largely because of the unexpected strong emphasis on the risk issue in the submissions received during the public information hearings and in the debate stage hearings. In the wake of the Three Mile Island accident, the Commission enlarged its assessment of nuclear risk in its final report in 1980. Meanwhile, the Ontario Legislative Select Committee, also sensing public unrest over the societal risks of an expanded nuclear program, turned its attention to future possible developments for nuclear power and their likely ramifications. Unfortunately, the latter study was never completed. The Select Committee was disbanded in March 1981 when the existing minority government was returned to power with a majority. These Ontario studies had a scope broader than the risk-related reports (with the exception of that of the Swedish Energy Commission) already discussed for the US, Sweden, and West Germany.

As Chapter 5 will make clear, the Commission never quite came to grips with the risk issue. Its interim report betrays a division on the matter of how broadly to consider the nuclear power question, with a narrow majority favoring a broad sweep of relevant issues but a significant minority preferring to confine the debate to technical matters. In the end, the Commission did acknowledge the methodological basis of the *Reactor safety study* and the criticisms of the Lewis group. Nevertheless, it did not consider a new analysis to be necessary. Rather, it concentrated on safety measures and component reliability testing, all the while stressing the importance of human error, particularly in its final report (Royal Commission on Electric Power Planning 1980), which appeared after the Three Mile Island accident.

The perplexing problem of safe disposal of high-level radioactive waste concerned the Commission enormously: its interim report advocated restrictions on nuclear development if the problem could not be satisfactorily resolved by 1985. But the final report moved this date to 1990. Nevertheless, the Commission remained suspicious of the risk question. It was anxious that adequate emergency procedures should be established as a matter of urgency, that worker radiation protection measures should be improved, and that a proposed 1,250MW CANDU reactor should not be completed (on the grounds that the existing 850MW design was well understood and hence more inherently safe). Ontario Hydro has since abandoned the 1,250MW design.

## Concluding note

The foregoing discussion demonstrates clearly that large-scale nuclear risk analysis has increased dramatically since the first limited consequence study performed in the United States in 1957. But the growth has been highly uneven; the United States, Sweden, and West Germany have been the major producers and users of such assessments, whereas Canada and the United Kingdom have been less convinced of their overall role and value. Even in the United Kingdom, however, the technical advances in probabilistic risk analysis since 1975 have been dramatic. What is different is that this progress is largely opaque to the public and does not appear in the form of a single, highly visible report.

The *Reactor safety study* emerges as a landmark document that has greatly influenced subsequent nuclear risk studies and risk discussion in all countries. The growth of probabilistic risk analysis (PRA) has occurred in a context of increasing public skepticism and concern, a situation that has constrained the impacts of PRAS on the public dimension. The motivations for conducting such major assessments are diverse, ranging from attempts to silence the nuclear debate, to adapt the *Reactor safety study* to a given country, or to overcome institutional or political limits to nuclear power. Meanwhile, recent experience suggests an emerging divergence in international risk assessment practice, with some countries according a very central role to comprehensive risk assessment and others according it a significant but less central place.

As a form of technology itself (which Ellul 1967 would term "technique"), comprehensive probabilistic risk analysis does not occur in a cultural or institutional vacuum. Indeed, the emergence and practice of risk assessment should be expected to vary with the relevant societal structures and institutions in which it is placed. The next chapter contrasts these cultural contexts.

## References

Åka (Åka-utredningen) 1976a. *Anvant kärnbränsle och radioaktivt avfall.* Statens offentliga utredningar (SOU) 1976: 32. Stockholm: Liberförlag.
Åka (Åka-utredningen) 1976b. *Spent nuclear fuel and radioactive waste: a summary of a report given by the Swedish government committee on radioactive waste.* Statens offentliga utredningar (SOU) 1976: 4. Stockholm: Liberförlag/Allmänna Förlag.

Boulten, J. (ed.) 1978. *Management of radioactive fuel wastes: the Canadian fuel disposal program.* Report AECL-6314. Mississauga, Ontario: Atomic Energy of Canada.
Bradford, P. 1980. *Condemned to repeat it? Haste, distraction, Rasmussen and Rogovin.* Remarks before the Seventh Annual National Engineers' Week Energy Conference, February 21.

Cluff Lake Board of Inquiry 1978. *Final report*, E. D. Bayda, Chairman. Regina, Saskatchewan: The Board.
Cohen, A. V. & D. K. Pritchard 1980. *Comparative risks of electricity production systems: a critical survey of the literature.* Health and Safety Executive, Research Paper 11. London: HMSO.
Cremer & Warner Ltd. 1980. *An analysis of the Canvey report.* London: Oyez Publishing.

EK-A (Energikommissionens Expertgrupp for Säkerhet och Miljö) 1978. *Miljöeffekter och risker vid utnyttjandet av energi* (Environmental effects and hazards of energy exploitation). D.s.I. 1978: 27, pts. 1–2. Stockholm: Allmänna Förlaget.
Ellul, J. 1967. *Technological society.* New York: Vintage.

Fremlin, J. 1985. *Power production: what are the risks?* Bristol: Adam Hilger.

GRS (Gesellschaft für Reaktorsicherheit) 1980. *Deutsche Risikostudie Kernkraftwerke: eine Untersuchung zu dem durch Störfalle in Kernkraftwerken verursachten Risiko.* Cologne: Verlag TÜV Rheinland.

Holdren, J. P., K. Anderson, P. B. Gleick, I. Mintzer, G. Morris & K. W. Smith 1979. *Risk of renewable energy sources: a critique of the Inhaber report.* Report ERG-79-3, Berkeley: Energy and Resources Group, University of California.

Inhaber, H. 1982. *Energy risk assessment.* New York: Gordon & Breach.

Kasperson, R. E. (ed.) 1983. *Equity issues in radioactive waste management.* Cambridge, Mass.: Oelgeschlager, Gunn & Hain.
Kasperson, R. E., G. Berk, D. Pijawka, A. Sharaf & J. Wood 1980. Public opposition to nuclear energy: retrospect and prospect. *Science, Technology, and Human Values* **5**, 11–23.
Kates, R. W. & J. X. Kasperson 1983. Comparative risk analysis of technological hazards (a review). *Proceedings, National Academy of Sciences USA* **80**, 7027–38.
KBS (Kärn–Bränsle–Säkerhet) 1977. *Handling of spent nuclear fuel and final storage of vitrified high level reprocessing waste.* Solna, Sweden: A. B. Teleplan.
KBS (Kärn–Bränsle–Säkerhet) 1979. *Handling and final storage of unreprocessed spent nuclear fuel.* Solna, Sweden: A. B. Teleplan.
King, F. K. & M. R. Vijay 1985. *The benefits of pre-operational risk assessment based on experience with the Darlington probabilistic safety evaluation.* Paper presented at the International ANS/FNS Topical Meeting, San Francisco, February 25–26.

Lewis, H. W. 1980. The safety of fission reactors. *Scientific American* **242**, 53–65.

Mazur, A. 1984. *Perception and communication of risk: sociological issues.* Paper presented to the US National Science Foundation/Environmental Protection Agency workshop on risk perception and risk communication, Long Beach, California, December 10–12.

Ministry of Agriculture and Environment 1978. *Energy, health, environment: summary of a report (sou 1977: 67) by the Swedish Governmental Committee on Energy and the Environment.* Stockholm: The Ministry.

Närförläggningsutredningen 1974. *Närförläggning av kärnkraftverke* (Close-siting of nuclear power plants). Statens offentliga utredningar (sou) 1974: 56. Stockholm: Allmänna förlaget.

National Research Council 1980. *The effects on populations of exposure to low levels of ionizing radiation.* Committee on the Biological Effects of Ionizing Radiation. Washington: National Academy Press.

Reaktorsäkerhetsutredningen 1979. *Säker Kärnkraft?* (Safe nuclear power? Report of the Swedish Government Committee on Nuclear Rector Safety.) Statens utredningar (sou) 1979: 86. Stockholm: Liberförlag.

Rijnmond Public Authority 1982. *Risk analysis of six potentially hazardous industrial objects in the Rijnmond area: a pilot study.* Dordrecht: D. Reidel.

Royal Commission on Electric Power Planning 1978. *A race against time: interim report on nuclear power in Ontario.* Toronto: The Commission.

Royal Commission on Electric Power Planning, 1980. *Final report.* Toronto: The Commission.

Royal Commission on Environmental Pollution 1976. *Nuclear power and the environment,* sixth report. Cmnd. 6618. London: HMSO.

Swedish Governmental Committee on Energy and the Environment (Betänkande av Energi- och Miljökommitten) 1977. *Energi, hälsa, miljö* (Energy, health, environment). Statens offentliga utredningar (sou) 1977: 67. Stockholm. sou.

UK Health and Safety Executive 1978. *Canvey: summary of an investigation of potential hazards from operations in the Canvey Island, Thurrock area.* London. HMSO.

UK Health and Safety Executive 1981. *Canvey: a second report.* London: HMSO.

US Atomic Energy Commission 1957. *Theoretical possibilities and consequences of major accidents in large nuclear power plants.* WASH-740. Washington, DC: The Commission.

US Environmental Protection Agency 1985. Environmental standards for the management and disposal of spent nuclear fuel, high-level and transuranic radioactive wastes: final rule, *Federal Register* **50** (18 Sept.), 38066–95; corrected by *Federal Register* **50** (1 Oct.), 40003.

US Nuclear Regulatory Commission 1975. *Reactor safety study.* WASH-1400, NUREG-75/014. Washington, DC: The Commission.

US President's Commission on the Accident at Three Mile Island 1979. *The need for change: the legacy of TMI.* Washington DC: Government Printing Office.

US Reactor Safety Research Review Group 1981. *Report to the President's Nuclear Safety Oversight Committee.* Washington DC: The Committee.

US Risk Assessment Review Group 1978. *Report to the us Nuclear Regulatory Commission.* NUREG/CR-0400. Washington, DC: The Commission.

# 2 The management of nuclear risk in five countries: political cultures and institutional settings

JAMES E. DOOLEY, BENGT HANSSON, JEANNE X. KASPERSON, ROGER E. KASPERSON, TIMOTHY O'RIORDAN, and HERBERT PASCHEN

As a new technology linked to matters of national security as well as energy production, nuclear power naturally shows a number of commonalities across countries. It is scarcely surprising to find cross-national similarities in the management of the risks attendant to this technology. Since nuclear power plants require a high technological proficiency, long planning horizons, and enormous capital investments, they generally also require centralized national institutions to shape policies and to regulate use. The high costs of research and development and the difficulties surrounding the assessment of ill-understood risks over the various stages of the nuclear fuel cycle have usually meant substantial national investments in risk assessment and research. But the precise role of risk assessment in the management process and its entry into policy making are intimately connected with the differing political cultures and institutional structures that prevail in the five countries studied in this volume. This chapter describes the overall contrasts in political culture and then reviews in greater detail each country's specific institutional arrangements for managing nuclear risk.

## A contrast in political cultures

The term "political culture" is used here to describe both the institutions and the accepted rules of conduct through which public policies emerge. The term relates to the "learned rules of the political and administrative game," with given relationships and expectations of participants. It is based on constitutional traditions, the law, and tacitly recognized codes of practice, all of which combine to provide order and an overriding sense of purpose to political and administrative activity. In this sense, the notion of culture or cultural approach contrasts with that used by other researchers (Douglas & Wildavsky 1982, Gross & Rayner 1985).

The countries studied reflect two paradigmatic styles of political culture – the *adversarial* style and the *consensual* style. The adversarial style entails decision making through dispute resolution, where all documentation is open and subject to full cross-examination. It is based on the principle of direct public accountability and legal challenge on all matters involving administrative decision. The adversarial style is most apparent in the United States.

American political culture is rooted in the inherent heterogeneity of American demography and in the Madisonian theory of democracy. In the *Federalist No. 10*, Madison (1911) noted the existence of factions which emanated from the nature of individuals – the differences of interest associated with differences in property, the attachment to various leaders, and the fallibility of human reason itself. Madison's central goal – which has become an article of faith in the American politial credo – is the achievement of a nontyrannical republic. Toward that end, the United States has erected a complicated network of constitutional checks and balances: the separate constituencies for electing a president, senators, and representatives; the presidential veto power; a bicameral Congress; presidential control over appointments; senatorial confirmation; and federalism itself. Other checks and balances have been added – judicial review, decentralized political power, the Senate filibuster, and indeed almost every organizational mechanism to provide an external check on any identifiable group of political leaders (Dahl 1956, pp. 14–15).

Central to this political culture has been the assumption of inherent conflict among the diversity of interests. The Constitution provides means for limiting and channeling conflict, not avoiding it. It is not surprising, then, that regulation in the United States is strongly adversarial in nature, comprising yet another arena for playing out social conflicts. Just as the constitutional founders feared the power of central government, so the populace at large has distrusted bureaucracy. A wary populace, more convinced of the pragmatic good sense of the individual American than of the wisdom and expertise of the public official, has always been suspicious of the expert in American culture. Thus President Reagan has skillfully tapped deep-seated aspects of American political culture with his program to deregulate economic and social activity and to "rescue" private initiative from the bureaucrats. The adversarial style, then, draws upon the twin concepts of conflict and suspicion, and is most clearly apparent in the United States, although there are some similarities in the West German political culture.

By contrast, the British operate through a consensual form of government, based on the principles of compromise, consultation, accommodation, and trust. This approach stems from a paternalistic view of government that commands limited accountability (basically only to Parliament, though even in Parliament accountability is very much subdued) and a strong belief in professional integrity. Safety regulation operates through a kind of club of specialists who are not only highly trained and experienced (and hence who share similar values), but who also espouse professional competence and high standards. This may result in an unintentional disdain of "lay" opinion and a difficulty in communicating with the ordinary public. The consensual approach in Britain also harbors official secrecy and a certain opaqueness regarding how decisions are actually reached. This consensual style is best developed in Britain, France, and Canada (although Canada now has a Freedom of Information Act).

The Swedish style is a different case again. It is basically consensual, though the pursuit of this aim occurs not in seclusion as in the United Kingdom, but out in the open and with active public participation. If the catchwords for the US style are conflict and suspicion and for the British style consensus and trust, one may say that the Swedish style embodies consensus *and* suspicion. Suspicion, because it is essential that all information be open, accessible to anyone interested, thereby making it possible to check the impartiality and competence of officials and experts – the public's right to information is a principle of wide applicability and of long standing in Swedish Public Law – and consensus, because it is supposed that the decision makers shall consider all sides of a case and decide fairly in the name of the whole nation and not in their own private interest or that of their organization. At root, this is also a paternalistic view of government (albeit of a collective kind), and, as one might expect in such a case, accountability is still very limited. Hardly any minister has left a seat as a result of revealed neglect, mismanagement, or incompetence.

Table 2.1 provides a summary of how these political cultures differ in key attributes. It is apparent that a continuum exists, on each dimension, with substantial variation. Moreover, not surprisingly, the attributes tend to group, with the United States representing one end of the spectrum and the United Kingdom the other.

These contrasting political cultures give rise to differing basic institutional structures. In the United States, the management of nuclear risk spreads over a large number of institutions and interests, including four major federal departments, at least two counterpart agencies in each of the 50 states, many local governmental bodies, some 44 private electricity supply companies (utilities), at least two dozen congressional committees, and the courts. This diffusion creates an organizational atmosphere that encourages conflict, allows the exploitation of uncertainty and delay, and enables numerous pressure groups to argue their cases. Decisions occur through a complex set of codes of practice and regulations, usually binding on the utilities and studded with quantified specifications, that allow for a thorough check on the performance of both the regulator and the regulated. Some critics (e.g., the Kemeny Commission and the UK Nuclear Installations Inspectorate) argue that this type of organization makes the utility more concerned with meeting safety standards than with actually ensuring safety.

In the United States, the electricity supply utilities are numerous, privately owned, and very variable in size and resources. In West Germany, more than 20 utilities (out of a total number of 1,000) use nuclear energy in varying degrees. The leader is the Rheinisch-Westfälische Elektrizitätswerke AG, which directly or through participation has about one-third of the installed and future nuclear capacity. In Sweden, the major supplier and owner of nuclear

**Table 2.1** Contrasting political cultures in the five countries: a summary.

| Country | Constitutional conventions for policy making | Policy-making style | Regulatory style | Main points of leverage for opposition |
|---|---|---|---|---|
| United States | polycentric – no single point of authority | open, accessible, accountable | formal, adversarial, open | legislative and judicial processes; public hearings |
| Sweden | central authority subject to local agreement | open, accessible, accountable | informal, cooperative, open | electoral, legislative, and administrative processes |
| Federal Republic of Germany | central authority, subject to local agreement/polycentric | partially open, partially accessible, partially accountable | formal, adversarial, open | judicial activity |
| United Kingdom | strong central authority | closed, mostly inaccessible, partially accountable | informal, cooperative, largely closed | legislative and administrative processes, public inquiries |
| Canada | central authority, strong provincial role | partially open, partially accessible, partially accountable | largely informal, largely cooperative, partially open | public inquiries |

reactors is state-owned. The other reactor owners are two major companies with a mixed ownership of local communes and private interests. In Canada and Britain, nuclear power is operated by monopoly public suppliers (Ontario Hydro in Ontario, the Central Electricity Generating Board (CEGB) in England and Wales, and the South of Scotland Electricity Board in Scotland), backed by large semi-public/semi-private manufacturing consortia.

Since the most formal approach to safety standards occurs in the United States, with West Germany and Sweden following thereafter and with Britain and Canada the least formal, though no less stringent in design and operating procedures, a connection may also exist between formal rules and the number and diversity of utilities. Central regulation through a rulebook may well be common where there are many different kinds of utilities, especially if some are small and privately run (as in the US). So the structure of the electricity supply industry is an important element in determining the form of safety standards, how such standards will be met, how licensing procedures will be followed, and hence the importance attached to formal risk analysis.

In Sweden, the licensing process splits into two phases. The first is what may be termed site-specific planning permission. As for all proposed buildings, the local commune has to grant a building permit to erect a building of specified size and construction at a specified site for a specified purpose. No risk assessment is formally necessary, although risk considerations inevitably play a major role in the present political climate (since the decision is primarily a political one). The second phase of the process is triggered only once communal approval is given. This is the permission which is granted by the State Nuclear Power Inspectorate after hearing testimony from a number of other state agencies (such as the State Radiation Protection Institute). The State Nuclear Power Inspectorate has no set rules of procedure (as in the United Kingdom) but requires both a preliminary safety report and a final safety report from the developer. These documents, like their counterparts in Britain, include subgeneric risk assessments, but, unlike Britain, do not formally require probabilistic risk analysis. Nevertheless, any application will draw heavily on existing comprehensive risk studies from both Swedish and foreign sources as contextual evidence for the detailed plant safety reports.

In the US, the picture is complicated by a federal standard-setting process and a federal/state/local licensing procedure. In general there is a complex, and sometimes inadequate, communication between the federal standard-setting process and the plant-level analysis report prepared by the constructing consortia, coupled with the architect engineers who must respond to federal, state, and local requirements. In recent years, the Nuclear Safety Analysis Center and the Institute for Nuclear Power Operations have played an enlarged role with the US Nuclear Regulatory Commission on the development of standards and related risk research (see Ch. 6).

In West Germany, the picture is even more complicated, owing to the rule of law and the role of the courts in interpreting it. Article 7, Paragraph 2 of the Atomic Energy Act of 1959 stipulates that in safety assurance, "every necessary precaution [must be] taken in the light of existing scientific knowledge and technology" to prevent damage (Bundesgesetz 1976). If they are not as yet technically feasible, the license may not be granted. Technical feasibility, thus, does not determine the appropriate measures of precaution. The courts are of the opinion that the determination of a "level of acceptance" on the basis of probabilistic risk analysis is a normative act that lies within the competence of the legislator and is not a question for scientists and engineers to decide. As in the United States, the German nuclear regulatory process is extremely complex, relying on numerous agencies at three tiers of government plus a variety of expert commissions. Public participation is built into the licensing procedure at different stages, but it is tailored to take into account only isolated or small numbers of protests. In the face of the broad opposition to nuclear energy that has developed during the 1970s and 1980s, this procedure has proved inadequate.

Plant licensing in Canada involves a mix of federal and provincial controls. The specific plant may be subject to an environmental assessment (conducted at the provincial level), although this is discretionary. Safety regulations are the responsibility of the Atomic Energy Control Board (AECB), the federal regulatory agency that must issue licenses for both construction and operation of new plants. Issuance of a construction license implies approval·of the general design of the plant but does not guarantee automatic granting of an operating license. In Canada, as in all of the countries studied, the primary responsibility for safety rests with the utility and the job of the regulator is to set safety objectives and some performance requirements and to ensure that reasonable levels of safety are met in both the provisional and post-construction safety reports. The Atomic Energy Control Board has issued only a few regulatory documents related to nuclear power plants and relies heavily upon consensus nuclear standards for particular topics (Atchison et al. 1983). No comprehensive generic risk study has been completed in Canada, where practice has favored "subgeneric plant appraisals" in the form of a series of safety reports using risk acceptibility criteria based on the work of relevant international committees. Ontario Hydro has under way a major risk evaluation, estimated to require 65,000 person-hours, for a 4 × 850 MWe nuclear power plant being developed for Darlington.

The British nuclear risk regulatory arrangements are not unlike those operating in Canada. The British rely extensively on a prolonged period of consultation among the plant designers, manufacturers, and the operators, with the onus for setting the safety standards and ensuring that they are met resting firmly on the shoulders of the operating utility. Despite the absence of comprehensive risk assessments, subgeneric studies of all aspects of accident sequences, component reliability, and engineering design come into play. In general, these documents are not made public, nor, until recently, has there been any opportunity for formal public examination of the safety case. The Nuclear Installations Inspectorate (NII) examines the case as it unfolds through four stages: the preliminary safety case, the pre-construction safety report, the plant completion report, and the integrated commission report. Each of these stages involves various kinds of probabilistic risk analysis, although the bulk of this work occurs for the pre-construction safety report. Recently there has been a change toward greater publicity. Both the Nuclear Installations Inspectorate and the Central Electricity Generating Board have been called upon to disclose details of their risk analyses and to defend their risk methodologies, the comprehensiveness of their analyses, and the regulatory procedures of the licensing process at the Sizewell Inquiry. In particular, the Nuclear Install-ations Inspectorate has drawn fire for failing to complete its licensing process, as originally intended, before the Inquiry began. Regardless of the outcome of the Inquiry, nuclear risk regulation is likely to be a much more public pro-cedure in the future – a prospect that is generally welcomed within the industry as a whole but likely less so by the fairly conservative Nuclear Installations Inspectorate.

With these overall contrasts in political cultures and institutional structures in mind, the specific nuclear risk management institutions and processes in each country may be treated in greater depth.

## United States

In the United States, the utilities and regulators share the major responsibility for protecting the public health and safety from nuclear power plants. Yet because of the adversarial nature of the regulatory process, legal restrictions limit the ready communication and degree of informality between regulator and regulatee. A complex system of rules and regulations, usually with exten-sive quantitative specifications and elaborate procedures, replaces decisions by informal negotiation.

The approval process (Fig. 2.1) occurs on two levels: (1) the federal structure of standards, rules, regulations, and assessment requirements, and (2) a utility planning effort that must meet state and local (as well as federal) requirements. The federal structure is shown here in sequential form, although of course the regulatory requirements are continually undergoing revision. Risk assessments enter into this process at a number of crucial junctures. The Environmental Protection Agency, using its contractors, conducts its own assessments of risks in setting environmental standards. With standards now in place for the nuclear fuel cycle and for exposure limitation, recent and current risk assessment efforts relate primarily to waste disposal and the issue of health effects of low-level radiation. As Chapter 1 notes, the Nuclear Regulatory Commission in the past has made only limited use of probabilistic risk assessment in formulating rules and regulatory guidelines, but the agency is currently rapidly increasing its use of this methodology in both the licensing and regulatory processes. Formal risk assessment is also an essential part of the preparation of the safety analysis report, usually conducted by contractors for the utility that is the applicant, but with the advice and review of the Nuclear Regulatory

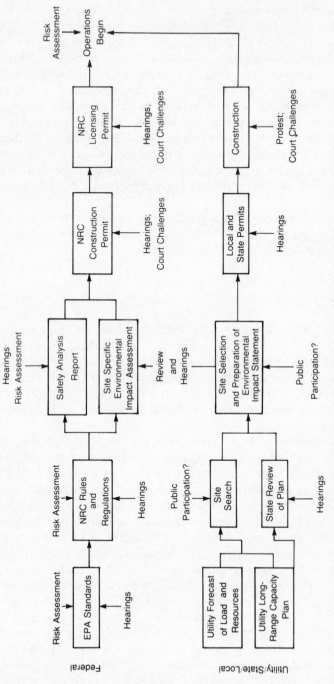

**Figure 2.1** Regulatory and licensing process for nuclear power plants in the US: the entrance of risk assessment and public participation.

Commission. Finally, risk assessment techniques are now being extensively applied to operating reactors, through the industry-wide Nuclear Safety Analysis Center and the Institute for Nuclear Power Operations and through the Nuclear Regulatory Commission's evaluation of safety performance and compliance with regulations. As Figure 2.1 shows, risk assessment is strongly oriented to the federal regulatory and licensing processes; little comparable activity occurs at the state and local levels.

Figure 2.1 also demonstrates the numerous points of potential public scrutiny and adversarial intervention into the process. Essentially all stages of the federal licensing and regulatory process require provision of information to and hearings for interested publics. This is not to say, however, that the public possesses adequate means to challenge decisions or to stimulate major changes. The deficiencies in such opportunities have been extensively detailed over the years by Green & Rosenthal (1967), Ebbin & Kasper (1974), and Stever (1980). Similarly, the utility planning and permit process allows for several points of prospective citizen involvement but generally not at the crucial early stage of consideration.

## Sweden

Sweden's nuclear power program involves 12 light-water reactors, 9 of which are Swedish-designed boiling-water reactors. The full program, to be completed in 1986, will supply an estimated 40–50 percent of the nation's electricity needs over the coming decade, making it one of the largest per capita nuclear programs in the world. A protracted debate over nuclear power led in 1980 to a parliamentary decision to limit the nuclear power program to the technical lifetime of the 12 reactors existing or in progress but to phase out nuclear plants over the longer term.

Basic safety policy, set out in legislation passed during the late 1950s, has been augmented by additional laws, design considerations, licensing requirements, operating experience, and public debate (Pershagen & Nilson 1984). The licensees are directly responsible for ensuring nuclear safety, with public authorities responsible for setting safety goals and assuring the implementation of safety requirements. A cabinet decision that takes account of relevant safety reviews must precede permission to build and operate new nuclear facilities. The government has overall responsibility for nuclear safety research, for the management of radioactive waste, and for ensuring the availability of funds to support these programs. It falls to the licensee, however, to undertake safety measures at his own expense.

The governmental authority with primary responsibility for regulating nuclear safety is the Swedish Nuclear Power Inspectorate. The approach to regulation is similar in a number of respects to those of Canada and the United Kingdom. The Inspectorate sets general goals for the safety work of the utilities, reviews the technical means adopted to realize these goals, and audits implementation and quality assurance programs. The detailed quantitative regulations and guides that characterize US nuclear regulation are eschewed. Resolution of safety issues typically occurs through direct negotiation and discussion between Inspectorate staff and the licensee. Perhaps because of the flexibility and discretion that characterize this approach, the Inspectorate is able to operate with a staff of only about 80 professionals (about the same size as that in the UK) and a simple organizational structure (Fig. 2.2).

The National Institute of Radiation Protection administers the Radiation Protection Act, establishing radiation protection standards and means for compliance. The Institute's Office for Nuclear Energy, with a staff of 30, conducts inspections of nuclear facilities and is responsible for emergency preparedness.

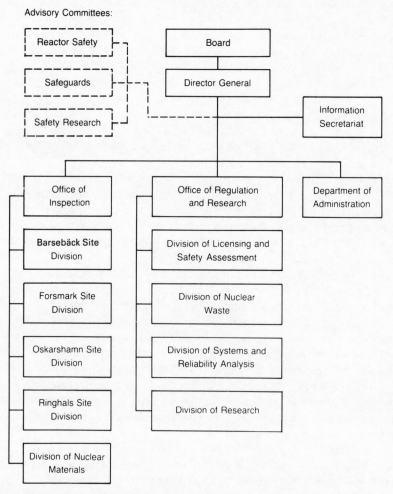

**Figure 2.2**  Organization chart for the Swedish Nuclear Power Inspectorate. *Source*: Pershagen & Nilson 1984, p. 5.

The three utilities that operate nuclear power plants have central safety departments that monitor safety issues. Each also has a central safety committee, reporting directly to top management, which evaluates all significant safety problems in the plant. The minutes of Swedish law require that the committee's meetings become public documents.

Supplementing the governmental and utility organizations are local safety committees at each of the nuclear sites. The Swedish government appoints these committees, upon the recommendation of local authorities, to review the current and planned safety work at the facilities. Law requires the licensees to provide the necessary information. The committees, in turn, are responsible for communicating the results of deliberations to the local publics.

The final institutional mechanism is the Nuclear Safety Board of the Swedish utilities, formed as a response to the Three Mile Island accident. The Board helps coordinate the reactor safety mark of the utilities and sponsors broad-based safety projects. In addition, it operates a computer-based information system for evaluating Swedish nuclear power operational experience and links with the Nuclear Safety Analysis Center and the Institute for Nuclear Power Operations in the United States.

In regard to probabilistic risk analysis, Sweden requires each nuclear power plant to undergo a complete safety review at least three times during its lifetime. Systematic reliability assessment forms a major basis for demonstrating safety performance and the appropriateness of the safety assurance program. A probabilistic risk analysis of the Ringhals 2 unit, completed in June 1983, predicts an annual mean core-melt frequency of about $5 \times 10^{-6}$ (Pershagen & Nilson 1984, p. 12), a level lower than that predicted for many other power plants. Plant-level probabilistic risk analyses are currently in progress for all other Swedish nuclear power plants. Meanwhile, scientists are actively pursuing research on an inherently safe nuclear reactor.

## West Germany

As noted above, all nuclear facilities in the Federal Republic of Germany must comply with a special federal law, the "Law on the Peaceful Utilization of Nuclear Energy and the Protection from its Dangers," as amended in 1976 (Bundesgesetz 1976). According to this Act, a license to build, operate, or modify a nuclear facility may be granted only if (among other things) "every necessary precaution has been taken *in the light of existing scientific knowledge and technology* to prevent damage resulting from the construction and operation of the installation" (Article 7, Paragraph 2, Number 3).

Statutory ordinances define more clearly the safety goals laid down in the Act and constitute a second level of regulations for the licensing of nuclear facilities. A third level consists of the Internal Administrative Regulation, which specifies concretely existing scientific knowledge and technology, including safety criteria issued by the Federal Ministry of the Interior and the recommendations of the Advisory Commission on Reactor Safety and the Advisory Commission on Radiation Protection. Technical rules are the fourth level of specification and, like the Internal Administrative Regulations, are not legally binding in the courts.

The licensing of nuclear facilities is extremely complicated, involving a large number of authorities, institutions, and the general public (Fig. 2.3). The licensing authority is a state (*Lande*) ministry which is, however, subject to instructions and control by the Federal Ministry of the Interior. The state ministry is responsible for consulting the affected communities. Experts

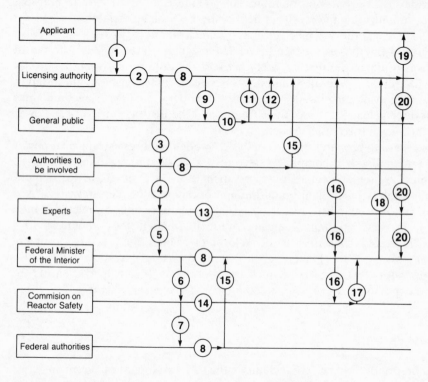

| | |
|---|---|
| 1 Applying for License | 11 Filing of interventions |
| 2 Checking application for completeness | 12 Conducting hearing |
| 3 Contacting authorities to be involved | 13 Preparing expert reports |
| 4 Commissioning experts | 14 Carrying through deliberation process |
| 5 Informing the Federal Ministry of the Interior | 15 Making comments |
| 6 Commissioning the Reactor Safety Commission | 16 Delivering expert reports |
| 7 Informing other Federal authorities | 17 Recommendations by the Commission on Reactor Safety |
| 8 Reviewing | 18 Instructions by the Federal Ministry of the Interior |
| 9 Publishing project and exhibiting application documents | 19 Making decision |
| 10 Public inspection period | 20 Informing objectors and others involved |

**Figure 2.3**   The nuclear licensing procedure in the Federal Republic of Germany.

representing a wide range of authorities and the general public also participate. Characteristically, licensing involves a whole series of permits for partial construction and partial operation. The nuclear facility application, safety report, and a brief description of the plant are exhibited publicly and are subject to the filing of interventions by third parties. Such interventions are dealt with in a nonpublic "hearing," involving those appealing, the license applicant, and the licensing authority. More important, after the granting of a (partial) construction or operating permit by the licensing authority, any citizen whose individual rights appear to be directly affected has the right to appeal to the administrative courts. In exceptional cases, constitutional complaints may even be brought before the Federal Constitutional Court.

These forms of intervention and public participation, constructed along constitutional principles, rest on the assumption that protests will be few and isolated. In the face of the broad opposition to nuclear energy that developed during the 1970s, they proved inadequate. Use of the right to intervene has flourished, hearings have often been turbulent and have failed to resolve underlying conflicts, and the filing of complaints against licensees before the administrative courts has occurred regularly.

Public disputes over the licensing of nuclear power plants in the courts have increasingly concentrated on risk issues. The legal basis (Article 7, Paragraph 2 of the Atomic Energy Act) for the controversy does not grant the applicant a legal claim to the issuance of a license. This licensing authority retains discretion to grant or deny the license, after due consideration, even if all of the conditions specified in the Atomic Energy Act are fulfilled.

This legal construction is intended to enable the licensing authority to consider carefully everything necessary for the licensing decision. Key here is that the concept "existing scientific knowledge and technology," from Article 7, Paragraph 2, Number 3 of the Atomic Energy Act, is an indeterminate legal term without administrative scope for discretion. Therefore, precautions passed to conform to the latest standards of scientific knowledge and technology, may, under existing law, be fully examined by the courts. Thus the courts must determine the current state of reactor safety research and enter the controversy between scientists and engineers on what is technically necessary, adequate, appropriate, or avoidable. Since neither laws nor ordinances provide sufficient normative evaluation criteria for the courts, each court must produce its own criteria to assess the necessity of precautionary measures; hence the heterogeneity of court rulings in West Germany and the partially contradictory results that have occurred. In short, the courts have a broader scope for review in West Germany than in the other countries studied in this volume. To assist them, the courts must themselves commission experts. This carries with it a danger that the courts may have to become specialized bodies on scientific and technological matters. Controversial court rulings may replace controversial administrative decisions. This has already provoked the charge that judges who are not publicly accountable and who lack sufficient specialized knowledge are altering political decisions in the energy field.

At the policy-making level, the governing parties, the Christian Democratic Union Christian Social Union (CDU/CSU) and the Free Democratic Party (FDP) basically favor the use of nuclear energy. Public controversy is, however, more strongly reflected in internal discussions within the FDP. Opposition within the respective parties to the pronuclear policy of the cabinet has often been strong and has appeared in the resolutions of party conventions since the mid-1970s.

In May 1984, the national convention of the Social Democratic Party (SPD) passed a resolution demanding that reprocessing of nuclear fuel must not be pursued in the Federal Republic of Germany, except for the prototype facility at the Karlsruhe Nuclear Research Center. The delegates decisively linked the expansion of nuclear power to waste reprocessing, branding further nuclear power development as unjustified and irresponsible unless:

(a)   safe isolation of waste from the biosphere is realized;
(b)   technology to support direct disposal is developed to maturity;
(c)   safe operation of the dry interim storage facility at Gorleben undergoes careful review;
(d)   an additional interim storage facility for nuclear waste is built (if required by the volume of waste).

## United Kingdom

Electricity provision in the UK nowadays is a highly centralized activity. The responsibility for determining future demand and guiding investment rests with an informal liaison of the main producers, known as the Electricity Council (though this primarily acts for England and Wales). In practice, the Council acts as part of the industry's lobby in Parliament and Whitehall (the Civil Service), coordinates the public relations for the industry, provides a forum for all electricity promotional groups (e.g., the Nuclear Power Information Group), and undertakes some research (though at a modest level compared with that of the CEGB).

Four generating boards, the CEGB, the South of Scotland Electricity Board (SSEB), the North of Scotland Hydro Electric Board, and the Northern Ireland Electricity Service handle actual electricity production in the United Kingdom. Only the CEGB and the SSEB have constructed nuclear stations. The CEGB, employing over 60,000 (of whom 15,000 are scientists and engineers) and with income in 1984–85 of £6.5 million (UK), is the largest energy supplier in the world outside the USSR. The CEGB has its own Health and Safety Division (Fig. 2.4), responsible for determining design and plant safety levels, a Generation Development and Construction Division where power stations are designed, and Central Electricity Research Laboratories responsible for basic research and all aspects of power generation and development. The SSEB is altogether a smaller concern, with only 12,000 employed and £1 million turnover in 1984–85.

(i) The Central Electricity Generating Board

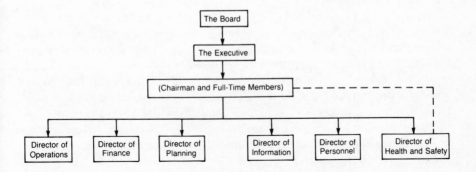

(ii) The National Nuclear Corporation

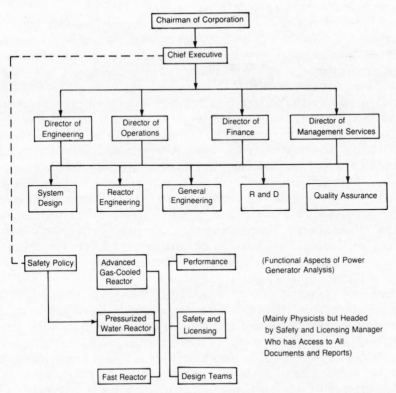

**Figure 2.4** The management of risk in two UK nuclear agencies.

The CEGB and SSEB provide, but do not sell, electricity. The selling occurs through 12 area electricity boards which handle day-to-day servicing and all accounts. The major generating boards, in league with the Electricity Council, fix prices. More recently, however, the government has (controversially) intervened in pricing by restricting the amount of borrowing available to the generating boards. The electricity consumer is, in effect, paying a tax as well as an electricity bill, and, in so doing, funds the government's economic strategies for tax cuts and reduces public sector spending.

The nuclear plant construction industry has passed through many years of administrative turmoil. The power plant industry as a whole (responsible for all electrical power) involves hundreds of companies, employs over 25,000 persons, and is worth £500 million in annual turnover. Before 1973, five consortia, none large enough to construct a sizeable nuclear plant or to possess adequate resources and coordination for plant design engineering safety standards, were responsible for nuclear plant design. In 1973, the merger of two of the major consortia formed the National Nuclear Corporation (NCC). For another eight years the picture remained confused, with the Nuclear Power Company (NPC) constituting a separate body responsible for plant design within the NNC. In 1981, the NNC became a single entity, although the old divisions of opinion remain and management problems persist.

The job of the NNC (Fig. 2.4) is to build nuclear plants to order – that is, to design criteria set by the CEGB or SSEB. Although the company has its own safety and plant design divisions, generating boards undertake most of the work. NNC engineers are part of a team, with a degree of independence but following the lead of the generating boards.

In 1984, however, following criticism of its project-management proposals at the Sizewell B Inquiry, the CEGB established a Project Management Board (PMB) for the PWR. The PMB is a wholly owned subsidiary of the CEGB, with a chairman who is also a member of the CEGB board. A project-management team (PMT), consisting of senior NNC personnel plus representatives from Westinghouse and Bechtel, will manage Sizewell B (and any additional PWRS). A new joint company, about 70 percent of which will be held by Westinghouse and 30 percent by the NNC, will handle the nuclear steam supply system of the Sizewell B PWR, if approved. This company will be wholly responsible for the component ordering, manufacture, and installation of the primary circuit and associated features, whereas design and safety considerations will be in the hands of the PMT.

These new arrangements, long desired by the CEGB but politically difficult to establish (because of the sensitivity over losing an independent design and management group), represent a significant development in the management of British nuclear power. The client is now totally responsible for all aspects of safety standards, design, and manufacture. The NNC is subsidiary to the process, being swallowed by the CEGB in the design side and by Westinghouse in the project management of the nuclear island (the plant inside the inner containment). This means that the operator, though working with American contractors, has complete control of the whole safety case of the PWR. This arrangement has numerous advantages: centralized and coordinated project management; clear line responsibility for plant-safety decisions; and the fusion of construction and operation with risk assessment and plant design. In short, safety considerations permeate the activities of the CEGB.

This all-embracing command structure does, however, have its drawbacks. The regulatory body (the NII) is relatively weaker in the face of such a coordinated organization. Public accountability for safety becomes even more difficult to establish, unless the Inspector in his Sizewell B Inquiry report makes specific recommendations to ensure a greater openness of safety assessment procedures. Without some illumination, there is the danger that self-confidence bred on complacency and insularity will produce variations in inadequately formulated safety criteria (especially if public opinion demands safety standards that are internally regarded as unnecessarily rigorous). Much depends, therefore, on the quality and competence of the various advisory bodies charged with reviewing safety considerations and the extent to which the plant licensing process is subject to open, independent review.

The major advisory and regulatory bodies involved in nuclear plant safety are as follows.

The *UK Atomic Energy Authority* (UKAEA) was established in 1954 with mandates to promote the peaceful use of atomic power, to educate the public as to the benefits of nuclear power, and to undertake research and development into all aspects of nuclear power. Accordingly, the Authority supplies essential information on reactor processes, and, through its subsidiary (British Nuclear Fuels), undertakes research on fuel reprocessing and radioactive waste disposal. The UKAEA has its own Safety and Reliability Directorate which has done much pioneering work on risk assessment and on aspects of risk probability analysis.

The *National Radiological Protection Board* (NRPB) is responsible for overseeing all aspects of radiobiological health and protection (both for workers and for the general public) and is attached to the International Commission on Radiological Protection (ICRP). The NRPB is responsible for research and advice on radiation exposure and injury and assists the safety analysts to devise means for controlling occupational and public exposure to radiation. It also advises the NII on the setting of quantitative standards for plant design and operation.

The official body responsible for nuclear plant safety is the *Nuclear Installations Inspectorate* (NII), now one of many industrial safety organizations embodied within the Health and Safety Executive. The NII consists of 98 employees, of whom 80 percent have experience (mainly on design and operation) in the nuclear industry. In 1985, the NII was short of about ten inspectors as a result of low morale (due to low pay scales relative to the private sector and to the impending move to Liverpool) and the poor quality of potential recruits. In response to parliamentary criticism, the government has reviewed the salaries of its inspectorates with a view to raising them by more than the national norm. The NII hopes to have a full complement of 108 inspectors. The government recognizes the dangers of adverse public reaction to an understaffed and overworked nuclear safety regulatory body. Nevertheless, NII salaries are still 15–20 percent below comparable specialists working for the CEGB, the NNC, or the new PMT (UK Nuclear Installations Inspectorate 1984, pp. 22–4).

Required to be independent of both the industry and the government, the NII enjoys absolute discretion over plant licensing. Its final judgments are not beholden either to the courts or to politicians, though clearly the Inspectorate cannot act arbitrarily or capriciously and must have regard for public and political opinion.

The Inspectorate's problem is how to command public confidence in the contemporary climate of public misgiving over the safety of nuclear power. It seeks to do this by two means. One is by hiring consultants for tasks that require specific expertise. These specialists cannot be employed by the generating boards or the NCC for a period of three years and must notify the NII when approached for employment elsewhere.

The other is to rely on the advice of an independent, quasi-scientific committee, the *Advisory Committee on the Safety of Nuclear Installations*, which reports directly to the Health and Safety Executive. The body also relies heavily on the advice of specialists for assessments of risk probability. The voluntary, part-time Committee comprises distinguished scientists and those associated with the nuclear industry. It could be argued that many of its members are not sufficiently independent of the industry to be truly inquisitive, a point closely examined in the Sizewell B Inquiry. The defense is that, in the UK, people act responsibly when they serve on such committees and are not necessarily slaves to their organizations or to a particular brief. Judging from the close cross-examination of the Health and Safety Executive at the Sizewell Inquiry, it is probable that the membership and the work of that Committee will be the subject of comment by the Inspectorate and that changes may be made to widen its membership and to make its deliberations and reports more open.

The government agency responsible for overseeing all energy matters, including plant safety (but not radioactive waste disposal), is the *Department of Energy*, headed by a Secretary of State who is responsible for licensing all new generating stations, allocating departmental budgets for both R&D and investment by the energy suppliers, and, in cooperation with the Treasury, providing the loan finances for major new stations. The Department of Energy oversees the work of both the UKAEA and the Energy Technology Support Unit responsible for general energy R&D work (plus scenarios of future energy demand); so it is both an advisory and an implementation body. In its Atomic Energy Division, the Department has no specialist advisors on nuclear safety, an omission viewed as a weakness by a parliamentary committee (UK Commons Select Committee on Energy 1981).

The character of the determination of nuclear safety in the United Kingdom is one of consultation, widespread discussion, and purposeful progress through a continual evolution of improved performance. This close network of advice and appraisal distinguishes the British process sharply from those followed in the United States and West Germany. The official view is not only that final responsibility for plant safety and design should rest with the plant operator (the self-regulation principle), but that formal requirements as to precise safety standards (as expressed either in specific numbers of unambiguous codes of guidance) are to be avoided in favor of a more flexible set of standards, constantly subject to review. This means that the plant designer/operator is part of a wide-ranging team of expert advisors, all of whom have a common interest in plant safety. Representatives of both generating boards talk of "quiet but constant pressure" imposed by the NII coupled with a "continuous grinding preoccupation with detail" on the parts of the plant safety teams and the NII.

## Canada

In Canada, the pursuit of nuclear energy as an option for energy policy has occurred primarily in the province of Ontario, although some nuclear capacity now exists in Quebec and New Brunswick. The first small-scale commercial reactor in Canada started operation in Ontario in 1962.

The political economy of energy in Canada and the relative resource endowments of the provinces have led to this concentration of nuclear power in Ontario. Under the British North America Act of 1867, the Canadian provinces own and have full jurisdiction over the resources within their boundaries and, by extension, over energy development within the province. When the Atomic Energy Control Act came into effect in 1946, however, the federal government assumed control of uranium, even though ownership still resided with the provinces. The provinces still, albeit mildly, dispute the federal takeover. This means not only that individual provinces develop their own energy policies but also that such policies tend to be directed to provincial rather than national goals. The federal government, for its part, is responsible for national energy policy planning, has full jurisdiction over any international or interprovincial flows of energy, and possesses several overriding powers of a general nature.

Most provinces have focused upon methods of increasing the degree of provincial self-sufficiency in energy. Ontario has water resources for the generation of hydroelectric power, uranium resources, but almost no hydrocarbon resources. Hence the early development of hydropower, followed by hydrocarbon thermal power and then nuclear power, reflects a conscious effort to remain self-sufficient at the generation level.

Since growth in hydroelectric capacity is approaching resource and economic limits, nuclear power has become the most promising indigenous source for increases in energy production. Moreover, since virtually the entire Canadian nuclear fuel industry is located in Ontario, powerful economic incentives exist to promote nuclear energy. The result has been generally strong provincial political support for the nuclear power program in Ontario.

With respect to the institutional setting for nuclear power, the military origins of the Canadian nuclear power program determined the relative juris-dictions of the federal and provincial governments. The nuclear program emerged out of a cooperative military nuclear research program involving Canada, Britain, and the United States during the 1940s. The result of the national security implications of that research program was that the federal government, under the Atomic Energy Control Act of 1946, asserted primary responsibility over all aspects of nuclear energy (Rowan 1980). Ownership, but not control, of uranium still remained in the hands of the governments of those provinces that contained uranium resources. Moreover, in Canada, the opera-tion and regulation of electrical utilities and electrical supply systems within provincial boundaries is a provincial responsibility (Barry 1981). As a result, two tiers of jurisdiction over nuclear energy developed, with the federal government primarily responsible for the development, demonstration, and regulation of nuclear power in Canada and the provincial governments respon-sible for the construction and day-to-day operation of the major commercial nuclear power plants.

The federal responsibilities are exercised through a number of agencies. Atomic Energy of Canada Limited, a Crown Corporation, is responsible for nuclear research, development, and international marketing. El dorado Nuclear Ltd. is a federally owned uranium exploration, mining, milling, and conversion (to $UF_6$) company. The Atomic Energy Control Board is the federal nuclear regulatory agency with responsibility for radiobiological matters. The relevant provincially owned electric utilities – Ontario Hydro, Quebec Hydro, and the New Brunswick Electric Power Commission – exercise provincial responsibilities. In addition, federal and provincial ministries – such as those for environment, fisheries, resources, and labor – have specific roles to play in regulating the industry.

Because of the dual nature of nuclear jurisdiction in Canada, proposals for nuclear power growth must pass through both federal and provincial regulatory processes. At the provincial level, the decision to build new capacity of any type begins with the Ontario Hydro load forecast. This is used to plan capacity, which in turn leads to a capital requirements forecast. Since new capacity is typically more costly than old, proposed changes in the rate structure usually emerge. As part of the approval process, therefore, Ontario Hydro prepares a rate proposal that the Ontario Ministry of Energy reviews and subsequently refers to the Ontario Energy Board. The Board then holds mandatory public rate hearings and makes recommendations to the Ontario Ministry of Energy. The government of Ontario makes the decision on how much capacity to add.

It is at the federal level that plant safety and nuclear risk issues are con-sidered, largely by review of the Atomic Energy Control Board (Fig. 2.5). The Board must license separately the construction and operating phases of nuclear plants. Issuance of a construction license implies approval for the general design of a plant but it does not imply the automatic granting of an operating license (Wyatt 1980).

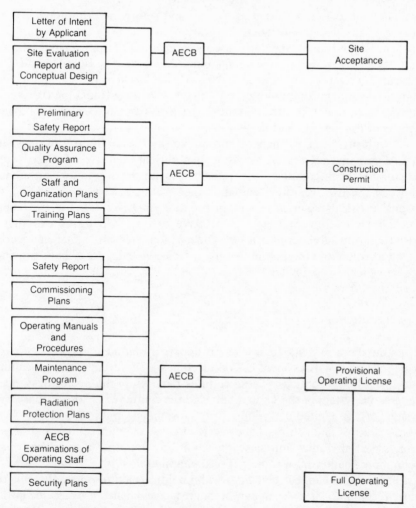

**Figure 2.5** The Atomic Energy Control Board (AECB) licensing process for nuclear power plants in Canada.
*Source*: Atomic Energy of Canada Limited 1982, p. 12; reproduced with permission.

The basic premise of Canadian reactor licensing, like that in the United Kingdom, holds that the nuclear industry is responsible for implementing adequate safety programs, subject to external review and regulation by the government. At the site acceptance stage, the Board's role is limited to indicating whether or not a proposed site is acceptable. At the construction permit stage, the AECB submits a detailed safety report, including design description and specifications on preliminary analyses of potential accidents. Since many design and engineering details of the proposed plant will not be finally determined until construction is actually under way, the safety report must be updated and revised as design progresses and before the provisional and full operating licenses can be issued.

AECB risk and safety standards used in regulation of the Canadian nuclear industry derive from the recommendations of the ICRP. The Board has adopted the estimates of the risks of nuclear exposure published by the ICRP, the United Nations Scientific Committee on the Effects of Atomic Radiation (UNSCEAR), and the US National Research Council's Advisory Committee on the Biological Effects of Ionizing Radiation (BEIR).

As with the United Kingdom, but unlike the United States, Sweden, and West Germany, no generic assessment of nuclear plant risks for the CANDU reactor has been completed in Canada, despite the substantial differences between the CANDU system and the other types of reactors elsewhere. An extensive risk assessment is now in progress, however, for the Darlington Nuclear Generation Station ($4 \times 850$MWe CANDU). Operating experience, based upon typical experience in non-nuclear industries with similar engineering characteristics, and the findings of the US *Reactor safety study* have provided the bases for risk estimates.

## Concluding note

From the discussion above, it is amply apparent that the emergence of large-scale nuclear risk assessment has occurred in widely varying political cultures and institutional contexts. These cultures range from the polycentric, open, adversarial system of the United States to the centralized, closed, consensual system of the United Kingdom, with substantial variation between them. These cultures and settings have surely affected the motivations and uses of large-scale risk studies, but these impacts are not uniform – they certainly have been more significant in some nations than in others. Interestingly, however resistant it would appear that a particular political culture is to embracing this new "technique," it is also apparent that risk assessment has overcome institutional barriers to register its imprint. Clearly this is the case with the notions of Farmer (1977) in the United Kingdom, the *Reactor safety study*, and (perhaps) the KBS studies in Sweden (see Ch. 3). The national studies that follow explore in depth both the effects that these institutional settings have had on risk assessment and the legacies that the large-scale assessments have left in their wake. The generic issues of social and institutional impacts of probabilistic risk analysis are taken up again in Chapter 8.

## References

Atchison, R. J., F. C. Boyd & Z. Domaratzki 1983. Canadian approach to nuclear power safety. *Nuclear Safety* 24, 439–58.

Atomic Energy of Canada Limited (AECL) 1982. *Nuclear reactor safety and related topics*. AECL-6685. Mississauga, Ontario: AECL.

Barry, L. 1981. Interprovincial electrical energy transfers: the constitutional background. In *Energy crisis: policy response*, P. N. Nemetz (ed.). Montreal: Institute for Research on Public Policy.
Bundesgesetz 1976. Gesetz über die friedliche Verwendung der Kernenergie und den Schutz gegen ihre Gefahren (Atomgesetz) von 23. Dezember 1959. In *Der Fassung der Neubekanntmachung*, October 31.

Dahl, R. 1956. *Who governs?* New Haven: Yale University Press.
Douglas, M. & A. Wildavsky 1982. *Risk and culture*. Berkeley: University of California Press.

Ebbin, S. & R. Kasper 1974. *Citizen groups and the nuclear power controversy*. Cambridge, Mass.: MIT Press.

Farmer, F. R. (ed.) 1977. *Nuclear reactor safety*. New York: Academic Press.

Green, H. P. & A. Rosenthal 1967. *Government of the atom*. New York: Atherton Press.
Gross, J. & S. Rayner 1985. *Measuring culture*. New York: Columbia University Press.

Madison, J. 1911. In *The federalist*, no. 10 (Everyman edn.). London: J. M. Dent.

Pershagen, B. & R. Nilson 1984. Nuclear safety in Sweden: policy and practice. *Nuclear Safety* **25**, 1–18.

Rowan, M. 1980. Nuclear policy and federal provincial relations. In *Canadian nuclear policies*, G. B. Doern & R. W. Morrison (eds.). Montreal: Institute for Research on Public Policy.

Stever, D. W. Jr. 1980. *Seabrook and the Nuclear Regulatory Commission*. Hanover, New Hampshire: University Press of New England.

UK Commons Select Committee on Energy 1981. *The government's statement on the new nuclear power programme*. HC Paper 114-1. London: HMSO.
UK Nuclear Installations Inspectorate 1984. *The relationship between NII's assessment principles and levels of risk*. NII/S/83(SAF). London: The Inspectorate.

Wyatt, A. 1980. The development of nuclear controls and licensing in Canada. In *Canadian nuclear policies*, G. B. Doern & R. W. Morrison (eds.). Montreal: Institute for Research on Public Policy.

# 3 *Major energy risk assessments in Sweden: information flow and impacts*

BENGT HANSSON

Sweden has been a leader in the production and use of large-scale assessment as a component of national energy policy analysis. Beginning in 1969, a number of major assessments have enjoyed wide circulation and coverage in the Swedish press; but the actual role and usefulness of major risk studies in the formation of societal opinion and decision making remain unclear. This chapter inquires into this issue. The scientific accuracy and technical quality of the studies are of interest only insofar as they affect political decision making or public opinion. The focus here, as in the volume as a whole, is upon major energy, and particularly nuclear power, risk studies.

The discussion that follows examines four aspects of social and governmental response:

(a)  How the studies were interpreted: What features did key groups advocate in the political process and in the mass media? What aspects did they mute or ignore?
(b)  The extent to which the studies served to clarify the risks.
(c)  The success of the studies in narrowing the scientific debate.
(d)  The impact of the studies upon safety measures and regulatory policy.

To address these issues, a number of specific projects were designed and implemented. A detailed report of the findings follows an initial characterization of the major Swedish risk studies examined. The chapter concludes with a discussion of the flows of risk communication and information and potential means of improving them.

## Seven energy risk studies and their receptions

This section presents a brief description of each of the seven major risk studies analyzed. Attention focuses upon the study objectives, approach adopted, major findings, and initial media and public response. The next section will then pursue, comparatively and in greater depth, the nature of the societal response.

THE *CLOSE-SITING* STUDY (NÄRFÖRLÄGGNINGSUTREDNINGEN)

In 1968, the Electricity Supply Authority of Stockholm applied for permission to erect a nuclear combined power and district-heating plant at Värtan, a site only a few kilometers from the center of Stockholm. Since there was no precedent for such an urban site, the safety authorities required further theoretical and empirical studies. Accordingly, in 1969, a broad study of the problems involved in close siting commenced, involving collaboration among governmental authorities, the utilities concerned, and AB Atomenergi, a state-owned corporation. The task of the study was to analyze both the economic and environmental justifications for such close siting and the attendant safety problems. In early 1970, the study was reorganized as a governmental committee.

The committee received a mandate to pursue the study in a general way, disconnected from any specific licensing matter. The environmental aspects included a comparison of the environmental effects of nuclear and oil-fired power stations during normal conditions, mainly with respect to airborne pollution in the form of radioactivity and fumes. The other main task concerned safety problems. The committee was required to analyze how distance influenced risk. Dispersion conditions during atmospherical releases were singled out for special study. Finally, the study was also to analyze the roles of reactor containment, emergency core-cooling systems, and other accident-preventing or consequence-mitigating features.

The members of the committee were all high officials with technical expertise from the utilities and governmental authorities. They published their report, *Close-siting of nuclear power stations*, in June 1974 (Närförläggningsutredningen 1974). Some 20 technical reports supplemented the main report.

After a short discussion of previously accepted criteria for the construction and siting of nuclear power plants, including the concepts of maximum credible accident (MCA), design basis accident (DBA), and maximum hypothetical accident (MHA), the committee argued that a more complete, quantitative analysis was needed. In support of this position, they offered three main reasons:

(a)  a cost–benefit analysis of nuclear power is desirable and requires a numerical analysis;
(b)  the DBA concept neglects the properties of the environment, particularly atmospheric conditions and patterns of habitation;
(c)  a detailed quantitative analysis could also be a useful tool in choosing optimal safety systems.

The committee used two reference constructions of nuclear plants, one pressurized-water reactor (PWR), and one boiling-water reactor (BWR), both basically corresponding to existing Swedish plants and assumed to be located in the vicinity of a model city with 1 million inhabitants. The committee considered four different sites, located 5, 20, 40, and 100 km from the center of the city. The model city comprised 60° sectors, with a population distribution modeled on the actual distribution for Stockholm.

The committee explicitly sought to calculate both the probability and the consequences of various types of accidents. The discussion of probability, however, is rather sketchy. It begins with a short survey of available empirical data concerning specific components used in a nuclear power plant and of generally applied methods of quality control and inspection. Although the discussion notes reservations concerning the accuracy of the figures used, the committee claims that the measures for estimation were consistent, so that the relative probabilities of different accidents should be more reliable than the absolute values. Despite an acknowledgment of the problems of common-cause failures and of human errors, no consistent way of treating them was indicated.

As for accident consequences, the committee first held that only the worst accidents carried any significant hazards to the environment. For each site, the study defines a number of release types, based on release height, released fractions of noble gases and iodine, and release time. For each combination of site, type of release, and type of injury (death, acute radiation syndrome, early disturbance of thyroid function, or indicated abortion), the number of injuries for each hour in the meteorological statistics were computed, taking into account population distribution, wind direction, and other dispersal data.

The results appear in a series of two-dimensional diagrams, relating magnitudes of consequences to frequencies of accidents. These diagrams reflected the same general idea as those used later in the *Reactor safety study* (us Nuclear Regulatory Commission 1975), but the curves were not smoothed but drawn stepwise for different categories of consequences. All the computed results from the many different combinations of site, type of release, and type of effect were placed as points against a constant background histogram. In this background histogram, the accident levels for other risks (road traffic in Sweden, commercial aviation, etc.) were drawn and displayed against two other levels, one reflecting the upper permissible limit for a single nuclear plant, and the other the complete Swedish nuclear program. These levels had been computed on the assumption that the long-term average effect should be at most one injury per year at a total installed nuclear program of 50,000 MWe.

Grouping the results of the computations according to the distance from the site to the center of the city reveals no significant difference between locations at 100 km and 40 km. At these distances, the figures estimate no deaths for any combination of release type and weather conditions. At a distance of 20 km, a small number of deaths occurs in some cases, and the number of other types of injury tends to increase about ten times in comparison to the site at 40 km. In the case of 5 km, finally, one combination of release type and weather conditions would cause some 400 deaths.

In its conclusion, the committee stated that economic reasons and the need to reduce airborne pollution argue that heat production in Sweden's metropolitan areas be based on nuclear power plants. Moreover, the expected number of fatalities and other injuries from releases during both normal and accident conditions is lower than that accepted for many other activities. Since most of the fatalities in the 5 km case occurred very close to the reactor, a restricted zone with a radius of 2 km around the reactor significantly reduced the number of fatalities, as did a specially designed containment building. It was further noted that economic considerations did not require *very* close siting, and that a distance of 20 km was also economically interesting. The committee recommended, therefore, the use of nuclear power for district heating in metropolitan areas but cautioned against very close sites pending the acquisition of further experience.

Press coverage of the study immediately applied the recommendations to a proposal to build a nuclear plant in Haninge, at a site that happened to be situated some 20 km from the center of Stockholm. News reports had it that the local government of Haninge opposed the erection of the plant. This opposition was probably seen as an embryonic popular fight against nuclear power (the nuclear question was about to become a crucial one in Sweden).

*Dagens Nyheter*, Sweden's largest newspaper, misquoted the study by concluding that nuclear power was so safe that an accident with severe consequences could not happen. This newspaper summarized only one part of the *Close-siting* study – the possibility of evacuating a large number of people in the case of an accident at a close site. The study concluded that no such evacuation is possible, and that a siting decision, therefore, had to be based on safety evaluations that did not presume any consequence reduction due to such a safety measure.

Most other newspapers followed the text of the Swedish news agency, Tidningarnas Telegrambyrå (TT), which allotted approximately equal attention to safety questions and economic and environmental effects. The agency categorically interpreted the recommendation to avoid pronounced close siting to mean that 5 km was too limited a distance, whereas 20 would be enough. The text stated that the worst possible accident would involve only some 10 fatalities within a radius of 2 km. In actual fact, the study itself admitted the possibility of accidents with some 400 fatalities. It was further stated that the risk for an accident in which persons might be injured was between $10^{-6}$ and $10^{-7}$ per 1,000,000 reactor–years. The correct figure, according to the study, is ten times larger.

The study produced some interesting findings, not observed in the media or in subsequent discussions, possibly because they received insufficient attention in the study's own summary. One significant finding suggests that the great gain in safety seems to lie in the step from 20 to 40 km, rather than in the step from 5 to 20. In the 20–40 km region, fatalities would be reduced to nil and other types of injuries reduced by a factor of about 10. The other interesting fact is that release height and fraction of iodine released were more important factors than the remoteness of the site. Indeed, the figures in the study suggest that a containment to force releases upward or a filter to reduce iodine releases would, from a safety viewpoint, be more efficient than moving the plant further away.

## THE ÅKA STUDY

The first Swedish research reactor came on line in 1954. For some time, Swedish nuclear ambitions were directed towards heavy-water reactors, one of which was in operation during 1964–74 in Ågesta, near Stockholm. During the latter part of the 1960s, several commercial light-water reactors were ordered. By 1973, one station was in operation, three were about to be started, and five more were on order or in different stages of construction. The owners of the first station had a reprocessing agreement with Windscale (now Sellafield) in the United Kingdom, but few other provisions addressed spent fuel and radioactive waste. Given a recognition that foreign countries might over the long run adopt more restrictive attitudes toward the reprocessing of Swedish fuel, it was important to investigate the possibilities for a Swedish reprocessing plant.

The Minister for Industrial Affairs therefore appointed, in 1973, a committee to analyze technical, economic, and safety-related problems connected with reprocessing of spent nuclear fuel, treatment and storing of radioactive waste, and the transport of radioactive material. More specifically, the committee was to find suitable methods for the handling of radioactive waste in Sweden, to investigate the possibilities of coordinating the handling of low- and medium-level wastes with high-level wastes, to study the possibilities of erecting a reprocessing plant in Sweden, and to review various organizational matters.

The report (Åka 1976a) was to a large extent a compilation of existing knowledge. Extensive surveys reviewed the current practices for handling radioactive waste in a large number of countries, the current state of reprocessing techniques, and of research and development both in international organizations and in individual countries. The most important empirical work initiated by the committee was a geological study in northern Sweden, which showed that existing technology was sufficient for locating a repository in rock free from cracks and containing only a minimum of groundwater.

The committee recommended that high-level waste should be vitrified or combined with ceramic materials and encapsulated in waterproof containers, to be stored in the primary rocks of Sweden. A qualitative examination of the risks connected with natural processes, such as volcanic activity, erosion, earthquakes, and glaciation, found them to be insignificant. Rather, the Åka study, pointing out the need for more basic data concerning the movement and composition of groundwater at deep levels, the solubility of the vitrified waste, the corrosiveness of various encapsulating materials, and various sorption processes in the surrounding materials, claimed that the unavailability of such data rendered impossible a detailed risk analysis.

As for reprocessing, the committee recommended the reprocessing of spent fuels from Swedish reactors and the initiation of studies to explore the erection of a Swedish reprocessing plant. It also recommended, however, the commencement of studies to examine the conditions for direct disposal, mainly by following developments in other countries. Insofar as the committee also noted that no detailed studies of direct disposal of unreprocessed spent fuel had been made anywhere in the world, the likelihood of direct disposal was minimal.

At the organizational level the committee recommended, successfully, the establishment of a special department in the Swedish Nuclear Inspectorate and a special governmental organization with responsibility for taking adequate measures to institute a plant for final disposal of radioactive waste. The organizations came to play important roles in the subsequent treatment of the waste problem.

The press paid little attention to the committee's report when it was published. The relative absence of "hard" facts, combined with the largely parliamentary membership of the committee apparently shaped a public perception of the report as more the manifestation of political will than a statement about factual matters. It seems fair to say that the lasting impact of the Åka study was that it served as a basis for the upcoming studies of nuclear reactor safety (KBS 1977, 1979).

### ENERGY, HEALTH, ENVIRONMENT

In the mid-1970s, the nuclear issue was rapidly commanding national concern. The proponents were driven less by a particular fondness for nuclear power than by the negative environmental effects of other sources of energy. It had been agreed for about a decade that the hydropower program should be halted for environmental reasons. Since coal- and oil-fired plants also adversely affected land use, notably through the $SO_2$ problem, it was natural that the first comparative study of different sources of energy be initiated, not by the Minister for Industrial Affairs, but by the Minister for Agriculture.

In February 1976, he appointed the Swedish Governmental Committee on Energy and the Environment to evaluate existing research results and present them in a way that facilitated comparisons of different energy sources. Since such comparisons were necessary for political decisions that lay a few years ahead, energy sources (e.g., oil, coal, nuclear power, and hydropower) already in use by industry were of special interest. Priority was to be given to potential health and environmental problems in Sweden.

The Committee made no attempt to develop a methodology for integrating the total risk picture for each energy source. Since it had no mandate to propose solutions to specific problems, it did not offer formal recommendations in its report (Swedish Governmental Committee on Energy and the Environment 1977, Ministry of Agriculture and Environment 1978). Rather, its findings describe the various types of negative health and environmental effects. Second, the committee describes for each energy source the most important health and environmental effects and provides a qualitative comparison among them. A coal plant, for example, might increase the cancer risk for the general public as much as, or even several times more than, a nuclear plant. Moreover, the health effects of nuclear power under normal conditions are small compared with those from oil and coal. Finally, the committee opines that the most important problems for nuclear power are the disposal of high-level waste, the risk of major accidents, and the uncontrolled proliferation of fissionable material that might be used for weapons.

Of all the studies treated in this chapter, *Energy, health, environment* received the least attention in the Swedish press. One possible explanation is that since the Committee had not been required to propose solutions to any current problems, its activities had a low news value. Another possible explanation is that the scope of the new Energy Commission, appointed while the Committee was working, encompassed the mandate of the previous Committee. The media officials may well have believed, therefore, that the committee's report was not the final word on the subject.

The news agency material, which was simply a slightly shortened version of the Committee's own press release, appeared in most newspapers. It is remarkable that all three of the newspapers selected for special study in this analysis chose to focus on the cancer risk. The headlines reflect confusion about what the study really said. One paper announced "Coal and nuclear give the same cancer risk"; another declared that "Cancer risk in Europe increases also with coal-fired power plants," and the third proclaimed "Coal plant increases risk for cancer." The interesting fact that the Committee found nuclear power to be superior to coal with respect to *all* health effects never made its way into either the headlines or the text. Almost nothing about the assessment, except the news agency material, ever came to the attention of the general public.

THE TWO KBS REPORTS

1976 was a dramatic year for nuclear power in Sweden. In May, the Åka Committee published its report, which recommended the erection of a reprocessing plant in Sweden, thereby supporting the development of the nuclear industry. In the general elections in September, the nuclear issue played a crucial role. The popular vote was for, rather than against, nuclear power: the two parties (the Centre Party and the Communists) that were openly against nuclear power lost in the election, but two other nonsocialist parties in the Parliament, the Moderates (pronuclear) and the People's Party (vaguely pronuclear) won enough votes to overthrow the Social Democrat government (strongly pronuclear) and to form a new government together with the Centre Party. Since the Moderates were not strongly pronuclear, the Centre Party became the most influential of the three coalition parties with regard to energy questions. So, despite the popular vote, the election brought, for the first time, antinuclear forces into a government position.

The government quickly passed the so-called "Stipulation Law" (SFS 1977, Sweden 1977), the second section of which reads:

If application at the State Nuclear Power Inspectorate for final permission for starting a nuclear reactor has not been requested before October 8, 1976 it is prohibited to load nuclear fuel into the reactor without special permission from the Government. Permission is only granted provided the owner of the reactor

(1)  has presented a contract, which in a reliable way covers the need for reprocessing of used nuclear fuels, and in addition has showed, how and where an absolutely safe final storage of the high active waste from the reprocessing can be achieved, or
(2)  has shown how and where an absolutely safe final storage of spent unreprocessed nuclear fuel can be done.

The nuclear industry immediately reacted by forming a project group called "*Projekt Kärnbränslesäkerhet*" ("nuclear fuel safety"), or KBS. Its task was simply to show that the requirements of the Stipulation Law were satisfied. In fact, KBS intended to satisfy both alternative clauses in the section quoted above. The organization of the work within KBS was determined by the requirements of the Stipulation Law: to show *how* final storage can be made, to show *where* it can be made, and to show that it is *absolutely safe*. The last part is the most interesting one in the context of this volume.

The basic idea adopted by KBS paralleled that of the Åka Committee. KBS assumed that disposal would be in Swedish primary rocks at a depth of about 500 m. The reprocessing case assumed that the waste was vitrified. In both cases, the spent fuel/waste was to be encapsulated in materials with high resistance against corrosion.

The main components of the safety analysis were calculations of the temperature and radiation levels in the waste, discussion of possible corrosion processes concerning the capsules, determination of the amount of groundwater and its chemical properties, determination of the permeability of the rock, and estimation of the effects of various sorption processes in the clay in which the capsules are embedded and in the surrounding rock. The most critical group of affected persons were identified as those who live close to the repository and who take their drinking water from a well in the neighborhood. The maximum radiation doses to the critical group occurred after 200,000 years and amounted to 10 millirem per 30 years under probable conditions (and up to 40 times that figure under unfavorable conditions). Comparisons with natural radiation, current limits for nuclear power plants, and the natural content of radium-226 in drinking water (all of which were found to be higher) put these figures into perspective.

The press showed relatively little interest in the actual contents of the KBS reports, except for the conclusion that the project considered the requirements of the Stipulation Law to be satisfied. Instead, the interest focused on the political implications of the study. The day the first KBS report was released, the nuclear industry, with the French company Cogema, presented a reprocessing contract and an application to start the Ringhals 3 nuclear plant. The government thus found itself having to take a decision that would become a precedent for the whole nuclear program. (The government finally approved the application for Ringhals 3, thereby admitting that the Stipulation Law was satisfied. However, the decision lost considerable importance when the nuclear issue was later submitted to a referendum.)

## THE ENERGY COMMISSION REPORT

Since the new government which assumed office in October 1976 comprised three parties with divergent views on energy in general and nuclear energy in particular, the energy issue was initially postponed. The mechanism chosen to do this was the appointment of a special commission, charged with preparing a policy for Sweden's future energy system, setting forth a number of major policy alternatives and assessing the risks, environmental effects, impacts on national security, and the costs associated with each.

The Commission's report (Energikommissionen 1978) consists of 12 chapters on different energy sources: coal, oil, natural gas, peat, shales, nuclear power, wind energy, solar energy, biomass, geothermic energy, and "others." Two chapters address special energy carriers: electricity and alcohols. The report also attempts to discuss, in a comparative manner, the waste problem and the risks of catastrophic accidents for *all* energy sources.

The Energy Commission submitted its final report in March, 1978, at a time when it had access only to a preliminary version of the report from its Subcommittee for Safety and Environment. Consequently, the conclusions and recommendations of the Commission were somewhat preliminary as far as they concerned safety and environmental effects. The subcommittee had initiated a number of studies of the probability and consequences of an accident in a nuclear power plant. In its final evaluation, the Commission concludes that the probability estimates for a core melt fall roughly within the uncertainty intervals of the studies made. The attempts to estimate the consequences, however, led to more divergent results, mainly concerning geologic disposal. The Commission points out that the probability of a core melt with very serious consequences is extraordinarily small and concludes that the decisive question is whether nuclear power risks are acceptable with regard to available alternatives and the social utility of the activity. Its answer is clearly in the affirmative.

However, a minority of three members disagreed, stating that they had found that the risks associated with nuclear power were generally correctly assessed by the Subcommittee on Safety and Environment but that the majority of the Commission had treated this background material in a misleading and incomplete way. When the final report of the Subcommittee became available, the majority, now only 10 out of 15 members, found no reason to change anything in its conclusions and recommendations.

The press focused on the antagonism within the Commission and largely ignored the factual content. An exception was *Dagens Nyheter*, the major morning newspaper in Sweden, which carried a very intensive debate about nuclear power. The newspaper printed most of the material on nuclear safety produced by the Subcommittee. Even in *Dagens Nyheter*, however, the need for collecting comparable data for all the various sources of energy was lost. Most of the systematic efforts of the Subcommittee went unnoticed by both the Commission and the public.

## *SAFE NUCLEAR POWER?* THE SWEDISH REACTOR SAFETY STUDY

A short time after the accident at Three Mile Island, the leader of the Social Democrat Party, Olaf Palme, announced that his party now favored a referendum on the nuclear issue, an idea which they had previously opposed. The other parties soon followed suit, and the referendum was set for March 1980. Soon after this decision, the Minister for Industrial Affairs appointed the Reactor Safety Committee, charged with considering whether there was reason to re-evaluate the risks associated with nuclear power and to analyze what measures should be taken to improve the security at Swedish nuclear power plants. The instructions were specific: investigate whether (a) the type of accident that occurred at Three Mile Island had figured in safety analyses of the Three Mile Island plant or similar plants, (b) the accident deviated essentially from what could be expected, (c) a corresponding accident could happen in a Swedish nuclear power plant (and how high the probability of such an event is). The Committee presented its report *Safe nuclear power?* (*Säker kärnraft?*), in November 1979 (Reaktorsäkerhetsutredningen 1979).

As to whether an accident similar to the one at Three Mile Island could happen in Swedish reactors, the Committee noted that most Swedish reactors are boiling-water reactors (BWRs) and thus less vulnerable to such an accident than are pressurized-water reactors (PWRs), such as the ones at Three Mile Island. At the time, only one Swedish PWR (Ringhals 2) was in operation, with two more under construction. The Committee concluded that accidents such as that at Three Mile Island could have happened and could still happen at Ringhals 2, but that the probability was lower than at Three Mile Island. This difference was due chiefly to better instrumentation but was also attributable to newly installed safety arrangements.

The report also reviewed previous safety studies. One of the technical appendices offers an evaluation of the general methodology of probabilistic risk analyses (PRAS). The main report focuses on previous Swedish studies (which, in turn, rely heavily upon foreign studies). The factual basis consists of the material collected by the Committee on Energy and Environment and the Subcommittee for Safety and Environment of the Energy Commission. (It is noteworthy that the Close Siting Committee received no mention.) The Swedish Reactor Safety Committee concluded that it had found no reason to re-evaluate the picture of nuclear risks that emerges from the reports of these two previous committees.

The Committee also evaluated the conclusions and recommendations of the

Energy Commission. It concluded that those who had founded their views on nuclear risks on the conclusions of the final report of the Energy Commission without having penetrated the background material had come away with an insufficiently modulated, incomplete picture of the safety questions of nuclear power. This was due principally to the uncertainties connected with the estimation of probabilities for a severe reactor accident. The Committee also concluded that substantially greater demands had to be made for the security of nuclear plants, from the construction of the reactors to daily maintenance.

When combined, these two answers from the Reactor Safety Committee to the question whether a need existed to re-evaluate the risks associated with nuclear power, give the conclusion that the nuclear industry, relevant authorities, and (perhaps) responsible politicians have not observed much of what has been known in principle. In particular, the conclusions of the Committee imply, albeit in very measured terms, a criticism of the Energy Commission which is quite unusual in Swedish committee life.

Reacting favorably to the study by the Swedish Reactor Safety Committee, both the nuclear industry and the authorities incorporated most of its 40 suggestions into their working plans. In addition, the press coverage was impressive, greater than for any of the other risk studies discussed here. The somewhat intricate character of the Committee's answer to the question of whether nuclear risks should be re-evaluated turned out to be a hotbed for miscellaneous interpretations. The study was cited in support for all sides in the referendum. "Confirms that an accident can happen," "Could happen also at Ringhals 2," "There are reasons to make greater security demands," and "False feelings of security" are some of the headlines that spotlighted the need for better safety, whereas "No new view of accident risks," "Harrisburg has made nuclear power safer!," and "Great concentration on increased safety" headlined a sense of complacency. But one newspaper, *Dagens Nyheter*, summarized the conclusion of the Committee rather well, though in language blunter than that in the Committee's report, in a sharp headline: "Accident risks known – politicians have closed their eyes."

## Uses and impacts of the risk studies

As noted above, various goals and aspirations accompany the initiation and conduct of major risk studies. The discussion that follows examines in comparative perspective the actual uses and impacts of the seven studies. Included are the responses of the press and politicians as well as the impacts on scientists and nuclear safety.

### THE INITIAL PRESS RESPONSE

Few technical issues have concerned the Swedish people as much as nuclear power. The mass media have obviously played an important role in the

**Table 3.1** The newspapers.

| Newspaper | Place | Covering | Circulation | Attitude |
|---|---|---|---|---|
| Svenska Dagbladet | Stockholm | national | 191,800 | pro |
| Dagens Nyheter | Stockholm | nat./reg. | 403,700 | con |
| Göteborgs-Posten | Göteberg | regional | 292,700 | pro |
| Sudsvenska Dagbladet | Malmö | regional | 115,100 | pro |
| Arbetet | Malmö | regional | 102,900 | pro |
| Skånska Dagbladet | Malmö | local | 29,500 | con |
| Uppsala Nya Tidning | Uppsala | local | 58,700 | pro |
| Barpometern/Oskarshamnstidningen | Kalmar | local | 54,100 | pro |
| Hallands Nyheter | Falkenberg | local | 28,200 | con |

formation of public opinion. This analysis sought, therefore, to document the role of the mass media in the initial reception of the published risk studies.

The research reported on here[1] examined nine daily morning newspapers (Table 3.1). *Svenska Dagbladet* is Sweden's only truly national newspaper, although *Dagens Nyheter* has the largest circulation. *Göteborgs-Posten* was chosen as a representative of the Press in Gothenburg, and *Sudsvenska Dagbladet* was chosen because it is the dominant newspaper in southern Sweden. *Arbetet* and *Skånska Dagbladet* were chosen because they are the main newspapers supporting the Social Democratic and Centre Parties, respectively. The three local newspapers are the ones with the greatest circulation in the localities where nuclear power sites are located. No such local newspaper could be chosen for the Barsebäck site near Mälmo, however, since *Sudsvenska Dagbladet* has by far the greatest circulation in that neighborhood.

For each of the seven risk studies, the nine newspapers were scanned for a period stretching from seven days before to seven days after the date of publication. Each article was coded on several indicators, some of a quantitative or formal character, others covering certain aspects of the content. The study found approximately 300 relevant articles, which filled a little less than 9,000 cm of text. Two-thirds was news material, one-quarter editorials, and the remainder mainly press releases and a few discussion articles. No significant differences emerged between the national/regional papers and the local ones, but papers that were against nuclear power tended to give more editorial space, proportionally speaking, to the risk studies. *Sudsvenska Dagbladet*, usually regarded as the most pronouncedly pronuclear paper, was extreme in the other direction: it published only one editorial on the risk studies (no other paper published less than five).

Figure 3.1 shows the amount of column space allotted to the different reports. Although no time trend is evident, it is apparent that the two reactor safety studies received the most attention (average = 950 cm), the three studies of radioactive waste commanded less interest (700 cm), and the two comparative studies were the least interesting (550 cm). It is worth noting that

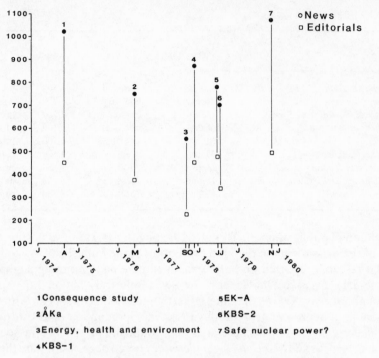

**Figure 3.1**  Press coverage of the major risks studies.

KBS-2 (KBS 1979) met the disadvantage of appearing during the holiday season when news coverage traditionally is less intense.

Another opportunity for comparison arises in connection with the referendum. The Swedish Reactor Safety Committee was only one of two committees charged with preparing a factual basis for the referendum. The other committee was charged with analyzing the economic consequences of abandoning nuclear power as a source of energy. The latter committee published its report – the *Consequence study* – at about the same time (November 1979) as the Reactor Safety Committee. The *Consequence study* (Konsekvensutredningen 1979) received twice as much attention as the *Safe nuclear power?*, commanded bigger headlines, and was more often on the front pages. This pattern holds when the papers are analyzed individually. In fact, the *Consequence study* caused quite a stir. Opponents of nuclear power branded it scandalous and biased in its choice of calculation parameters. So, although the *Safe nuclear power?* was the *risk* study that attracted the most attention, it was not the most noticed study of *nuclear power*.

The news media are obviously sensitive to different sources of information. The present study examined six categories of "participant" – the committee, politicians, environmentalists and antinuclear groups, scientists, utilities, and others – for their treatment by the media. Generally speaking, the committee and politicians were those most frequently cited, but the relative frequency of citation differs from one risk study to another. The press betrayed a clear tendency to regard some studies as "political" and others as "expert," a classification that does not always correspond to the actual composition of the committee. The most "political" study is Åka, with 63 percent of the space given to the comments made by politicians (and only 26 percent to the committee – including summaries of the content). But in the case of the report of Subcommittee A of the Reactor Safety Committee (EK-A 1978) and *Safe nuclear power?* (Reaktorsäkerhetsutredningen 1979), the Press also quoted politicians more frequently than the Committee itself, even though the Reactor Safety Committee was a typical expert committee.

On the other hand, for the *Close-siting, Energy, health, environment*, and the two KBS studies, the Press allocated less than half the amount of space to comments of politicians than to those of the committee itself. Somewhat surprisingly, the Press was interested only in comments from scientists in connection with the two KBS reports.

The picture that emerges is a press interested in interviewing or obtaining comments from politicians when a study contains results of immediate importance, as in the case of the *Åka study* (Åka 1976a, 1976b), EK-A (1978), and *Safe nuclear power?* (Reaktorsäkerhetsutredningen 1979). Comparatively more attention is given to the factual content of the study when the study has a more compilatory or theoretical character, as in the cases of the *Close-siting* study (Närförläggningsutredningen 1974), *Energy, health, environment* (Ministry of Agriculture and Environment 1978), and the two KBS (1977, 1978) reports.

Finally, in regard to various types of issues posed for society, safety questions have dominated. About 40 percent of the editorial material dealt with accident risks and about 10 percent with siting and emergency plans. Thus, safety in a broad sense was the topic of approximately 50 percent of the editorial material. This percentage stayed fairly constant over time, with a low of 37 percent for the *Close-siting* study to a maximum of 61 percent for *Safe nuclear power?* A slight increase observable over time, is too small to exclude chance. The same trend was observable in the news material, although the percentages were slightly higher throughout. Only for the *Close-siting* study and *Energy, health, environment* did the press discuss economic matters to a significant degree (19 percent). Surprisingly enough, ecology and environment attracted even less discussion (the average figure was only 3 percent).

Breakdown of these figures for each of the separate newspapers indicates a surprising uniformity in the broader categories. Upon closer examination, however, certain differences between pro- and antinuclear newspapers emerge. The editorials of the antinuclear Press seem to avoid the topic of reactor safety, whereas the pronuclear papers eschew emergency planning. Both sides obviously recognized their weaknesses.

USE IN THE REFERENDUM DEBATE[2]

When it was decided to hold a national referendum on nuclear power, Sweden had six nuclear power plants in operation, four more ready to start, and two

under construction. The referendum posed three alternatives, none of which
was unrestrictedly pronuclear. Alternatives 1 and 2 – in this connection called
"lines" – called for using all 12 plants for their full economic life, estimated to
be 25 years. Line 2 had a number of additional clauses which called for the
stimulation of energy conservation, an intensification of research and development about renewable energy sources, special safety studies for each reactor,
and, in principle, state or local ownership of facilities for nuclear power
production. Line 3 prohibited the starting of any new plants and provided for
those already in operation to be shut down within 10 years. Line 1 was officially
supported by the Moderates, line 2 by the People's Party and the Social
Democrats, and line 3 by the Centre Party and the Communists. (None of the
lines, it should be noted, won an absolute majority: line 2 received 39.1
percent, line 3 38.7 percent, and line 1 18.9 percent of the votes.)

To analyze the treatment of the risk reports in the referendum coverage,
three newspapers and a TV news program were examined during the five weeks
immediately preceding the March, 1980 referendum on nuclear power. *Dagens
Nyheter* is Sweden's largest morning paper, published in Stockholm, not formally connected to any political party but with liberal traditions, which supported line 3. *Aftonbladet*, the second largest evening paper, also published in
Stockholm, represents the Social Democrats and supported line 2. *Borås
Tidning* is a fairly large local newspaper, published in Borås; it represents the
Moderates and supported line 1. In addition the TV news program "Rapport"
was studied. According to current Swedish rules, news reporting on radio and
TV should be objective and impartial. The objective was to study *all* types of risk
reports, not only the major Swedish ones. The adoption of a broad definition of
"risk study" included university research reports and some economic studies
concerned with nuclear power.

The most striking result (Table 3.2) is the large number (64) of references to
the study *More efficient emergency planning*, performed by the State Radiation
Protection Institute (Statens Strålskyddsinstitut 1979–80). Two probable
reasons may account for this spotlight. The first concerns timing – the main part
of the study was published in December 1979, but one part, which contained a
scenario of a large reactor accident at the Barsebäck site, was not published
until February 1980 (i.e., a month and a half before the referendum). Therefore, this study had a news value that most of the other studies lacked.

It is also worthwhile to note the extensive citation, greater than any of the
proper risk studies, of the *Consequence* study. This agrees with the findings
reported above and is not surprising for a study published only four or five
months before the referendum.

More remarkable is that neither the Åka study nor *Energy, health, environment* was mentioned at all during the period studied. The oldest study, the one
on close siting, was almost totally neglected, and it seems clear that the older
studies have been superseded by the newer ones (*Safe nuclear power?*, the Åka
study, the two KBS studies, and *Energy, health, environment*) in the public
consciousness.

**Table 3.2**  References to risk studies.

| Risk study | Number | "Rapport" (%) | Dagens Nyheter (%) | Afton-bladet (%) | Borås Tidning (%) | Total (%) |
|---|---|---|---|---|---|---|
| Energy Commission | 16 | 0 | 4 | 2 | 2 | 3 |
| *Close-siting study* | 2 | 0 | 1 | 1 | 0 | 1 |
| *Safe nuclear power?* | 23 | 0 | 4 | 8 | 4 | 4 |
| *Consequence study* | 64 | 9 | 12 | 10 | 13 | 11 |
| Åka study | 0 | 0 | 0 | 0 | 0 | 0 |
| *Energy, health, environment* | 0 | 0 | 0 | 0 | 0 | 0 |
| *More efficient emergency planning* | 110 | 32 | 17 | 27 | 14 | 20 |
| war risk study | 10 | 5 | 2 | 1 | 1 | 2 |
| other studies by authorities | 45 | 0 | 9 | 8 | 13 | 8 |
| KBS 1 & 2 | 20 | 0 | 5 | 2 | 3 | 4 |
| local consequence studies | 29 | 5 | 4 | 0 | 11 | 5 |
| other commercial studies | 7 | 1 | 3 | 1 | 1 | 1 |
| Becker study | 13 | 1 | 4 | 1 | 1 | 2 |
| other university studies | 34 | 8 | 8 | 0 | 3 | 6 |
| US *Reactor safety study* | 19 | 3 | 5 | 1 | 2 | 3 |
| Kemeny report | 8 | 1 | 1 | 3 | 1 | 1 |
| Rogovin report | 4 | 1 | 1 | 1 | 0 | 1 |
| other Three Mile Island reports | 14 | 6 | 3 | 2 | 0 | 3 |
| Hiroshima report | 4 | 3 | 1 | 4 | 0 | 1 |
| Sternglass report | 1 | 0 | 1 | 0 | 0 | 0 |
| other foreign studies | 32 | 6 | 9 | 1 | 3 | 6 |
| party studies, lines 1 & 2 | 27 | 4 | 2 | 13 | 5 | 5 |
| party studies, line 3 | 51 | 12 | 5 | 12 | 13 | 9 |
| *"Kalla"* ("source") | 14 | 0 | 3 | 0 | 4 | 3 |
| other studies | 15 | 1 | 1 | 1 | 7 | 3 |
|  | 562 | 98 | 104 | 99 | 101 | 102 |
| Number of references |  | 66 | 252 | 92 | 152 | 562 |

Official studies (i.e., studies performed by governmental committees or initiated by standing committees, agencies, or other authorities) played an important role, accounting for about 50 percent of the total number of references. Reports from private trade and industry accounted for another 10 percent, university studies for 10 percent, and foreign studies for 15 percent. It is remarkable that studies performed or initiated by the parties involved (i.e., the organization committees for the three lines), accounted only for 15 percent of the total number of references. Thus although three lines were unable to set the agenda for the referendum debate, the risk studies themselves had already defined that agenda.

Special attention should be given to a series of booklets, collectively called *"Kalla"* ("Source"). Initiated by a standing committee for the dissemination of scientific information in the Swedish Council for Planning and Coordination of Research, these booklets were based on mediation principles. Two scientists with diverging opinions presented their views and a third person, the mediator, helped to put presentations into a uniform format with an eye to removing uncontroversial material from the agenda and identifying as precisely as possible the remaining points of actual factual disagreements. This ambitious and imaginative attempt to provide the public with reliable scientific information in a popular form nevertheless failed to play an important role in the referendum debate.

Concerning the distribution of references among the media, *Dagens Nyheter* has the greater number by far, thereby confirming the generally held opinion that *Dagens Nyheter* was a driving force behind the nuclear debate in Sweden. That *Dagens Nyheter* had a much more varied pattern of references than any of the other media also supports this opinion. Many reports received mention only in *Dagens Nyheter*, which also made proportionally less use of otherwise "popular" reports (e.g., *More efficient emergency planning* and the line 3 party studies), although these studies were generally considered to be the most influential ones against nuclear power.

As expected, an evening paper such as *Aftonbladet* did not give as much attention to the nuclear issue as the morning papers. Further, many of the references in *Aftonbladet* occurred in very short news items, whereas the references in the morning papers usually appeared in the context of longer articles. It is noteworthy that *Borås Tidning*, a local paper, gave special attention to the local consequence studies performed by various regional chambers of commerce.

"Rapport" is a half-hour television news program. It has less space than the news pages of a daily newspaper, so the smaller number of references to risk reports is only natural. It also probably explains why many reports that received limited attention in the newspapers were not even mentioned in "Rapport." Nevertheless, the column for "Rapport" shows a rather different pattern. *None* of the major proper risk studies which are the subject of the present study was mentioned in "Rapport." Instead the program concentrated on two of the most popular studies – *More efficient emergency planning* and the line 3 party studies – both of which were played down by *Dagens Nyheter*. Those, if any, who received the major part of their information about the nuclear issue through "Rapport" received a rather narrow and superficial picture.

**Table 3.3** How the studies were used.

|  | "Rapport" (%) | Dagens Nyheter (%) | Afton-bladet (%) | Borås Tidning (%) | Average (%) |
|---|---|---|---|---|---|
| mentioned | 12 | 8 | 18 | 9 | 10 |
| summarized | 32 | 28 | 20 | 23 | 26 |
| criticized | 21 | 24 | 24 | 22 | 23 |
| used as support | 35 | 40 | 38 | 46 | 41 |
|  | 100 | 100 | 100 | 100 | 100 |
| Number of references | 66 | 252 | 92 | 152 | 562 |

**Table 3.4** How different participants used the studies.

|  | Line spokesmen (%) | Authorities (%) | Experts (%) | Comm. spokesmen (%) | Journalists (%) |
|---|---|---|---|---|---|
| mentioned | 6 | 10 | 5 | 3 | 20 |
| summarized | 4 | 10 | 7 | 8 | 66 |
| criticized | 30 | 31 | 36 | 29 | 3 |
| used as support | 60 | 49 | 52 | 60 | 11 |
|  | 100 | 100 | 100 | 100 | 100 |
| Number of references | 142 | 49 | 104 | 38 | 184 |

Risk studies may be used in many ways. Here we distinguish among four major uses: the study is only mentioned, the content of the study is summarized but no attitude is expressed, the study is criticized, and the study is used to support an argument.

As Table 3.3 makes clear, the risk studies are mentioned largely in controversial contexts. It is also more common for them to be used as support than to be criticized. The pattern is remarkably stable across media, but it does not reflect a uniform policy or outlook on energy risk studies. Rather, it arises from the averaging effect of looking at many such studies.

Finally, it is useful to distinguish among different categories of participants (line spokesmen, authorities, experts, commercial spokesmen, journalists, and others) to determine how each used the risk studies (Table 3.4). Journalists largely served as transmitters of information and avoided taking a stand of their own. Perhaps one would have expected that commercial and line spokesmen, who are expected to defend their interests, would show a different pattern from authorities and experts, who are supposed to be more impartial. But this was not the case.

When the figures are analyzed, however, the uniformity collapses. In the case of *More efficient emergency planning* (Statens Strålskyddsinstitut 1979–80), it is obvious that it came to be regarded as possessing an unambiguous message (Table 3.5). It was either accepted or rejected as a whole. Only the

**Table 3.5** How the participants used *More efficient emergency planning*.

|  | Line 1 (%) | Line 2 (%) | Line 3 (%) | Authorities (%) | Experts (%) | Journalists (%) |
|---|---|---|---|---|---|---|
| mentioned | 0 | 0 | 0 | 5 | 0 | 12 |
| summarized | 0 | 10 | 0 | 9 | 0 | 77 |
| criticized | 100 | 90 | 0 | 32 | 89 | 0 |
| used as support | 0 | 0 | 100 | 54 | 11 | 11 |
|  | 100 | 100 | 100 | 100 | 100 | 100 |
| Number of references | 4 | 10 | 18 | 22 | 18 | 26 |

**Table 3.6** How the participants used the *Consequence study*.

|  | Line 1 (%) | Line 2 (%) | Line 3 (%) | Authorities (%) | Experts (%) | Journalists (%) |
|---|---|---|---|---|---|---|
| mentioned | 0 | 0 | 5 | — | 0 | 13 |
| summarized | 0 | 0 | 5 | — | 0 | 83 |
| criticized | 20 | 20 | 28 | — | 25 | 0 |
| used as support | 80 | 80 | 62 | — | 75 | 4 |
|  | 100 | 100 | 100 | — | 100 | 100 |
| Number of references | 5 | 5 | 21 | — | 4 | 23 |

authorities were more moderate, whereas almost all the experts lined up behind the pronuclear spokespeople. For the *Consequence study* (Närförläggningsutredningen 1974), however, a very different picture emerges (Table 3.6). All sorts of people, except journalists, found in the study something that they could use to support their own case. Obviously, the study was sufficiently many-sided to permit a number of conclusions, and, as in so many other cases, the strategy of selecting suitable facts got the upper hand over straightforward argument.

RISK INFORMATION AND THE POLITICIANS[3]

To trace the pathways of information from source to responsible politician, a series of in-depth interviews was conducted with ten members[4] of the Swedish parliament, two from each of the main parties.

The politicians were selected according to the following criteria: the first respondent for each party should be a person who had a leading role within the party with respect to energy questions. No ministers or party leaders, however, should be included (to ensure a certain openness). The second respondent should be a person who had not specialized in energy questions to such a degree as to stand out as the party's main spokesperson.

The politicians were first asked to characterize their most important sources of information about nuclear power. Most frequently, they referred to direct contacts (i.e., talks and discussions with representatives of authorities and companies, scientists and technicians, fellow party members, and environmentalist groups). Other frequent answers included research reports (Swedish and foreign), governmental committee material, pamphlets (Swedish and foreign), seminars and lectures, and popular science books (including the series "*Kalla*"). When the politicians were asked to give a critical assessment of their sources, half answered that they were by and large satisfied with the amount and quality of information. However, several emphasized the low credibility of the mass media and sometimes even expert statements, including those made in governmental committee reports.

But several persons also indicated that they had had problems. The sheer amount of information was mentioned as an obstacle by some, and the pronounced polarization of the nuclear issue made it difficult to find exactly the information needed. Deciding between opposing expert opinions was a particular problem. One of the politicians called for more "abstracts" of information – short and objective summaries of facts on central questions. Several mentioned the "*Kalla*" series as an example of how to present information that suits politicians.

Another question asked whether the politicians had experienced any noticeable failures of information. The answers fell into two categories. The first addressed questions of particular facts, such as the gas bubble in the Three Mile Island reactor, which threatened to explode, and the risk of steam explosions, where expert opinion seemed to be divided. The second category concerned not particular facts, but how different problems were seen and experienced as important. One person indicated that awareness of risks connected with other sources of energy came much too late. Another pointed to the underestimation – which even nuclear disarmament activists were guilty of during the 1950s and 1960s – of the risks of nuclear power.

In regard to familiarity with the major risk studies, roughly equivalent numbers of respondents indicated that they had read the whole study, had read parts of the study, had read only the summary, or had received information from members of the relevant committee. As the energy questions grew more important politically, an increasing number of the politicians seem to have attempted to acquire continuous information from members of the committees.

"To what extent has your party organization furnished you with information about nuclear power?" The unanimous answer to this question was that the role of the party organization was minor. The information distributed through the parties originated for the most part from those members who had special responsibility for energy questions. Several of those interviewed had had such assignments. The parties also served their members by distributing summaries of ongoing committee work, sometimes prepared by the party's energy specialist but often simply photocopies of the summaries prepared by the committees themselves.

Four out of the ten politicians had established personal contacts with qualified scientists and other energy experts. These channels served as sources of new information at an early stage and for checking information obtained from other sources. The remaining six interviewees all indicated that they regularly took advantage of the opportunity to discuss issues directly with scientists and experts whom they met or telephoned.

All of the ten Members of Parliament agreed that information acquired through the media played a very important role, and some even mentioned the media as one of their most important information sources. But they all made clear that it was not factual information that they sought from the media, but rather information about opinions and the focus of debates. The lack of objectivity and impartiality of the media drew criticism from several quarters (this applies particularly to *Dagens Nyheter* and television programs).

What had politicians learned about obtaining information on technically complicated questions? Most tried to abstract from the special features of the energy question and saw parallels to questions about computer technology, recombinant D.N.A., weapons technology, and news media. Some representative answers were: politicians must learn to criticize expert statements, to analyze arguments, to consult sources to a greater extent, to seek criticism at an early stage, and to initiate debates. Politicians found it difficult to handle scientific questions after they had become matters of faith, because experts used their prestige to make statements about matters on which they were not experts.

What should be done for the future? It was generally agreed that a continued division of responsibility for politicians and experts is inevitable; politicians, therefore, to a large extent will have to trust information that they receive from fellow party members. Against this background, they suggested: more frequent personal contacts with scientists and politicians, more objective publications (such as "*Kalla*"), increased demands on scientists to participate actively in the dissemination of information about research, augmented resources for research, a more secure working situation for scientists (which would increase their willingness to acknowledge and discuss controversial issues), and a clearer division between factual issues and political values in committee work. They also believed that limited funds to individual members of Parliament to initiate smaller studies would be helpful.

In conclusion, most politicians seem to prize verbal contacts and then the importance of second- and third-hand information from specialists among fellow party members. Only the specialist in a party entertains any real possibility of going directly to the sources, and usually there is only one such specialist for each question. As for written sources, selection was a matter of chance when the energy question was new. But as the energy issue grew more important, politicians became more sophisticated and systematic in their selection of sources.

## IMPACT ON SCIENCE AND THE SCIENTIST

Nuclear power depends on a highly complex technology, so qualified engineers and scientists play an important role in risk studies. It is therefore important to know not only how science affects risk studies, but also how risk studies affect science and the scientists. To what degree do risk studies contain scientific research and do they solve any scientific problems?

To answer these questions, ten leading Swedish scientists were interviewed.[5] The selection process involved several criteria: the scientist should be a recognized leader within his or her field in Sweden, have a field of speciality of essential importance to the risk studies, and should have taken an active interest in some of the risk studies. Some attention went to achieving breadth over different specialities as well, including persons known for an optimistic attitude towards technological development as well as some with a more critical or reserved attitude.

As to whether the risk studies or their technical appendices involved scientific research, the majority of the scientists were doubtful. However, one was anxious to point out that the refusal to use the label "scientific research" does not imply a negative view of the quality of the work done within the risk studies. Rather, it means that the activity is of another kind, with different aims and methods. But some scientists wished to classify parts of the KBS work as real scientific research, pointing out that KBS stands in a class of its own among the Swedish risk studies. This view also has support from those who did not wish to classify KBS as scientific research – they were asked to rank the studies with respect to degree of "scientificness," and they all agreed that KBS was at the top of that ranking. Independent of their views on the quality of the research, the scientists agreed that KBS was far more ambitious than the other studies and that the activity within KBS was scientifically relevant in a way that put KBS in a class of its own.

One of the scientists had thought in more general terms about why large goal-directed projects, such as KBS, so often (in his view) were found wanting in scientific quality and so seldom discovered anything significant. The reasons he suggested concerned in part the organization of Swedish universities and authorities, but had also to do with the ways in which such projects are organized. Working under a tight time schedule, a scientist is seldom able to contribute anything significantly new, because what is new is not that which is planned. It is impossible, therefore, to hatch scientific progress in a tight time schedule. The fact that it is the principal investigator who determines which problems will be attacked also results in the most qualified scientists often choosing not to take part or, if they do, not working at the peak of their ability. Another contributing factor is that the project organizers often feel compelled to cooperate with authorities whose scientific competence is sometimes insufficient or limited.

The scientists, asked whether the methodology of the risk studies had any scientific value, interpreted this question in two ways. The first interpretation viewed the methodology of the risk studies as event- and fault-tree analysis, as it was used in, for example, the *Reactor safety study* (US Nuclear Regulatory Commission 1975). Such methods have, to some extent, penetrated scientific research. In many cases, the work has increased the emphasis on the probabilistic aspects of a subject (e.g., in solid mechanics) where deterministic thinking was dominant before. The other interpretation equated methodology with "methodicalness," with the ambition to cover all aspects of a research area in a systematic way.

In this sense, the risk studies have had a clear scientific impact because they have directed attention to a number of research areas that were previously neglected (e.g., in destructive testing in solid mechanics, studies of corrosion, and a number of statistical problems). And, even more important, it has become clear that a number of interdisciplinary problem areas need attention. Cooperation among geologists, chemists, and experts in solid mechanics was noteworthy in the KBS project. In other cases, cooperation has occurred between engineers on the one hand and social scientists and humanists on the other, concerning the human factor in safety analysis and the factors which determine the risk perception of different individuals.

As to whether the risk studies solved any scientific problems, unanimity prevailed, even among those who held that KBS in part was genuine scientific research, that none had. On the other hand, the scientists did believe that the risk studies had raised important scientific problems. Most respondents cited the systematizing aspect of the risk studies, which has led to the discovery of the new problem areas mentioned above.

In response to whether they felt that their competence, collectively speaking, had been utilized in an optimal way in relation to the risk studies, the answer was a hesitant yes. The scientists believed that, given the level of ambition, the risk studies were competent but would have been more effective if they had aimed a little higher and had made more use of qualified scientists. As to providing politicians with a basis for their decisions and the public with general information, however, the studies were deficient.

One of the scientists with extensive experience in committee work concluded that *ad hoc* committees of scientists and politicians are effective in informing politicians about complicated technical matters – through the process of working together and not through the contribution of the final published report. Several others emphasized the importance of meeting politicians face to face, to allow for the immediate clarification of obscure points and for the avoidance of misunderstandings. Although the scientists value personal contacts with politicians, they hesitate to assume any special responsibility for initiating such relationships because they feared that a few unscrupulous scientists would use the opportunity to blow their own trumpets. Therefore, they preferred to advise politicians to acquire better training in technical and scientific matters, both to take the initiative when needed and to withstand attempts to manipulate them.

As for risk communication to the public, the scientists believed that much is inadequate. Ambitions are often high, but suitable channels to the public are missing. The most natural channel would be the media, but many doubted their competence and willingness to disseminate objective information. Many of the scientists' comments faulted *Dagens Nyheter*, particularly for editorials that were far from consistently competent and for frequently using basically correct data in deceptive ways. Another widely endorsed claim held that it was almost impossible to get informative articles about nuclear power published in *Dagens Nyheter*. Should this claim be generally true (an issue beyond the scope of this chapter), it suggests a possibility for bias that cannot be verified exclusively by examination of the paper itself but only through substantially more complicated investigations.

IMPACT ON THE NATURE OF SAFETY STUDIES

The ultimate goal of safety studies is, of course, to improve safety. It is beyond the scope of this analysis to evaluate the *extent* to which safety has actually increased as a result of the risk studies. Nevertheless, the analysis has examined *how* these studies have influenced the safety work at Swedish authorities, utilities, and reactor manufacturers. A series of interviews was conducted with leading representatives of these groups.[6] The criteria for selecting interviewees were: they should hold a position that rendered them well acquainted with safety questions concerning nuclear reactors or radioactive waste, and they should have been directly affected by some of the major Swedish risk studies. The sample also aimed at balance in two respects: it should contain representatives of authorities, reactor manufacturers, utilities, and other organizations related to nuclear power, but it should also include directors with a responsibility for policy and qualified officials with more direct connection to production, construction, or similar activities.

To assess the impact of the risk studies on safety work, it is necessary to distinguish between reactor safety and waste management. Although the Åka and KBS studies betray the tentative character of pioneer work, they have nonetheless set the scene for all future thinking about the safety of nuclear waste. Everyone in the sample testified that these studies had had extraordinarily great importance, not only in the quality of the work but also in filling a major void in knowledge. From industry came the admission that they were ill prepared for the waste problem and that the Åka study functioned as an alarm clock and provoked good solutions. Moreover, the extensive scientific discussion about the KBS proposals furthered their technical quality. A few voices, however, expressed a more reserved attitude: KBS was a hypothetical study in the sense that its only task was to prove that something *could* be done. It was not a proposal to go out and actually do it. Only when such a proposal exists will the influence of the risk studies become known.

The other risk studies, by contrast, address an industrial activity (nuclear power production) that has enjoyed a long history. It is appropriate, therefore, to ask whether any concrete measures have been taken, in the form of technical devices, routines, or instructions, which can be directly traced to recommendations or results in any of the risk studies. If by new safety measures one means concrete actions, then the answer is in the negative. No one in the sample could remember any specific measure that had been taken directly because of any risk study. Whereas one cannot categorically deny that such measures have occurred, they can hardly be important ones. This result is not surprising. It was not the task of the risk studies to make detailed recommendations but rather to contribute more generally. One future concrete measure of considerable importance, which might be attributed to a recommendation in *Safe nuclear energy?* is the filtered-vented containment at the Barsebäck plant.

Almost everyone agrees that the *Safe nuclear energy?* was the one Swedish risk study that really penetrated into practical security work. For the first time, safety questions, together with systems design, training of operators, formulation of instructions, adminstrative rules, and the like, came to be regarded as an integral part of nuclear engineering. The committee's discussion of person–machine problems has influenced both utilities and the Nuclear Inspectorate, but this also applies more or less to all its recommendations. The study was also a strong contributing factor in the creation of the Council for Nuclear Safety.

One interviewee referred to the report of subcommittee A of the Energy Commission (EK-A 1979) as a study that had practically no effect whatsoever, although it was probably the one that produced the most interesting and useful background material. This was cited as an example of how inefficient committee work sometimes is and how the success of a committee study depends more on the manner of its preparation and the openness of its recipients than on the novelty and quality of the facts set forth.

Most respondents agreed that the US *Reactor safety study* (US Nuclear Regulatory Commission 1975) had had a great influence, both directly and through its methodological influence, on the Swedish risk studies. The Lewis report (US Risk Assessment Review Group 1978) which criticized certain aspects of the methodology of the *Reactor safety study* should, according to one member of the sample, have received more attention. It was misinterpreted in the general debate, which stressed its critical sides at the expense of the constructive ones (a criticism frequently expressed in the US, as noted in Chs. 1 & 6 of this book).

Thus, even in the face of general agreement on the importance of the risk studies for general safety philosophy, a differing attitude clearly prevails as to their contribution to detailed safety changes. Most impulses for concrete safety improvements come from the feedback of operational experience. This view is particularly noticeable among those who work close to actual production. They emphasized the importance of assiduous work with small improvements, based on collective operational experience. They saw the recommendations of committee reports as often theoretical or somewhat out of touch with reality. This applies primarily to accident-preventing measures; for consequence-mitigating measures, they acknowledge the importance of risk studies.

General attitudes towards safety have changed in several ways as a result of the risk studies. First, whereas the previous safety philosophy aimed almost entirely at the prevention of major accidents, more attention now addresses the limitation and mitigation of the consequences of a core melt should it occur. Second, it is realized that the combination of several routine failures can pose as important a risk as large pipe breaks or leaks. A special case of the latter is the awareness of the mixed blessings of extensive testing. Previously, the view prevailed that "the more tests, the better." But through systematic analyses, industry has become aware of the risks of *introducing* faults in connection with tests.

As noted above, a certain tension exists between those who stress the importance of feedback from operational experience and those who advocate theoretical probabilistic risk analyses. However, the trend seems to be toward a narrowing of the gap. As the risk studies become more detailed and more site-specific, they approach the level where meaningful comparisons can be made with real incidents. Moreover, as operational experience moves toward more systematization, it becomes more accessible to theoretical analysis. In

Sweden, probabilistic risk analyses, now under way at Oskarshamn 1 and Ringhals 1 and 2, are filling this gap. Since the studies are site-specific, it is possible to go deeper into details, to examine human errors, and to test the analyses against a number of real incidents.

It is easy to take for granted that safety work always adds new things to all the old ones and that an ever-increasing set of requirements comes forth from the authorities. The question was raised, therefore, as to whether anyone had experienced the opposite trend in any connection. As expected, most answers were in the negative, but some pointed in another direction. These all had to do with uncertainty: in many cases, safety requirements were defined in situations with considerable uncertainties and were, therefore, based on unfavorable assumptions and contained large safety margins. But new knowledge may, of course, reduce uncertainties, so that what was once commendably cautious becomes unnecessarily restrictive.

The indirect effects of the risk studies have been mainly organizational. No one in Sweden has complained about a lack of money for safety purposes. The State Nuclear Inspectorate and the State Radiation Protection Institute have received several rounds of new funding. The State Power Board has set up a permanent section on reactor safety, and two of the more recent organizations – the Council for Nuclear Safety and the Board for the Handling of Spent Nuclear Fuels – owe their existence largely to the risk studies.

When asked to evaluate the usefulness of the major risk studies as a basis for political decision making, the members of the sample offered both negative and positive viewpoints. It was a good thing, in their view, that committee work *forced* the political representatives in a committee to penetrate technical problems from a factual stance. Also the requirement that a committee take a stand and offer recommendations made politicians focus on concrete problems. All this implies that it is the *process* of working within the committee, and not the product ultimately produced by the committee, that is important. The negative viewpoints, however, referred specifically to the risk studies. The studies, some interviewees argued, often overlapped and were poorly coordinated. New committees were appointed too often and there was no time to let the findings ripen into a carefully prepared action program. The great haste with which most of the committees worked also contributed to their low cost-effectiveness.

These interviewees highlight three key points:

(a)  The risk studies have had an extensive and deep influence on safety work at Swedish nuclear power stations. Their methods penetrate safety thinking. Concretely, they have caused organizational changes within both public authorities and the industry. They have not only affected the design of the plants planned and built during the latter part of the 1970s but also produced certain more extensive changes in plants already in operation. For the great number of smaller technical safety improvements in plants in operation, however, the feedback of operational experience is the more important source of inspiration.

(b)   No persisting difference between representatives of public authorities and the industry is noticeable. But certain signs indicate that persons who work more concretely with safety questions have somewhat different attitudes, experiences, or both, mainly concerning the relative importance of theoretical safety studies and feedback of operational experience, than persons in more general positions. This distinction can be made within both public authorities and the industry. But the size of the difference should not be exaggerated.

(c)   As might perhaps be expected, experts consider the solution to the problem of public distrust to consist of improved education of politicians, the public, and the mass media. This view regards committee work (as distinct from published reports) as a good thing, since it forces politicians to penetrate factual problems and also necessitates other contacts with the public and the mass media.

## Improving risk communication and information flow

Although certain general conclusions stand out in this chapter, an obvious prerequisite to bringing some semblance of order to the complexity of the research results is a unifying idea. The concept of information flow in society offers some potential. Indeed, most of the results lend themselves to a description or evaluation of flows of information from one type of participant to another.

To this end, Figure 3.2 identifies seven idealized participants: the company, the authority, the political specialist, the general politician, the scientist, the journalist, and the public. The *political specialist* denotes a person in a party who has been assigned a special responsibility for a certain area or problem and who serves as the main source of information about that area to fellow party members. For the energy question, it is possible to identify such persons in all the major parties in Sweden, even if the degree of formal responsibility varies and several such persons exist in a certain party. The *general politician* is someone who is a politician at the national level (usually a Member of Parliament), but who does not belong to the category of political specialist. The *journalist* is assumed to work on a daily morning newspaper or in television. It should be emphasized that the diagram in Figure 3.2 applies only to the case concerning information about nuclear power.

The figure depicts two kinds of commuication connections. Solid lines represent an information *process*, which is continuous, formalized to a certain extent (and therefore of a certain durability), and which allows immediate feedback. A typical example would be a committee that meets regularly. The broken lines, by contrast, represent regular *flows* of information. Such flows, which may consist of regular production of written material, have indirect and slow feedback mechanisms and are usually receiver-initiated. Since all the processes in the figure also have supporting flows, there is no need to draw double lines

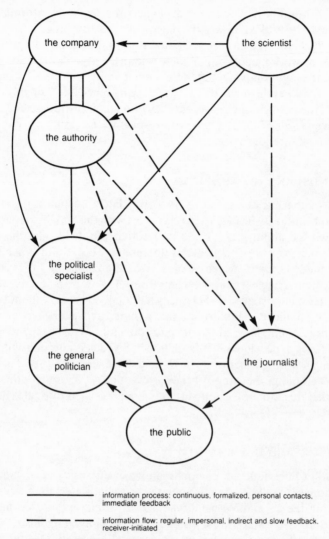

**Figure 3.2**   Idealized risk information flow in society.

(but a solid line is assumed to include both categories). It is intended that the vertical position of the participants should indicate their average level of technical competence. At the two uppermost levels, individuals freely use technical jargon internally and are professionally engaged in nuclear power.

THE SCIENTIST

The role of the scientist is to be at the forefront of basic knowledge. Scientists regard themselves as the real contributors to committee work. Consequently, all the arrows are directed away from the scientist, who usually disseminates results in written form. The scientist, then, is the source of information flows (as illustrated by broken lines in the diagram). The only process (i.e., the solid line) in which the scientist participates is with the political specialist in a committee or working group. For some scientists, a similar relation may hold with respect to the company, but there are not many such cases. Scientists feel that their views get through and that their competence is reasonably utilized in relation to the political specialist, but they often feel frustrated about the small penetrative power of their results with respect to the company, the authority and, above all, the journalist.

## THE SCIENTIST AND THE AUTHORITY

The task of the nuclear authority is to regulate a certain kind of activity. Because the authority has such a close contact with this activity, it develops the best knowledge about present and past activity. But, ideally, the authority should also foresee possible new developments. To this end it needs a more abstract understanding, which is of a scientific character (at least in such complex cases as nuclear power). Therefore, the flow from the scientist to the authority is an important one. Scientists habitually complain about the lack of scientific competence of authorities, and, as noted above, one representative of an authority has emphasized the need for the authority to keep an open mind and to encourage new ideas. The situation in Sweden is now unusual, since the two main authorities in the nuclear field have extremely strong scientific competence among their top officials. Nevertheless, there is little reason to suppose that this situation is self-sustaining, and contacts must also be made at lower levels.

## THE COMPANY AND THE AUTHORITY

Several solid lines link the company and the authority, indicating that the cooperation is very close. As this volume clearly indicates, the Swedish model differs from the US and West German cases in that authorities and utilities cooperate in their safety work instead of occupying antagonistic roles. The Swedish, British, and Canadian models have all drawn fire for interlacing of authorities and companies into a nuclear industrial complex, which tends to isolate itself and which is difficult to control through ordinary political channels. It is not possible to discuss the accuracy of that view here, except to point out that some structural features of the diagram promote the emergence of such isolated communities. Solid lines unite stronger ties than do broken ones, and both the company and the authority receive information through information processes limited virtually to each other. So, even if the fear of isolation is unfounded at present, some structural driving forces bear watching. In fact, the only external source from which the company and the authority receive information is the scientist, and that is the channel to strengthen if one wants to counterbalance the isolating forces.

## THE SCIENTIST AND THE POLITICAL SPECIALIST

It is clear that all parties consider the process of committee work involved in a risk study as much more important than the written report. The scientist was quite happy with such work because it forced the politician to face the technical problems. For their part, politicians preferred to learn about risk studies through personal communication with those involved. But risk studies do not last forever. If this highly valued form of information process is to continue, some new mechanism must be found. It is not likely, however, that seminars, information meetings, and the like will suffice, because they lack the imperative dimension.

It is interesting that politicians would like to impose on the scientist the obligation to inform the public about potential hazards, whereas the scientist opposes that idea for fear that some colleagues may abuse the opportunity. Instead, scientists recommend that the politicians themselves acquire better training in scientific matters. Observations about the relation between the political specialist and the scientist also apply to some extent to the relations of the political specialist to the company and the authority.

## THE GENERAL POLITICIAN

The political specialist is perhaps the best informed of all the people in the system, not because of a depth of information but because of the large number of different sources from which the information emanates. The general politician occupies a much more isolated position and receives information from a single institutional source – the party specialist. Apart from that, the general politician must exercise initiative. The information that comes from the journalist and the public emphasizes people's attitudes to the problem.

Given an information structure such as that in Figure 3.2, the political specialist should be a valuable source of information for the general politician. What is precarious is that the specialist is the *only* source. If the party specialist misunderstands something, receives a biased impression, or succumbs to manipulation, then it will affect *all* party members.

## THE JOURNALIST

The journalist is in a difficult position. Although the recipient of several flows of information, the journalist is not a participant in any communicative process (at least in regard to technical information). Much depends, therefore, upon the initiative and ability to utilize the information generated by the scientist, the company, or the authority. In addition, the journalist – whose sources occupy the top levels of the diagram and whose own position is only one step above the public (although there are exceptional cases) – has a wide gap to bridge. This leads to a high dependence on summaries from other sources, usually news agencies or the secretariats of the risk study committees. News reporting thus becomes highly uniform and sometimes bears the stamp of the engineer (who produced it!) and not the journalist.

In principle, the journalist should be much freer in other capacities than as a pure news reporter. But as we have seen, the risk reports set the scene for the nuclear debate and afford the journalist little opportunity to do other than explain complicated technical matters. A newspaper or a television program owes its image more to the editor than to any individual journalist. Different media have in fact adopted different policies. Most newspapers, for example, openly supported one of the three lines in the referendum, whereas this road was not open to the TV program "Rapport." We have also seen different selection principles at work. Discussion of the risk reports often occurred in controversial contexts and sometimes in highly selective ways.

## THE PUBLIC

Unless the public takes its own initiative, it is usually limited to information received from the mass media and occasionally from some authorities. Since we have seen that the information about technical risks in the media is often stereotyped and inaccurate, one can scarcely expect the public to have a particularly clear or accurate picture of technical risks unless it takes some active steps to obtain and study more qualified information. In this way the public becomes stratified: a few laypersons with power of initiative, education, and library resources acquire an impressive degree of knowledge; others gather bits and pieces that are seldom put into proper context and are expressed in a language that is difficult to comprehend.

## THE AUTHORITY AND THE PUBLIC

One of the most striking features of all the risk studies is that they invariably deal with the public in a collective way. The studies rarely address the distribution of risk over sexes, geographical areas, age groups, occupations, personal habits, and other factors. In this connection, it is useful to remember the complaints of some representatives of the nuclear industry that the public never showed any interest in risk questions until its own private spheres were threatened. In comparison with other interesting political problems (e.g., taxation), it is surprising that so little attention is paid to how the individual is affected. If it is desirable to increase the public's knowledge and understanding of risk and to make decisions in a democratic manner, then current risk studies need to be supplemented with studies that demonstrate the interconnections between abstract calculations and individual cases.

## THE NEED FOR AN INTERMEDIATE LEVEL OF INFORMATION DISSEMINATION

An idea that cropped up repeatedly in our work was the need for some sort of "qualified journalism" in scientific and technical matters. Scientists, meaning that their own capacity is not utilized, bemoan the ignorance of journalists. Representatives of authorities and utilities complain that "qualified journalists with recognized integrity" are nonexistent. The high regard accorded the series "*Kalla*" by practically everybody also lends support to the idea.

Undoubtedly, many arguments counter the creation of some sort of new organization, but the research results point to a potential innovation. Figure 3.3 introduces a new actor, one who sits at a fairly high level of competence between the scientist and the journalist. This person would work predominantly through information *processes* and would have close contacts with the

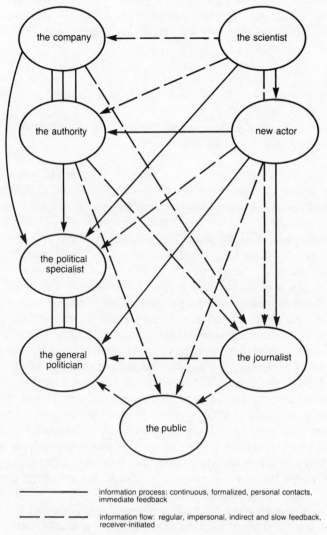

information process: continuous, formalized, personal contacts, immediate feedback

information flow: regular, impersonal, indirect and slow feedback, receiver-initiated

**Figure 3.3**   Idealized information flow with a new actor.

scientist. Dissemination of information would occur in somewhat formalized and continuous forms, connected mainly to the journalist, the general politician, and the authority. The new participant would not replace the scientist as a contact for the political specialist, because this might risk making the information too uniform. (But the political specialist should, of course, receive any sort of written material from the new source.) Such a new participant would counteract the tendency of the authority and the general politician to move toward isolation.

The series "*Kalla*" played a role similar to that of the new actor in Figure 3.3, but, apart from its uncertain future, its written form means that all contacts are flows rather than processes. It is important to notice that these functions would not be satisfied by just another journal or generally increased support for popular science, since they would require an organization with some permanence of staff.

## Conclusions

The analysis of Swedish energy risk studies and the various responses to them suggest a number of key conclusions:

(a)  Public presentation of the risk studies received a fair amount of press coverage, but the presentation of the content was strikingly uniform, and relied, directly or indirectly, very heavily on the summaries prepared by the committees themselves. Much attention was also given to the potential impact of the studies on political decision making.

(b)  The risk studies had the effect of tuning in the whole nuclear question to the problem of risks in general and reactor safety in particular. The economics of nuclear energy received some attention, but environmental questions related to energy production were almost totally neglected. Within the safety category, antinuclear papers tended to avoid reactor safety and pronuclear ones shunned emergency planning.

(c)  When the period preceding the referendum in Sweden in March 1980 was singled out for study, it was remarkable how safety questions dominated the debate. Here, too, the environment received negligible attention.

(d)  Clear differences were discernible between different newspapers. *Dagens Nyheter*, a major morning paper, devoted considerably more space to nuclear energy than did any other newspaper, and it referred to many otherwise little-noticed reports, most of which had a clear antinuclear tendency. It also avoided excessive use of otherwise popular or spectacular reports, thereby differing from *Aftonbladet*, an evening newspaper, and "Rapport," a television news program.

(e)  The risk reports were predominantly used in argumentative contexts, in most cases as support for particular views, but also as objects of criticism. Some risk reports became very closely attached to one side, which used them only as support, whereas the opposing side only criticized them. Meanwhile, other reports were both criticized and used as support by both sides.

(f)    Parliamentarians interviewed considered personal contacts with informed persons, rather than official risk studies, to be their best source of information about the risks of nuclear power. Scientists and representatives of utilities, the nuclear industry, and nuclear-related authorities who had been involved in the many Swedish risk studies doubted the value of the risk studies as documents. They did emphasize, however, their value as processes that forced the different parties to penetrate each other's standpoints.

(g)    All parties interviewed expressed dissatisfaction with the media, which they think failed to supply factual information. Scientists felt that their competence could have been used more efficiently, both in the risk studies as such and in the dissemination of information to politicians and the public.

(h)    Although the risk studies were not considered to have added anything new to scientific knowledge, they had a profound effect on the engineering sciences. These contributions manifested themselves mainly through more frequent contacts among different research areas, new ways of posing problems in the individual disciplines, and the emergence of new research areas.

(i)    The risk studies wielded an extensive influence on safety work, and their methods permeate safety thinking about nuclear power in Sweden. They have also caused organizational changes and have generally strengthened the internal position of safety and quality-control activities.

(j)    The picture that emerges is thus one of success in relation to the effects on the nuclear establishment, including nuclear-related authorities and certain engineering sciences. On the other hand, as attempts to settle disputes and inform the public, the studies are largely failures. Shortcomings in informing the public are attributable to the lack of an intermediate level of information dissemination.

## Notes

1    The research was conducted by Stephen Schmidt of the Department of Political Science, Lund University.
2    The research was conducted by Kent Asp and Christina Valdensjo of the Department of Political Science, Gothenburg University.
3    The research was conducted by Peter Palmkvist.
4    The ten politicians were: Ingvar Carlsson and Lennart Pettersson from the Social Democrats; Per Unckel and Lars Tobisson from the Moderates; Birgitta Hambraeus, a member of the Energy Commission; Bertil Fiskesjo from the Centre Party; Kerstin Aner and Gabriel Romanus from the People's Party; and C. H. Hermansson and Per Israelsson from the Communists.
5    The ten scientists were: Kurt Becker, Professor of Nuclear Reactor Engineering at the Royal

Institute of Technology in Stockholm (KTH); Janne Carlsson, Professor of Solid Mechanics at KTH; Jan Hult, Professor of Solid Mechanics at Chalmers University of Technology, Gothenburg (CTH); Sven Johansson, Professor of Nuclear Physics in the School of Engineering, Lund University (LTH); Ingvar Jung, Emeritus Professor of Thermal Engineering at KTH; Karl-Erik Larsson, Professor of Nuclear Reactor Physics at KTH; Jan Rydberg, Professor of Nuclear Chemistry at CTH; Torbjorn Westermark, Professor of Nuclear Chemistry at KTH; Frans Wickman, Emeritus Professor of Mineralogy, Petrology and Geochemistry at Stockholm University; and Gustaf Ostberg, Professor of Engineering Materials at LTH.

6    Those included in the sample were: Bengt Ahlman, Head of Production at the Barsebäck plant; Per-Eric Ahlstrom, Chief Engineer and Head of the reactor safety section of the State Power Board in Stockholm; Anders Björgerd, Director at Sydkraft in Malmö (the utility which owns the Barsebäck and part of the Oskarshamn plant); Thomas Eckered, Director of the Council for Nuclear Safety in Stockholm since April 1980, before that Assistant Director for the State Nuclear Inspectorate in Stockholm; Erik Jansson, Reactor Inspector at the State Nuclear Inspectorate in Stockholm; Bo Lindell, Professor and Director of the State Radiation Protection Institute in Stockholm; Lars Nordström, Professor and Director-General of the State Nuclear Inspectorate in Stockholm; Stig Rolandsson, Head of the section for reactor safety at Asea-Atom in Västerås; Nils Rydell, Chief Engineer at the Board for the Handling of Spent Nuclear Fuels in Stockholm; Sten Salomonsson, Head of Production at the Oskarshamn plant, Cnut Sundqvist, Head of the technical department of Asea-Atom in Västerås; Gunnar Tedestål, Director at OKG AB in Stockholm (the consortium which owns the Oskarshamn plant); and Ingvar Wivstad, Technical Director at the State Power Board in Stockholm.

## References

Åka (Åka-utredningen) 1976a. *Använt kärnbränsle och radioaktivt avfäll.* Statens offentliga utredningar (SOU) 1976: 32. Stockholm: Liberförlag.
Åka (Åka-utredningen) 1976b. *Spent nuclear fuel and radioactive waste: a summary of a report given by the Swedish government committee on radioactive waste.* Statens offentliga utredningar (SOU) 1976: 4. Stockholm: Liberförlag/Allmänna förlag.

EK-A (Energikommissionens Expertgrupp for Säkerhet och Miljö) 1978. *Miljöeffekter och risker vid utnyttjandet av energi* (Environmental effects and hazards of energy exploitation). Ds.I 1978: 27, pts. 1–2. Stockholm: Allmänna Förlaget.
Energikommissionen 1978. *Energi: betänkande av energikommissionen.* Statens offentliga utredningar (SOU) 1978: 17. Stockholm: Liberförlag.

KBS (Kärn–Bränsle–Säkerhet) 1977. *Handling of spent nuclear fuel and final storage of vitrified high level reprocessing waste,* Vols. 1–4. Solna, Sweden: AB Teleplan.
KBS (Kärn–Bränsle–Säkerhet) 1979. *Handling and final storage of unreprocessed spent nuclear fuel,* Vols. 1–2. Solna, Sweden: AB Teleplan.
Konsekvensutredningen 1979. *Om vi avvecklar kärnkraften: konsekvenser för ekonomi, sysselsättning och miljö: betänkande av Konsekvensutredningen.* Statens offentliga utredningar (SOU) 1979: 83. Stockholm: Liberförlag. Appendices (Bilagor) 1–10, Ds.I. 1979: 10–15, 18–21. Stockholm: Industri-departementet.

MHB Technical Associates 1978. *Swedish reactor safety study: Barsebäck risk assessment.* Ds.I. 1978: 1. Palo Alto, Calif.: MHB Technical Associates for the Swedish Energy Commission.

Ministry of Agriculture and Environment 1978. *Energy, health, environment: summary of a report (sou 1977: 67) by the Swedish Governmental Committee on Energy and the Environment.* Stockholm: The Ministry.

Närförläggningsutredningen 1974. *Närförläggning av kärnkraftverke* (Close-siting of nuclear power plants). Statens offentliga ütredningar (sou) 1974: 56. Stockholm: Allmänna Förlag.

Reaktorsäkerhetsutredningen 1979. *Säker kärnkraft?* (Safe nuclear power? Report of the Swedish Government Committee on Nuclear Reactor Safety.) Statens offentliga utredningar (sou) 1979: 86. Stockholm: Liberförlag.

sfs (Svensk författningssamling) 1977. *Lag om särskillt tillstånd att tillföra kärnreaktor kärnsbränsle m.m.: utfärdad den 21 April 1977.* sfs 1977: 140. Stockholm: Liberförlag.

Statens Strålskyddsinstitut 1979–80. *Effektivare beredskap mot kärnkraftolyckor* (More efficient response to nuclear emergencies; English summary: *More efficient emergency planning*). Stockholm: Statens Strålskyddsinstitut.

Sweden 1977. *The Stipulation Law: law regarding special conditions for charging nuclear fuel into nuclear reactors.* sfs 1977: 140.

Swedish Governmental Committee on Energy and the Environment (Betänkande av Energi- och Miljökommitten) 1977. *Energi, hälsa, miljö* (Energy, health, environment). sou 1977: 67. Stockholm: Statens offentliga utredningar.

us Nuclear Regulatory Commission 1975. *Reactor safety study.* wash-1400, nureg 75/014. Washington, dc: Nuclear Regulatory Commission.

us Risk Assessment Review Group 1978. *Risk assessment review group report to the us Nuclear Regulatory commission.* nureg/cr-0400. Washington, dc: Nuclear Regulatory Commission.

# 4 *The* German risk study *for nuclear power plants*

HERBERT PASCHEN, GOTTHARD BECHMANN,
GÜNTER FREDERICHS, FRITA GLOEDE,
FRIEDRICH-WILHELM HEUSER, and HELMUT
HÖRTNER

In the Federal Republic of Germany, nuclear facilities have to comply with a special federal law, the "Law on the Peaceful Utilization of Nuclear Energy and the Protection from its Dangers," the Atomic Energy Act (Bundesgesetz 1976). With regard to damage, danger, and risk, the Atomic Energy Act claims that existing (i.e., state-of-the-art) scientific knowledge and technology are the criteria for judging adequate prevention of damage and risk. Consequently, safety requirements for the design, construction, and operation of nuclear facilities are major elements of the regulatory process. Detailed descriptions of these requirements appear in the *Safety criteria for nuclear power plants* issued by the Federal Minister of the Interior (Bundesminister des Innern 1977) and in additional guidelines and regulations.

In accordance with this framework of safety criteria and guidelines, safety assessments for nuclear power plants in Germany were originally based on a deterministic approach. Requirements for quality assurance, design of engineered safeguards, and measures for consequence mitigation, were worked out as principal guidelines. Extensive safety evaluations and accident analyses relied on the concept of a design basis accident (DBA); that is, a certain DBA is selected by engineering judgment.

As well as the evolution of this deterministic safety approach, early efforts addressed the effects of severe accidents beyond the DBA concept, judged to be "not credible." As noted earlier (Ch. 1), the first and best known study of this type was WASH-740 (US Atomic Energy Commission 1957) prepared by Brookhaven Laboratory in the United States. Since the primary objective of this study was to estimate the consequences of the most severe accidents, probability evaluations played only a subordinate rôle in the assessment.

The first proposals for nuclear risk assessment that explicitly considered probability values occurred in the mid-1960s. A particularly strong impetus came from the suggestion by Farmer (1967) to use a quantitative risk assessment to set up siting criteria for nuclear power plants. These ideas were taken up in Germany, and recommendations emerged to base not only site selection but also safety assessment as a whole on a quantitative probabilistic concept (Lindackers 1970). Although these proposals stimulated further developments, at that time they could only be discussed as concepts. Analytical methods, especially the techniques for predicting the likelihood of failure of engineered systems and adjoining accident sequences, were not well developed. Furthermore, the data base available from operating experience of nuclear plants was insufficient to estimate risk accurately. In the following years, however, probabilistic methods, especially reliability analysis techniques and their application to safety issues in reactor technology, made substantial progress.

In recent years, the executive and legislative branches of government have increased their efforts to conduct "special projects" aimed at clarifying nuclear risks. The major projects involved are:

(a)  generic studies of the risks of different reactor types and of alternative waste-management and disposal systems;
(b)  the so-called "Gorleben hearings" on the German Nuclear Reprocessing and Waste Disposal Center that was to be built in Lower Saxony;
(c)  the Federal Parliament's Special Commission of Inquiry, "Germany's Future Nuclear Energy Policy."

This chapter examines one of these projects, the *German risk study for nuclear power plants* (GRS 1980). Phase A of this study was carried out by the *Gesellschaft fur Reaktorischerheit* (Association for Reactor Safety, or GRS) as the main contractor (with several other institutions) between 1976 and 1979. Initiated and supported by the Federal Ministry for Research and Technology, it aimed to assess the collective risk involved in potential reactor accidents. To make possible a comparison of results, the methods and assumptions of the German study largely followed those of the *Reactor safety study* (US Nuclear Regulatory Commission 1975). The nuclear power plant Biblis B, which has a typical pressurized-water reactor (PWR) of German make, was chosen as the reference facility. To assess the risk, the analyses considered 19 sites with a total of 25 reactors. A general conclusion of the study is that risks caused by accidents in nuclear power plants do not differ significantly between the two countries. Phase B of the *German risk study* is still in progress.

The treatment to follow inquires into the objectives and results of the study, influences on licensing and reactor design, the "official" response by government and the courts, and the response of environmentalists and antinuclear groups. Particular attention focuses on the reactions of the media. Finally, concluding observations address the general relationship between risk analysis and the public acceptance of nuclear power. An initial overview of the use of reliability analysis in the Federal Republic of Germany provides the context for this discussion.

## The use of reliability analysis

High demands on reliability, especially for the engineered safety features of nuclear power plants, have always characterized nuclear engineering. Specified demands on safe design and on safety-related components and systems have, however, been derived mostly on the basis of deterministic criteria. Examples include the single-failure criterion, the fail-safe principle, and the redundancy of safety systems. In some instances, however, probabilistic methods were incorporated into official rules and regulations. The safety criteria, for example, demand that: "To verify the balance of the safety concept and to supplement the deterministic methods of safety assessment of reactors, the reliability of safety-related systems and main components should be evaluated using probabilistic methods as far as this is possible, according to the state of art, with sufficient accuracy" (Bundesminister des Innern 1977).

Paralleling the evolution of the deterministic safety approach in Germany, efforts attempted to assess quantitatively the reliability of emergency safety features. First, probabilistic analyses were performed for special systems of process engineering, for mechanical systems, and for the electric power supply (Bastl & Gieseler 1970, Balfanz *et al*. 1974). Further analyses addressed such special design features as the reliability characteristics of electronic circuits in the reactor protection system (Nieckau 1974). These analyses were used mainly to guide plant safety design, in that they were performed to demonstrate that the design and the demands on engineered safety equipment comply with general safety requirements. Mostly, however, the respective systems underwent study in isolation, without detailed consideration of their interactions with other systems. Also, the specific demands on the system functions with regard to potential accidents often received only very rudimentary consideration. More advanced analyses have taken into account demands with respect to specific accident sequences and the interaction of different safety functions. A typical example of such broader efforts is an investigation of the engineered safety features installed in a PWR in order to ensure emergency cooling of the reactor core in the case of a large loss-of-coolant accident (Hörtner *et al*. 1976).

Currently, reliability analyses are routine in the reactor licensing process. The main objectives of these analyses are:

(a)  To detect weak points in the design of emergency safety features by identifying the component failures that contribute dominantly to the failure probability of the overall system. In such cases improvements can often be achieved through slight system modifications, such as additional instrumentation or increased maintenance (Bastl *et al*. 1978).

(b)  To perform comparative investigations on alternative system variants. The quantitative analysis allows selection of those system variants which can be expected to meet best the required safety demands.

(c)  To determine admissible repair and maintenance times that can be tolerated for further plant operation in the case of failed components or subsystems.

(d)  To optimize strategies and procedures on functional testing in order to obtain a high availability of the safety system. It has been shown, for example, that staggered testing of redundant subsystems increases systems reliability considerably as compared to simultaneous testing of all subsystems (Dressler & Spindler 1974).

Reliability analyses for complex systems rely predominantly on fault trees, which reflect the logical connections and interdependencies among the elementary inputs (component failures and other influences) that contribute to overall system failure. Since construction of a fault tree requires a comprehensive systematic procedure, fault trees provide detailed insights into the structure of a system even without quantitative calculation. For numerical evaluation, system failure probabilities are calculated on the basis of component input data (component failure rates, test intervals, etc.) according to the logical structure of the fault tree. The process entails the application of computer codes that are based on analytical or simulation methods or a combination of both (Kotthoff & Otto 1976). The development of more advanced codes also allows the calculation of confidence limits of the results due to uncertainties in the input data (Schlösser 1978).

Reliability analyses require a broad database for all components that influence system reliability. Because of the limited experience available in the nuclear field, reliability data, especially on process engineering and structural components, still harbor considerable uncertainties. To some degree, one may circumvent these uncertainties by means of parametric sensitivity calculations showing the effect of component data uncertainties on the overall system reliability. On the other hand, during the last few years the database has been improved substantially by systematic collection and evaluation of operating experience from nuclear power plants in several countries.

Following a pilot project in a conventional plant, systematic data collection from nuclear operating experience (nuclear power plant Biblis, units A and B) commenced in Germany in 1977 (Hömke *et al.* 1978). Component failure rates emerging from this work in most instances were found to be lower than values gained from non-nuclear experience. Also, as may be expected, uncertainty ranges for reliability data are smaller than those for data from various non-nuclear industries (Lindauer 1981). To some extent even data for system failure rates have been evaluated from operational experience and compared to calculated system reliability values. A reasonable agreement has been found between analytical and empirical failure probabilities for selected subsystems (e.g., for parts of the emergency core-cooling system of a PWR). Although this comparison has been made only for single trains (*Stränge*) of redundant systems, it can help to check the validity of calculated system reliability values.

Besides random failures of single components, system reliability can be affected significantly by the possibility of common-mode failures. Such simultaneous failures of redundant components – due to a common cause (e.g., design error, manufacturing deficiency, or environmental impacts) – counteract the redundancy of a system. Obviously, this type of failure becomes more important the less sensitive a system is to random failures. To cope with common-mode failures, systems analysis has to be supported by a thorough check of the plant design. Even with the identification of possible common-mode failures, however, their rare occurrence renders it difficult to quantify their probability values.

As experience has shown, operator actions in nuclear power plants demand particular attention. In some cases, human intervention has exacerbated or even caused incidents. On the other hand, human adaptability, which cannot be provided by automatic systems, has prevented adverse effects in several cases. In principle, reliability analysis can take both aspects into account, although it is still difficult to quantify the influence of human error through probability values.

Thus far, reliability requirements (i.e., quantified reference values attached to individual systems) have not enjoyed formal introduction into the licensing process. Instead, they emerge as a matter of practice. If reliability demands are to be quantified, they cannot be unrealistically high. Unavailabilities (i.e., failures to perform) well below $10^{-4}$ per demand (i.e., 1 system failure per 10,000 demands) can hardly be realized for individual systems. Above all, it is questionable whether extremely low probability values can be proven analytically. In any case, reliability requirements should relate not only to the availability of individual systems but to the frequencies of accident-initiating events and the failure probabilities of all system functions involved in an accident sequence.

This review shows that the possibilities for applying reliability analyses in reactor licensing are not yet exhausted. The risk studies performed in the last few years have led to further improvements and to a widening of the objectives of reliability analyses. In the context of a comprehensive probabilistic risk analysis, reliability investigations give detailed insights into plant reliability, including all types of relevant accident-initiating events and correlated accident sequences. Thus, reliability analysis has become an increasingly efficient tool for further improvement of overall safety design and development of general safety strategies (see Ch. 8).

## *The* German risk study *of nuclear power plants*

Publication of the US *Reactor safety study* (US Nuclear Regulatory Commission 1975) raised the question of its applicability to conditions in the Federal Republic of Germany. Although both countries use mainly light-water reactors (LWRS) for commercial generation of nuclear power, a direct transfer of the results of the *Reactor safety study* seemed to be unjustified, primarily for the following reasons:

(a)    Several important differences separate the reference plants (Surry 1, Peach Bottom 2) of the American study and the nuclear power plants erected in the Federal Republic of Germany. These differences concern primarily the design and functioning of several emergency safety features.

(b)  The population density in the Federal Republic of Germany and in central Europe is higher than in the United States.

These important differences led to the decision to conduct a separate large-scale risk study in the Federal Republic of Germany.

As in the *Reactor safety study*, the main objective of the *German risk study* (GRS) was to assess the societal risks associated with potential accidents in nuclear power plants. Other objectives were to find starting points for further improvement of the methodology of risk assessment and to support safety research. The study comprised two phases. Phase A applied, as far as possible, the basic assumptions and methods of the American study to German conditions. Phase B, which is still ongoing, seeks to intensify work within certain areas found to be problematic during phase A.

The steps within the *German risk study* are the same as in the *Reactor safety study*. For the first three steps (i.e., the plant-oriented analysis), the Biblis nuclear power plant unit B was selected as the reference plant. It has a pressurized-water reactor and was constructed by Kraftwerk Union (KWU) with an output of 3,750 MW of thermal power (1,300 MWe). In the subsequent steps, the potential consequences of a radioactive release outside the plant were calculated and related to the respective frequencies of occurrence. Then the corresponding risk levels were assessed. These calculations included all sites in the Federal Republic of Germany where nuclear power plants with LWRS producing at least 600 MW of electric power were in operation, under construction, or undergoing the licensing procedure in July 1977. Thus, the study eventually covered 19 sites with a total of 25 units.

As to the choice of initiating events to be investigated, the *German risk study* follows closely the example of the *Reactor safety study*. With all relevant contributions summed, an overall core-melt frequency of about $9 \times 10^{-5}$ per reactor-year is calculated as a mean value (expected value). The median is $4 \times 10^{-5}$ per year.[1] Table 4.1 compares these values with the corresponding values calculated in the *Reactor safety study*.

Figure 4.1 summarizes the results of event-tree and fault-tree analysis, showing the relative contributions of the different initiating events to the core-melt frequency. According to the *German risk study*, a loss of primary coolant through a small leak in a reactor coolant line dominates all other contributions. The second largest contribution comes from transients and from a small leak through the pressurizer relief valve, as a consequence of transients. This

**Table 4.1**  Comparison of the assessed core-melt frequencies.

|  | Core-melt frequency per reactor year | |
|---|---|---|
|  | *German risk study* | *Reactor safety study* |
| median | $4 \times 10^{-5}$ | $5 \times 10^{-5}$ |
| mean | $9 \times 10^{-5}$ | $1 \times 10^{-4}$ |

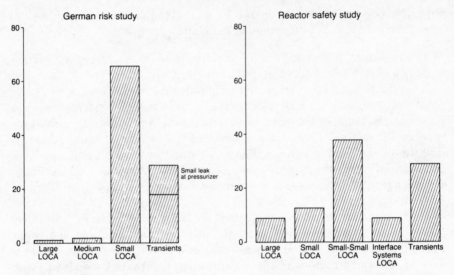

**Figure 4.1** Relative contributions of various accident-initiating events to the core-melt frequency.
*Source*: after GRS 1980, pp. 243–4.)

accident sequence roughly corresponds to the first phase of the accident at Three Mile Island. Such a transient, leading to a loss of coolant, was discussed and analyzed at an early stage of the study (Bastl *et al.* 1978). It resulted in various system improvements which were made one year before the Three Mile Island accident.[2] In most cases, the containment structure strongly limits the release of radioactive material into the atmosphere. Major releases would occur only if the containment were to leak or fail early in an accident sequence.

Combining the results of core-melt analysis and containment-failure analysis gives the amount and frequency of fission product release from the plant into the atmosphere. Thus, accident sequences that result in the same containment failure mode all fall into the same release category. Eight release categories are distinguished in the *German risk study*, whereas there are nine in the *Reactor safety study*.

In both studies the last two categories describe controlled loss-of-coolant accidents, whereas the other categories comprise core-melt accidents. Category 1 contains the most severe releases, caused by a steam explosion with damage of the reactor pressure vessel and the containment. This type of accident was taken into account in both studies as a cautious assumption, whereas current analysis shows that such an event is extremely unlikely. Categories 2 and 3 of the *Reactor safety study* describe early overpressure failure of the containment; such a failure is not possible for the German plant. But if the containment did not fail by leakage, a late overpressure failure of the containment would occur for the German reference plant (categories 5 and 6 of the *German risk study*). For the US reference plant, core-melt accidents are possible, and the containment barrier would retain its integrity until the molten core proceeded through the concrete containment floor (categories 6 and 7 of the *Reactor safety study*). It was estimated that such a melt-through would occur some 10 hours after core melt for the US reference plant, and some 100 hours after core melt for the German plant.

A set of best-estimate values of the physical parameters and the distribution of the frequency of occurrence describes each of these release categories. A re-evaluation of these frequencies entails adding 10 percent of the frequencies in the adjacent larger and smaller categories (i.e., probability "smoothing"). In the *Reactor safety study*, probability smoothing produces no large numerical effect on the overall results, whereas in the *German risk study* the frequency-of-release category 7 is enhanced by a factor of 500. This release category yields by far the largest contribution to the averaged risk of late fatalities.

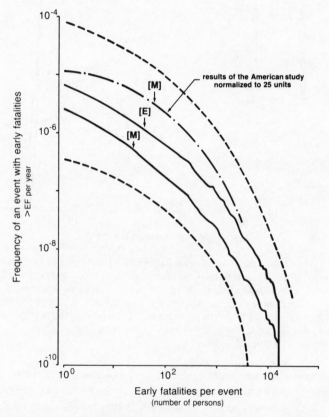

**Figure 4.2** Complementary cumulative frequency distribution of early fatalities (collective damage) of the German study and the American study (US Nuclear Regulatory Commission 1975) corresponding to 25 reactor units. Curve E, reference curve of the German study, determined on the basis of the expectation values of the frequency of release (categories). Curve M, curve determined on the basis of the median values of the frequency of release (categories); analogous to the American study.
*Source*: after GRS 1980, pp. 204–9.

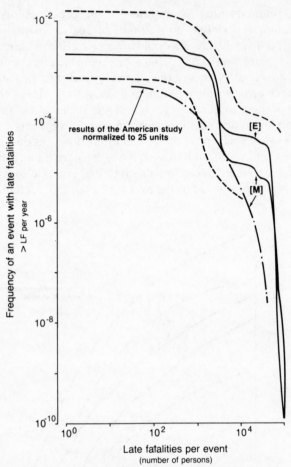

**Figure 4.3** Complementary cumulative frequency distribution of late fatalities (collective damage) of the German study and the American study (US Nuclear Regulatory Commission 1975) corresponding to 25 reactor units. Curve E, reference curve of the German study, determined on the basis of the expectation values of the frequency of release (categories). Curve M, curve determined on the basis of the median values of the frequency of release (categories); analogous to the American study.
*Source*: after GRS 1980, pp. 204–14.

Accident consequences were assessed for 19 German sites with a total of 25 reactor units. In conformance with the procedure in the *Reactor safety study*, the *German risk study* assessed the consequences for an area of up to 2,500 km in diameter and an overall population of about 670 million (the total population of Europe). Calculations indicate that early fatalities are possible up to a maximum distance of about 20 km, but the analysis shows that even a core-melt accident carries a probability lower than one percent of causing early fatalities. This is due to the containment-retention function regarding the release of fission products into the environment. A large number of early fatalities is possible only if:

(a)  large amounts of activity are released (i.e., early containment failure), and

(b)  the wind blows in the direction of a highly populated area, and

(c)  rain causes high ground contamination.

The study estimates a maximum number of 16,600 early fatalities, at a frequency of $5 \times 10^{-10}$ per year.

Late fatalities are not restricted to vicinities of nuclear power plants, and they were assessed wherever the transport of radioactive materials might expose the public to radiation. The linear dose–risk relationship used in the *German risk study* recognizes the possibility of an increased risk of cancer and leukemia at the smallest level of radiation exposure. The German study assessed a maximum number of about 100,000 fatalities at a frequency of $5 \times 10^{-10}$ per year.

Complementary cumulative frequency distributions describe the risks of early and late fatalities. Figures 4.2 and 4.3 show the results of the *German risk study* and the *Reactor safety study*. For the purpose of comparison, both curves of the *Reactor safety study* were first normalized to 25 units and then, in the case of the late-fatalities curve, the figure for collective damage per year was multiplied by the idealized plateau period of 30 years to obtain the total number of late fatalities per event. It should be mentioned here that the American study obtained its results by using medians of the release frequencies instead of expected values.

As the figures demonstrate, the curve for early fatalities of the German study is generally somewhat lower than the corresponding curve of the American study, but the curve for late fatalities is higher than the American curve. This is mainly due, as noted above, to the use of the linear dose in the *German risk study* and the higher population density in Europe. These differences between the German and the American study also show up in the average values for the collective risks due to accidents in nuclear power plants (Table 4.2).

Probabilistic risk analysis (PRA), a rather new, yet effective, way to assess the safety of large technological systems can lead to a deeper understanding of safety. On the other hand, at the present state of the art, PRA is still subject to considerable uncertainties and some major restrictions. These issues receive full discussion in Chapter 8. The limitations have to be taken into account when interpreting the results of risk analyses. The *German risk study* deals only with

**Table 4.2**  Comparison of expected values of collective damage corresponding to 25 reactor units.

|  | Fatalities per year | |
|---|---|---|
|  | *German risk study* | *Reactor safety study* |
| early fatalities | $5.1 \times 10^{-4}$ | $7.5 \times 10^{-4}$ |
| late fatalities | 9.3 | 0.5 |

risks from accidents. It does not consider contributions to risk from normal and abnormal operation of nuclear plants and from other parts of the fuel cycle or contributions to risk that are due to the impacts of war and sabotage.

When interpreting the results, one should note that the study does not deal with exact calculations of risk but with risk assessments that are subject to considerable uncertainties. To the extent that a basis exists, an attempt was made to quantify these uncertainties (e.g., uncertainties of component reliability data). Uncertainties of modeling remain and were not quantified within the framework of the study. To cover such uncertainties, simplifying assumptions were made which generally led to a pessimistic assessment. In many instances, the study relies on results of previous investigations. The simulation of accidents as performed within the framework of licensing, for example, constitutes the basis for establishing the minimum requirements for the demands on emergency safety features.

Only a limited data base was available to evaluate common-mode failures, which were quantified only in cases where operational experience indicated that such failures might exist. As for human error, only scheduled manual interventions (e.g., operator action according to the operator manual) were taken into account. Unscheduled interventions, and especially human adaptability, were not considered, a limitation in large-scale probabilistic risk analysis (Ch. 8).

The design conditions of the reference plant constituted the basis for the plant system analysis, although data for the most part were not derived from the reference plant. The investigation of the reliability of plant design had to rely on data obtained from comparable components in other industrial plants. Furthermore, the calculations of consequences were based on typical German site conditions, represented by a number of actual sites in the Federal Republic of Germany. The results therefore do not relate to a particular plant at a real site but are only representative of plants of a particular type at comparable sites.

The findings of the *German risk study* indicate that weak points often tend to occur at interfaces between different systems and between different technical disciplines (e.g., coupling between mechanical systems and adjoining electronic control devices). A thoroughgoing PRA can identify such weak points with a greater degree of certainty than the usual deterministic approach. In most cases, minor modifications of system design can eliminate these weak points. Investigations of the plant response to core-melt accidents (e.g., the containment–retention function to a radioactive release), permit the drawing of conclusions about potential means for mitigating consequences even in severe core-disruptive accidents. As for the consequence analysis, the calculations performed in the *German risk study* allow an assessment of various accident parameters that can significantly influence the extent of damage resulting from a radioactive release. Moreover, the insights gained from these calculations can assist in planning adequate emergency protection measures.

All in all, the *German risk study* has indicated a number of starting points for further improvements of the risk assessment methodology and for system improvements that may lead to a reduction of risk.

## *The* German risk study, *phase B*

The work for phase B is intended to contribute primarily toward a deeper understanding of different problem areas. This will include, as already mentioned, the further development of mathematical modeling techniques and due consideration of the present state of the art of safety research and its contribution to risk estimation. The work for phase B of the study, then, bears a close relationship to other projects within the framework of the Ministry of Research and Technology's research program on reactor safety.

To encourage broad participation of different working groups in the further work on the *German risk study*, the German Minister for Research and Technology in 1981 invited tenders for the work planned for phase B. Based on the investigations performed within the framework of phase A and the related commentary, the tender comprises approximately 20 single projects in the following subject areas:

(a)    accident analysis and systems analysis;
(b)    core meltdown and activity discharge;
(c)    accident–consequence models;
(d)    methods and instruments.

The following discussion outlines the main activities within the framework of the above topics.

### ACCIDENT ANALYSIS AND SYSTEMS ANALYSIS

As in the US *Reactor safety study*, the accident analysis in phase A often rested on conservative requirements stipulated in the licensing processes. This applies above all to the determination of the efficiency requirements for safety systems. Phase B, however, requires more exact accident analyses on the basis of so-called "best-estimate" conditions in order to reduce conservative assumptions and attain a less pessimistic description of possible accidents. In addition, events (e.g., steam pipe leaks, steam-generator/heating-pipe ruptures, earthquakes) not analyzed in detail in phase A will be examined in phase B. From the systems engineering aspect, the insecurities in the results of the reliability analyses for safety systems will require further reduction. To achieve this, analyses of operating experience will continue, in parallel with the work for the *German risk study*, in order to specify failure rates of plant components more exactly and to reduce the inadequacies in data needed for the reliability analyses. Considerations of human failure in phase B will entail attempts to analyze the consequences of human interventions which are *not* prescribed (i.e., are not specified in the operating manual). Also, phase A considered only operator errors during *foreseen* behavior. The analysis for the reference facility Biblis B shows that those errors contribute about 60 percent of the frequency of core meltdowns. Automation aimed at reducing precisely these human errors has been a result of phase A conclusions.

## CORE MELTDOWN AND ACTIVITY DISCHARGE

Knowledge about a core-melting event and its consequences has increased substantially during recent years. Of special importance is the conclusion that the core-melting events that might lead to early and large radioactive discharges will contribute considerably less to overall risk. In fact, recent investigations show that, in most cases, exceeding the conservative upper safety limits does not lead to core melt. Consequently, the actual occurrences of meltdowns for the cases dealt with in phase A are much fewer than those presented in the results of phase A. In addition, phase A utilized very simple – and mostly pessimistic – models of release of radionuclides from the melt as well as the behavior of these radionuclides in the containment vessel. To supplement these new insights into the calculations of core melting and radioactive releases, phase B is exploring in greater detail the releases of radioactive material from the fuel, its fate in the atmosphere of the containment, and the retention capability of the containment. But it is already apparent that, because of the transport behavior of the radionuclides, releases are less than assumed in earlier models. Accordingly, phase B results will almost certainly lower the risk probabilities estimated in phase A.

## ACCIDENT–CONSEQUENCE MODELS

Accident–consequence models, which underwent further developments and improvements immediately after the conclusion of phase A, are being used directly for the calculations in phase B. This applies equally to improvements in the atmospheric dispersion model (e.g., inclusion of changes in wind direction) and to the determination of damage. An important point will be the extension of the model, developed in phase A, for preventive measures and countermeasures in the event of an accident.

## METHODS AND INSTRUMENTS

As well as more detailed specifications and improvements of the model, attempts will be made in phase B to treat systematically and thoroughly the statistical issues connected with the partial and overall risk results. To this end, the mathematical-statistical methods used in phase A for determining the reliability of the results of the accident–consequence calculations will be extended to the investigations of the technical aspects of plants, the description of core-melting events, and subsequent discharges. Overall, phase B will attempt to improve the presentation of the results and to reduce considerably the uncertainties associated with the results of the investigations.

## The official review

After the completion of phase A of the study, the Federal Minister for Research and Technology called for a comprehensive review. A working group that had not participated in the work for phase A of the study received the assignment of conducting a review that was to emphasize:

(a) a critical evaluation of the investigations performed for phase A and of the results obtained and, based on this,
(b) the formulation of a program for the investigations planned for phase B.

The completed review (Dornier System GmbH 1981) notes that the investigations for phase A drew largely upon the methodological bases of the US *Reactor safety study*. The objective of phase A was to determine, for German conditions, the risk from accidents in nuclear power plants in accordance with the *Reactor safety study*. At the same time, however, the limits observed in phase A were precisely where future work had to start. Corresponding proposals for phase B should, on the one hand, include methodological improvements; on the other hand, the more recent results of reactor safety research should be considered in the formulation of the program.

According to the review, the plant-specific investigations, especially the analyses of event progression and systems analysis, are treated in greater detail than in the *Reactor safety study*. Thus, the technical reliability analyses have greater detail and the computer programs used have a larger capacity and a broader scope of application than those used in the *Reactor safety study*. With a view to the future scope of activities, however, the study calls for checking – and, if necessary, supplementing – the list of "triggering events" considered so far. In addition, attention is directed to the still limited database for reliability analyses as well as to the difficulty of evaluating possible common-mode failures and human errors.

The description of core-melting accidents and subsequent releases of radioactive material relies closely on the *Reactor safety study*. In this context the review report emphasizes that this procedure failed to take into account important recent results of reactor safety research. It recommends, therefore, that phase B of the study describe core-melting accidents more realistically on the basis of these new research results. A similar criticism is advanced against the accident–consequence model without discussing in greater detail the deviations from the *Reactor safety study*. The review also contains a number of proposals for further activities, including those that are directly related to phase B of the study.

The broad participation of groups having different attitudes toward nuclear energy has been an objective of the work for the *German risk study*. In this context, a two-year research project of the Ecological Institute at Freiburg, financed by the Federal Ministry for Research and Technology, was intended as a contribution from the critics of nuclear energy. Based on a critical discussion of the state of the art as represented in the *German risk study*, the analytical methods for risk analyses were to be improved further within the framework of this research project.

Not unexpectedly, the main criticisms voiced in the United States over the *Reactor safety study* were advanced (in almost the same words) in this case as well. Thus, an interim report on the project (Öko-Institut Freiburg 1981) raises a number of critical points that the Union of Concerned Scientists had already raised in its review of the *Reactor safety study* (Kendall 1977). The methods used in the *German risk study*, especially fault-tree and sequence analyses, are considered as altogether insufficient. In this context, reference is also made to the critical statements of the Lewis report (Risk Assessment Review Group 1978) without, however, also noting the positive judgment the Lewis Commission makes on the use of probabilistic risk analysis. Additional criticism includes objections to the mathematical-statistical bases and to the question of whether the *German risk study* considers all aspects of the event's progression in the case of an accident.

Several arguments in the critique of the *German Risk Study* show that important preconditions and interrelationships either have not been recognized or have been misrepresented by the critics. Thus this review claims that both the *Reactor safety study* and the *German risk study* calculate the risk of accidents in nuclear power plants merely as expected value (risk = frequency of occurrence × damage). Closely related is the statement that the *German risk study* used inadmissible selection and cut-off criteria for event progression and thereby neglected major risk contributions. As concerns specific items, the criticism focuses primarily on checking individual data and the calculations performed in the *German risk study*. To the extent that the review makes recommendations for future work, they correspond largely to proposals in the *German risk study* itself or to those in the comments on the work for phase B.

The Institüt für Energie- und Umweltforschung (IFEU) at Heidelberg (Franke & Steinhilber-Schwab 1981), an antinuclear group, studied the consequences of accidents in the nuclear power plant at Grafenrheinfeld for the town of Schweinfurt. Starting from a few selected partial results of the *German risk study*, the IFEU attempts to question the present safety concept for nuclear power plants (i.e., the proof of the safety of the facility required in the nuclear licensing procedure). Thus it argues that the existing safeguards cannot guarantee that the precautionary measures against possible accidents are sufficient. It emphasizes the maximum possible damage due to serious accidents as the decisive indicator for risk evaluation, without taking account of the extremely low probabilities of occurrence. The calculation of the damage itself is based on now unjustifiably pessimistic assumptions regarding important influences. As a consequence, the damage is considerably overestimated. The critique thus proceeds from assumptions which, on the whole, are not appropriate for a realistic risk assessment.

## *Influence on reactor licensing and design*

As pointed out earlier, the application of reliability analyses has recently become common practice for safety assessments within the licensing process. Although formal requirements have so far not been introduced, quantitative reliability analyses increasingly supplement the existing framework of safety criteria and guidelines.

In the Federal Republic of Germany, risk analyses are not a formal part of the licensing procedure. The main purpose of the *German risk study* was to provide a first assessment of accident risk from nuclear power plants and to gain experience with risk assessment methodology. It is likely, however, that risk assessment will play an increasingly important role in licensing, although it may take a long time until risk assessment procedures or even quantified risk criteria are *formally* introduced into the licensing process. An important condition for such an enlarged role would be a further reduction of uncertainties. In any case, all experts agree that risk analysis provides important background information for the licensing procedure for nuclear power plants. It is also noteworthy that requests for risk analysis and the quantification of safety are increasingly common for non-nuclear technologies as well.

Probabilistic methods of reliability and risk analysis are obviously more effective than current procedures for providing quantitative measures for safety evaluation. Applying advanced probabilistic techniques will lead to a broader base for safety judgments. First, probabilistic methods may aid the review of the deterministic basis, for instance, of the DBA concept, especially with regard to its overall consistency and completeness. Second, in a more refined step, risk analysis methods may help to define quantitative demands for safety equipment and minimum safety factors for structures. Thus, deterministically fixed criteria and delimitations may give way to the results of more extensive quantitative investigations. Risk analysis also yields all advantages of a comprehensive reliability analysis, but on the broader scale of an overall plant system and accident analysis. As discussed more fully in Chapter 8, this can help to optimize plant design with respect to accident prevention, thereby minimizing the frequency of severe accidents. From the investigations of plant response (e.g., in the case of a core-melt event that leads to radioactive releases into the environment), it is possible to draw conclusions with respect to mitigating potential consequences by further improvements of technical systems or other effective countermeasures.

The *German risk study* has significantly influenced special design features, especially for the reference plant Biblis B. Thus, analyses of technical systems and potential accidents led to several modifications in the design of engineered safety features. One example relates to the finding that operator errors can

contribute significantly to risk. Therefore, in the reference plant, the installation of automatic control devices for cooling down the plant has reduced the
influence of complicated human intervention for coping with a small loss-of-
coolant accident. Improvements of the pressurizer system offer another
example. According to the interim results of the *German risk study*, a small
leak through a stuck-open pressurizer relief valve significantly contributed to
core-melt frequency. Several improvements (for instance, emergency power
supply of the redundant block valve in the blow-down line and monitoring of
the positions of the control and relief valves) have significantly reduced the
probability of the corresponding accident sequence. Besides system improvements performed in the reference plant, the results of the study also promoted
additional improvements of engineered safety features in newer plants.

## The official response of the government and courts

A review of the relevant documents suggests a dearth of "official" reactions by
ministries, parliamentary committees, and courts to the presentation, or the
results, of the *German risk study*. Some general observations, however, are
possible.

Volker Hauff, the Federal Minister for Research and Technology, presented
the *German risk study* at the Federal Press Conference on August 14, 1979. The
Minister's positive evaluation of the study and the methodology of risk analysis
in general emphasized the following points:

(a)   As far as he, the Research Minister, was concerned, the study contained
      nothing that would induce him to change his (positive) attitude toward the
      peaceful utilization of nuclear energy. He saw no reason to dramatize the
      risks of nuclear energy, but neither should one play down these risks. As
      far as possible, factual and informed discussion of the risks and benefits of
      nuclear energy would be necessary. In his judgment, the study made a
      valuable contribution to such a discussion.
(b)   The study would be an important aid in the further planning and pro-
      motion of reactor safety research. It pinpoints the areas in which
      additional knowledge and further development of safety technology
      would be especially valuable.
(c)   Furthermore, the study and the methodology on which it rests provide a
      rational basis for further measures and technical requirements for licens-
      ing procedures under the German Atomic Energy Law for improving
      safety, as well as an aid for the planning of precautionary measures in the
      event of an accident.
(d)   The study should be continued with a phase B, which, among other
      things, should further develop the methodology of risk analysis. In addi-
      tion, the cooperation of scientists skeptical of nuclear energy will be
      sought during phase B to guarantee a comprehensive discussion.

(e)   In his ministry, he would promote the further development and broad use of risk analysis and hoped that a thorough discussion of the study would stimulate corresponding analyses in other fields of technology.

The Federal Ministry of the Interior (Bundesministerium des Innern, or BMI), which until the formation in 1986 of the Ministry for the Environment, Protection of Nature, and Reactor Safety, was responsible for questions of reactor safety, has, to our knowledge, never issued an official statement on the *German risk study*.

The German Parliament (*Bundestag*) never debated the merits of the study, nor was there any deliberation of the results by the Committee of the Interior of the Bundestag. The results of the risk study were put on the agenda of the Committee for Research and Technology of the Bundestag on October 17, 1979 (Deutscher Bundestag 1979). Representatives of the Federal Ministry for Research and Technology and of the Ministry of the Interior commented on the study, but Members of Parliament largely refrained from its evaluation. In a statement to the Press on August 14, 1979, Albert Probst, the Chairman of the Committee for Research and Technology, characterized the *German risk study* as a thorough and well balanced piece of work that certified the high safety standards of German nuclear power plants and provided the basis for a rational discussion. It also proved, according to Probst, that this was not the time to call for further dramatic safety regulations. Yet, in spite of the proven high reliability of German nuclear power plants, Probst argued, new and exaggerated discussions repeatedly challenged their safety. These discussions brought no significant improvements in safety but did impair the expansion of nuclear energy, thereby assuring either an insecure energy supply or the risks associated with other energy sources (Probst 1979).

The parliamentary Commission of Inquiry on "Germany's Future Nuclear Energy Policy" viewed the *German risk study* as an "important contribution toward a better description of the technical risks of nuclear power plants and as an important step in the scientific development of quantitative risk assessment" (Deutscher Bundestag 1980, p. 147). According to the Commission, the second phase of the risk study should emphasize further development of risk assessment methodology and improvement of the calculation models, taking due account of the more recent findings of risk research. The Commission made the following recommendations:

(a)   to investigate the extent to which the results of the *German risk study* were applicable to existing older nuclear power plants in the Federal Republic of Germany;
(b)   to investigate the risk of fire within the plant and impacts from outside (earthquakes, airplane crashes, chemical explosions);
(c)   to investigate the impacts of compact storage on the damage potential and on the risk;
(d)   to make an attempt at improved quantification of the risk contribution

from human failure and from nonprescribed interventions on the part of the operating personnel;

(e) to investigate whether the risk contributions from sabotage or acts of violence in the case of war could be quantified;

(f) to include the risk due to a failure of the planned measures for preventing a catastrophe in the probabilistic considerations;

(g) to attempt a more detailed description of the detrimental effects in the surroundings of nuclear facilities in the case of accidents (e.g., radioactive pollution of large areas of land), considering also interrelationships according to the laws of nature and organizational measures. (Deutscher Bundestag 1980, p. 147)

The majority of the Commission endorsed a proposal that would subject controversial cases to analysis by at least two different working groups, representing different opinions on the problem. The majority of the Commission proposed the continuation of the *German risk study*, with the inclusion of differing expert opinion and taking special account of the views of opponents to nuclear energy – a recommendation that echoed that already proposed by the Federal Minister for Research and Technology in presenting the study. Such an approach, it was believed, could increase the sought-after public acceptance of the study. A minority of the Commission, however, insisted that expert knowledge should be the only relevant criterion and that one's position on nuclear energy should not be considered.

Thus far, in the German administration of justice, rulings have made no direct reference to the *German risk study*. One must recognize, however, that the major judgments on the Atomic Law were passed in the period between 1975 and 1979, when work on the *German risk study* was still in progress. On the other hand, in the relevant literature as well as in judicial decisions, a certain reservation prevails against the applicability of risk studies to concrete decision making (Lukes 1978, Wagner 1981).

Risk assessments can be drawn upon only in the context of the concept of danger, as specified in nuclear energy law. This concept of danger is – as in other fields of technological safety jurisdiction – determined by the extent of the damage and the probability of occurrence. The administrative court at Münster, in its judgment (February 20, 1975) on the nuclear power plant Würgassen, expressed the qualitative concept of danger in terms of the quantitative (that is, in principle, measurable) concept of risk. This judicial formulation is now widely followed (Oberverwaltungsgerichte Münster 1977).

The relationship between the two factors, probability of occurrence and extent of potential damage, is established by the condition that, with increasing extent of the damage, the still tolerable probability of occurrence would have to diminish steadily. This means that cases where the potential damage is very high would require certification of the existence of a "danger" even if the probabilities of occurrence are extremely low (Lukes *et al.* 1980). Parliament has not settled the issue of where to draw the line between a danger that is so minimal that the citizens can be expected to accept it and a danger that is considered to be so serious that precautions have to be taken in order to reduce it significantly or to mitigate its harmful effects. Parliament has left the settlement of this highly political issue to the authorities and the courts.

In their attempts to demarcate danger, the courts appear to vacillate between two strategies: (a) greater emphasis on the extent of the potential damage, as in the Freiburg administrative court's demand for protection against the potential bursting of the reactor pressure vessel of the nuclear power plant at Wyhl in spite of the extremely low probability of such an accident (Verwaltungsgericht (vG) Freiburg 1977, p. 626), and (b) greater emphasis on the probability of occurrence, as in the Würzburg administrative court's dismissal of such a requirement for the Grafenrheinfeld nuclear power plant (Verwaltungsgericht Würzburg 1977, pp. 444ff.).

In its hearings on the nuclear power plant at Würgassen, the administrative court at Münster was the first to consider, with reference to the us *Reactor safety study*, a quantitative safety analysis for determining the probabilities of occurrence. The court did not consider it necessary to perform, as demanded by the plaintiff, a quantitative analysis of the safety standards.

The judgment of September 15, 1978, on the nuclear power plant Unterweser passed by the administrative court at Oldenburg, was partly based on quantitative probability estimates. In a number of questions, the court referred in its argumentation to the (preliminary) results of the *German risk study* (Verwaltungsgericht Oldenburg 1979, pp. 651ff.).

In general, court decisions show a tendency to incorporate a quantitative probabilistic approach into their decisions. Whether the deterministic safety concept that plays an important role in legal practice will finally be replaced by a comprehensive "probabilistic licensing" cannot yet be decided. What is important is that, on the legal side, virtual unanimity exists that the determination of a "level of acceptance" on the basis of quantitative probabilistic analyses is a normative act that is the responsibility not of the technician but of the legislator or those who issue ordinances (Lukes *et al.* 1980, pp. 205ff.).

## Response of environmentalists and nuclear opponents

The evaluation and critique of the *German risk study* by the environmentalists ("*Grüne*") and other antinuclear groups occurred in two steps. In a first phase, they reacted to the summary version of the study, its presentation, or both, by the Federal Minister for Research and Technology. The main thrust of the criticism at this stage was, understandably, directed against the political use of the study and, as concerns its contents, the omissions and intentional limitations of the study as well as the concept of risk used. The scientific discussion entered a second phase with the publication of the complete study – especially when the technical volumes, published during 1980–81, became available to the public. The controversy still rages and has gained new momentum from the participation of the nuclear energy critics in the study for the fast breeder reactor at Kalkar on the one hand, and their collaboration in phase B of the *German risk study* on the other. Thus, two levels of criticism can be differentiated: the sociopolitical and the scientific.

The main arguments advanced in the statements by the BBU (Bundesverband Bürgerinitiativen Umweltschutz 1979b, 1979c) largely represented the sociopolitical reactions of the antinuclear groups to the *German risk study*. These statements contended that the risk study provided no evidence that would induce the BBU to change its negative attitude toward nuclear energy. The BBU also claimed that the study had from the start set out to confer scientific legitimacy on political interests: namely, to make the public believe that nuclear risks are controllable because they can be quantified. The BBU criticized the way the study was "sold" to the public and declared that, as in the *Reactor safety study*, an attempt was being made to convey the erroneous impression that a nuclear catastrophe can occur only in thousands of years and that the present hazards of nuclear facilities are negligible. Indeed, the "catastrophe at Harrisburg" had demonstrated unmistakably that these "statistical games" did not have much value.

Another important criticism related to the selectivity of the analysis. The major shortcomings of the *German risk study*, according to the BBU, were that the study "cannot quantify human failure; it does not take into account the manifold impacts from outside a reactor, such as war, sabotage, etc.; it is limited only to the traditional light water reactors and considers neither new reactor types – the Fast Breeder and the High Temperature Reactor – nor the remaining parts of the nuclear fuel cycle, including uranium enrichment, fuel transport, reprocessing and final disposal of the nuclear waste." A "remarkable" result of the study was, in BBU's view, that, "in spite of the much vaunted German reactor technology," the conclusion is reached that German reactors represent a greater risk than the facilities assessed for the United States (Bundesverband Bürgerinitiativen 1979b, 1979c).

The scientific discussion of the *German risk study* began slowly because the technical volumes, the actual nucleus of the study, were published rather late. In September 1980, the Federal Minister for Research and Technology granted approximately 1.6 million DM to the Öko-Institut Freiburg for a two-year project, "Further development of the analytical tools for the German risk study for nuclear power plants." According to the work program, this study was to include an overall criticism of the *German risk study* and, based on this, a more detailed analysis of specific aspects. The application of the Öko-Institut was made independently of the invitation for tenders for phase B of the Risk Study (issued in spring, 1981). The project (Öko-Institut Freiburg 1981), carried out by a group composed mainly of three subgroups in Heidelberg, Darmstadt, and Bremen, was intended to furnish a comprehensive and critical analysis of the approaches, methods, models, and assumptions of the *German risk study*. Proposals were to be made for a more realistic calculation of the risk from reactor accidents. In addition, it would address more general items, such as a critical discussion of the concept of risk used, the general function of risk studies, and the determination of (social and health) effects which were not considered in the *German risk study*. Moreover, the approach presented in the *German risk study* was to be compared with those developed by the Öko-Institut itself (Hahn 1981).

Another study (Franke & Steinhilber-Schwab 1981), conducted by opponents to nuclear energy, which (in connection with assessing the consequences of accidents in the nuclear power plant at Grafenrheinfeld for the town of Schweinfurt) also critically discussed the *German risk study*. Finally, mention should be made of the extremely critical reaction to the *German risk study* by the "Bremer Arbeits- und Umweltschutz-Zentrum" (Danzmann 1981) which is, however, based only on the summary version of the study, as well as a "countercriticism" presented by the GRS, the main contractor of the *German risk study*.

## Reactions of the media

When the Federal Minister for Research and Technology presented the *German risk study* at the Federal Press Conference, extensive coverage of the main volume of the study was not possible. So, on short notice, the GRS's "Information Department" took on the task of preparing selected information for distribution to the Press and interested public. The department prepared three main items:

(a) a brief (1.5-page) press release, *German risk study published* (GRS 1979b);
(b) a lengthy (6-page) press release, *The German risk study for nuclear power plants* (GRS 1979c);
(c) a 50-page abridged version of the *German risk study* (BMFT 1979a).

The press statements, in German and English, went to 350 national and over 200 foreign addresses. Preparations for the press conference on August 18, 1979 also involved the compilation of a catalog of questions and answers on the risk study and a list of keywords from the section on results (GRS 1979d). Additional sources for reports in the Press were:

(a) the speech (5 pages) of Federal Research and Technology Minister V. Hauff to the federal press conference (Hauff 1979);
(b) a press statement from the Federal Ministry for Research and Technology: *Research Minister Hauff: risks from nuclear energy should neither be explained away nor dramatized* (3.5 pages), which is largely a summary of the above speech (BMFT 1979b).

The Association for Reactor safety, or GRS, collected for documentation reports on the presentation in the daily and weekly press during the period from August 15 to 30, 1979 (Pollmann 1979). The documentation, which was limited to publications in German, includes about 250 articles from the Press.

During the period from August 15 to 18, media reporting focused largely on three events:

(a) the *German risk study* press releases (or, in the best case, the 50-page abridged version of the study);
(b) the speech by Federal Research and Technology Minister V. Hauff and the corresponding press releases, in addition to comments made during the press conference;
(c) first reactions on the part of the "interested public" – political parties, the KWU (Kraftwerk Union), the BBU (Bundesverband Bürgerinitiativen Umweltschutz, or Federal Association of Citizens' Committees for the Protection of the Environment), individual scientists, etc.

Articles stating opinions in comments or editorials after August 18th comprise only about 5 percent of the 250 articles. The evidence suggests that "a lasting interest, at least of the press, on the subject of reactor safety" (Pollmann 1979, p. 2) did not materialize (a finding which parallels that of the Kemeny Commission response; see Ch. 6). In any case, at least 40 percent of the newspapers surveyed presented both news and an editorial on August 15, 1979 on the subject of the presentation of the *German risk study*. This fact, and the overall "outstanding presentation" (Pollmann 1979), suggest that the media treated it as an important event, largely against the background of the persistent problem of the acceptance of nuclear energy.

METHODOLOGY AND DATABASE

The basis for our assessment of press reporting on the *German risk study* is the previously mentioned GRS documentation of 250 German-language articles (among them, roughly 20 percent comments and a number of readers' letters). Because of its incompleteness, the documentation does not permit a rigorous quantitative analysis of press reaction, even for the period from August 15 to 18, 1979. First, the documentation omits relatively large daily newspapers (such as the *Hannoversche Presse*) but includes small provincial papers. Second, news articles from several large papers (such as the *Frankfurter Allgemeine Zeitung* and the *Hannoversche Allgemeine Zeitung*) have been omitted, but the corresponding editorials have been included. Finally, readers' letters to several periodicals are often included, but all remaining reporting is missing. Even so, the documented articles were subjected not only to a qualitative, but also to a quantitative, evaluation. The number and diversity of the daily and weekly papers appear sufficiently significant to provide a reasonably comprehensive "review of the Press."

QUANTITATIVE ANALYSIS

The examination of the structure of press coverage entailed the identification of four main features – the political–administrative framework of the study, the methodological approach, the study results, and the consequences and usefulness of the study.

To begin, the structure of press reporting was measured in terms of the frequency with which the aspects referred to above were mentioned or reproduced in the articles reviewed. These frequencies are then related to the total number of articles reviewed, so that the result may be viewed as a kind of "issue density" per article for the different aspects. A comparison of "densities" permits the estimation of the weight assigned by press reporting to each of the aspects.

Table 4.3 presents a general overview of the distribution of the issue densities. One may draw the following initial conclusions:

(a) Reporting concentrates mainly on the results and the approach of the study (a total of 6.6 mentions per article), with results at the center of attention. Within the reporting on results, the figures on the extent of damage and on risks dominate.

**Table 4.3** Issue densities of aspects of the *German risk study* (overall and by type of article*).

| Aspects | Positive evaluation of study | No evaluation | Negative evaluation of study |
|---|---|---|---|
| political-administrative framework of the study (total) | 1.9 | 2.0 | 1.7 |
|   chronology and participants | 1.3 | 1.4 | 1.1 |
|   aims of the study | 0.6 | 0.6 | 0.5 |
|   distortion/influence on the study | 0.03 | 0.0 | 0.06 |
| approach of the study (total) | 2.8 | 3.0 | 2.7 |
|   subject of the study | 0.9 | 1.2 | 0.7 |
|   methods of the study | 1.0 | 0.9 | 1.1 |
|   exclusions from the study | 0.9 | 0.9 | 0.9 |
| results of the study (total) among these: | 3.8 | 4.7 | 2.9 |
|     topology of accidents | 0.3 | 0.4 | 0.2 |
|     probability of accidents | 0.6 | 0.7 | 0.5 |
|     consequences of accidents/magnitude of damage | 2.0 | 2.8 | 1.3 |
|   evaluation of results | 0.9 | 0.8 | 0.9 |
| consequences and use of the study (total) | 2.0 | 2.3 | 1.8 |
|   consequences for safety research | 0.5 | 0.6 | 0.4 |
|   consequences for the political-administrative area | 0.5 | 0.6 | 0.5 |
|   sociopolitical consequences | 1.0 | 1.1 | 0.9 |
| all aspects of the study | 10.5 | 12.0 | 9.1 |

* "News item" also refers to detailed reports; "comment" refers both to opinion-containing reports and letters (from readers) containing comments.

(b)   Aspects of the consequences and the practical use of the study receive only minor attention. They do not receive significantly more mentions than comparatively "formal" aspects of the "framework" for the study. Among the aspects of the usefulness of the study, those in the "sociopolitical" area distinctly dominate (this area is mentioned as frequently as the other two areas combined).

(c)   Aspects of bias or influence on the study on account of the participation or nonparticipation of certain groups are clearly nonissues. Also, results on the topology of accidents are mentioned relatively seldom.

(d)   Differences in the distribution of mentions between "news items" and "comments" are small.

More precise conclusions emerge from a detailed evaluation of individual issue densities or of the frequencies of mentions. If we focus our attention on those ten aspects of the study receiving most frequent mention as an issue (expressed, in this case, as the percentage of articles mentioning the aspects in question) and exclude the two formal aspects regarding the administrative framework of the study (Table 4.4), a number of important features relating to content emerge.

If a distinction is made between news items and comments, the following aspects, in addition to the above eight, should be mentioned for *news items*:

(a)   exclusion of the fuel cycle from the study – 31.3 percent of articles;

(b)   damage-risk figures for reactor meltdown accidents are below those for "natural radiation" and "radiation from medical therapy" – 37.5 percent of articles;

**Table 4.4**   Individual issue density.

| Aspect | Mentioned in % of articles as a whole | Mentioned in % of news items | Mentioned in % of comments |
| --- | --- | --- | --- |
| specific accident probabilities | 57.6 | 68.8 | 47.3 |
| immediate damage | 57.6 | 56.3 | 58.8 |
| delayed damage | 51.5 | 56.3 | 47.1 |
| study provides no arguments against nuclear energy | 39.4 | 43.8 | 35.3 |
| study was designed to adapt results of the *Reactor safety study* | 39.4 | 37.5 | 41.2 |
| results on topology of accidents (small leakages, safety containments) | 30.3 | 43.8 | 17.6 |
| plant technology considered in the study | 27.3 | 31.3 | 23.5 |
| need for international negotiation for prevention of accidents, safety standards, etc. | 27.3 | 37.5 | 17.6 |

(c)   the study provides an objective basis for the discussion of nuclear energy and could be used by both opponents and advocates – 31.3 percent of articles.

With respect to comments, only one frequently featured aspect merits additional mention:

(a)   knowledge of the results of the study is not a sufficient condition for the acceptance of nuclear energy: "Acceptance is a process within the framework of the formation of political opinion:" 29.4 percent of articles.

The failure to mention certain aspects is revealing. The following aspects receive no mentions at all (either in the news items or in the comments reviewed):

(a)   the study was designed to contribute to the optimization of the reactor safety research program;
(b)   the study was designed to contribute to the analysis of weak points in plant technology;
(c)   critics of nuclear energy with professional competence did not participate in the study;
(d)   the issue of the participation of physicians and biologists in the study;
(e)   the issue of the participation of Norman Rasmussen and the US Nuclear Regulatory Commission in the study;
(f)   failure to deal with boiling-water reactors and underground construction;
(g)   exclusion of the problem of demolition of reactors;
(h)   the study did not address transfer factors in the food chain;
(i)   the study did not consider contamination of groundwater and soil;
(j)   no statements were possible on specific sites;
(k)   consequences of the study for the licensing procedure.

This statistical evaluation suggests that, other than the formal aspects of presentation, the features chiefly treated were the more striking results of the *German risk study* along with a somewhat less frequent discussion of method and of political consequences (acceptability and acceptance of nuclear energy). In the areas of safety research and of political–administrative consequences, only the aspect concerning the transnational effects of nuclear power plants and the "need for international negotiations" received attention. On the other hand, critical aspects (e.g., bias, exclusions) of the study were largely neglected. Moreover, the consequences of the study for the licensing procedures for nuclear power facilities and its relevance for the Commission of Inquiry were hardly discussed at all.

Of greater importance than the distinction between news items and comments were differences in the structure of reporting resulting from positive, neutral, and negative evaluation of the study (and, for the greater part, of

nuclear energy). The results of the corresponding analysis (Table 4.3), rein-
force the foregoing discussion. *Negative statements* were a distinct minority
among the 250 articles in the documentation. Articles in which *no evaluations*
of the risk study are discernible were obviously mainly news items and reports
on the presentation, but some were comments that focused on the questionable
value of the study. Articles *favorable* to the study were, once again, largely
comments. But some are reports, whose selection of headings and style of
reporting clearly reveal a positive evaluation.

If one refers once again to the *frequencies* of features and examines only
those aspects mentioned in 40 percent or more of the articles, there was no
difference in reporting by attitude for the aspects "probability of accidents,"
"immediate damage," and "delayed damage" – the figures on these subjects
were mentioned with similar frequency in all articles. The only additional
aspect receiving equally frequent mention in the positive and neutral reports on
the study noted that the study provided no arguments against nuclear energy.

The same aspect, however, received far less mention (in only about 25
percent of the articles) in unfavorable reports. These emphasized the problems
of the analysis of the course of incidents, the probabilistic approach, the
exclusion of threats from outside the plant (such as sabotage and war), and the
problems involved in emergency measures and plans for evacuation.
References to the (usually negatively judged) *Reactor safety study* as a model
and basis for comparison occurred with similar frequency (>40 percent) in the
unfavorable reports. Finally, it is noteworthy that, compared with other
aspects (especially the sociopolitical consequences), the consequences for the
area of safety research and safety technology and for the political–administrative area received less frequent coverage in all three groups of articles.

QUALITATIVE ANALYSIS

The following examination of arguments supplements the quantitative assessment and employs the same structure of analysis.

*The political–administrative framework of the study*     The quantitative analysis
suggested that the negative evaluation of the *German risk study* focused upon
the "framework" of the study. This corresponds to the fact that only detractors
addressed this aspect, focusing on two points:

(a)  The emphasis on the model character of the *Reactor safety study*, which
     had already been withdrawn in the United States, and the use of methods
     that had long ago been rejected as inadequate by the National Aeronauti-
     cal and Space Administration (NASA) were an "insult" to the public by the
     nuclear industry and permitted conclusions about its underlying
     intentions.
(b)  The interests of the *German risk study* were "not beyond suspicion"
     (*Frankfurter Rundschau*, August 8, 1979: Hollenstein 1979a). The study

was not "independent," its "partisanship on behalf of the nuclear industry" was documented (Barthel 1979). Statements by the author, Professor Birkhofer, indicated his attitude totally in favor of nuclear energy (Borsche 1979, of the BBU).

*The methodological approach of the study*   Both advocates and opponents of the study stressed that it considered "human error" only insufficiently or that this factor could be quantified only with great difficulty (if at all). Significantly, *Unsere Zeit*, the newspaper of the German Communist Party, added that the study was confined to technical laws, neglecting *societal laws* (Bubenberger 1979), which are, however, unpredictable. A second basic argument, discussed mainly by the critics but also by some of the advocates, was that probability calculations had only limited or no value for the study conclusions. Development and documentation of this argument proceeded in several ways:

(a)   *Harrisburg* showed that a core meltdown was by no means merely a hypothetical case (Rudzinski 1979, Hofmann 1979).
(b)   Although an American scientist had classified the midair collision of two jumbo jets as even less likely than a core meltdown, this very accident occurred shortly after the statement was made (*Tageszeitung* 1979).
(c)   *Vorwarts* quoted Ralph Nader, who claimed that experts had classified as "unlikely" no less than 35 percent of the breakdowns occurring in nuclear power plants (Fischer 1979).
(d)   On an even more general note, Lorenz Borsche (1979) of the BBU writing in the *Stuttgarter Nachrichten* emphasized that *statements on probability* include the *possibility of accidents*, which could occur equally well tomorrow or in a thousand years' time.
(e)   In this context, several authors simply described "games with numbers" (Bundesverband Bürgerinitiativen Umweltschutz 1979a, Hollenstein 1979a, 1979b, Fischer 1979).

These arguments on the methodology of the study contributed to a more negative final assessment of its value. A third criticism centered on *omissions or deliberate exclusions* in the material or the presentation:

(a)   The exclusion of *advanced reactor designs*, and especially the problem of *waste management*, led to an underestimation of danger.
(b)   The study failed to examine accidents below the level of the maximum credible accident (MCA).

Closely related were arguments criticizing the selection of subjects for examination in the study:

(a)   The examined reactor of type Biblis B was not representative of nuclear power plants in the Federal Republic of Germany in that it incorporated the most advanced safety standards.

(b)   The method employed for the selection of representative accidents was not valid. For instance, the study claimed that Harrisburg fell within the group of representative accidents, but considered its occurrence as much less likely than critics felt correct (Borsche 1979).

(c)   In the absence of practical experience, the *estimated values* were only *makeshift* (Rudzinski 1979); the large number of possible combinations of accidents prevented complete examination and analysis.

(d)   The *database* for the study contained "inconsistencies" and partly contradicted previous publications by the GRS (Barthel 1979).

An extremely important factor in the reception to the study was its assumption of the existence of evacuation plans of a scale that did not exist anywhere. For instance, the occurrence of a maximum credible accident at Biblis would necessitate the evacuation from the Frankfurt–Darmstadt area of 2.9 million people. The authorities, however, tacitly regarded this as impossible, and recommended, therefore, that those affected in the "inner circle" should seek shelter in cellars. Finally, the general question was raised as to whether the term "safety" used in the study had been modified for compatibility with the interests of the nuclear industry, just as it was in the *Reactor safety study* (Fischer 1979).

*On the results of the study*   Neither advocates nor opponents of the study proposed additions or changes regarding the presentation of results. The advocates of the study, of nuclear energy, or both stressed the small likelihood of accidents and consequences of accidents:

(a)   It is a well established fact that death from a traffic accident is more likely than death in a reactor accident (a statement of Birkhofer that received extensive Press coverage) (*Neue Hannoversche Presse* 1979).

(b)   Serious consequences of an accident, such as Three Mile Island or similar incidents, properly belong to the realm of "adventurous improbability calculations" (*Frankfurter Neue Presse* 1979).

Using identical results, the critics of the study emphasized the opposite aspect:

(a)   The accident proneness of German reactors was, surprisingly, estimated by the study to be *greater* than that of American reactors.

(b)   According to the study, the likelihood of a maximum credible accident was greater than had previously been assumed.

(c)   Taking into consideration the margin of error, in the worst case a core-meltdown accident could occur every 40 years in the Federal Republic of Germany.

In connection with the last-mentioned figure, it should be pointed out that critics generally chose to omit one result of the study which stated that immediate damage (acute fatalities) occurred in far less than 1 percent of all core-meltdown accidents. A remarkable phenomenon is that, despite numerous political and methodological reservations concerning the risk study, the results were described positively when they supported the commentator's point of view.

Several additional points concerning the reproduction and evaluation of results stressed by the study's supporters were:

(a)  the significance of common-mode accidents and the difficulties in quantifying them (Rudzinski 1979);
(b)  the difficulties in communicating the results, given the backdrop of the different everyday experiences of politicians and the general public (von Randow 1979);
(c)  many periodicals argued that the "residual risks" that existed could scarcely be reduced by even the best safety technology and thus had to be accepted in the politicians' considerations.

*On the consequences and the usefulness of the study*  With regard to safety research and technology, the study's supporters emphasized that since it provided nothing new for the improvement of safety, which was already high, no additional requirements were necessary. To make this point, they quoted a GRS statement that the safety conception of German nuclear technology had proved its worth. For their part, the critics complained that the "safety" of the fast-breeder and high-temperature reactors was apparently not scheduled for examination before they would be put into service. They announced a counter-study to be conducted by the Öko-Institut.

As for the political–administrative consequences, the relevance of risk studies to other fields (including the projected extensions to petrochemistry or other energy technologies) attracted considerable skepticism (Schütz 1979). According to this view, the "practical consequences" of a study of this kind confronted all kinds of opposition and conflicting interests. Most of the additional arguments on the consequences of the study addressed effects in the sociopolitical area. First came the arguments of those in favor of the study:

(a)  Many were very skeptical of the effect of the study on the public acceptance of nuclear energy. Complaints were made over "the powerlessness of mathematics against ignorance" (Bruns 1979), the "innate fear" of complex technologies, and games with numbers. In short, the study would not solve the problem of acceptance (Jansen 1979).
(b)  The influence of the study on politicians was thus of far greater importance. On the one hand, proponents appealed to politicians to make clear decisions, taking into account (residual) risk to safety and risks for the future (shortage of energy). On the other hand, special reference was made to controversy in the Social Democratic Party (SPD), where the pro-nuclear-energy group was on the offensive due in no small part to the study (especially at the SPD Party Convention in Berlin).

(c)   The study could, in a certain sense, conclude the long public discussion on nuclear energy.

(d)   The "residual fear" of the public had been a truly productive corrective factor for the "decision makers" (Piel 1979).

(e)   The "horrifying figures" (with regard to extent of damage) in the study could lead to public misunderstanding, in as much as they were separated from the likelihood of their occurrence or in their drawing attention to risks of nuclear energy in the first place.

(f)   In view of the considerable risks to safety revealed in the study, "problems of the atom state" had not been averted (Jansen 1979) and democratic (and not authoritarian) enforcement of the expansion of nuclear energy was currently the main political task (Rudzinski 1979).

The opponents to nuclear energy and the critics of the study expected it to have greater effects on acceptance, in that:

(a)   a warning was given not to "abuse" the results of the study by playing down the risks of nuclear energy and thereby create a biased picture for the public (*Wirtschaftswoche* 1979), as happened with the *Reactor safety study*;

(b)   it was assumed that the strength of the pronuclear energy group (in the SPD) would increase (*Der Spiegel* 1979) despite the assumption that the "residual energy demand philosophy" would be retained as the official party line for some time yet (Rudzinski 1979). In this respect, the assessment corresponded to that of the advocates.

The environmentally oriented critics of the study saw no reason to change their attitudes to nuclear energy. On the contrary, several readers complained in letters about the moral insolence that tolerated tens or hundreds of thousands of dead whether by "nuclear accident" or by the "traffic accidents" used as a basis for reference but that rejected abortions on religious or constitutional grounds.

SUMMARY

The results of the quantitative and qualitative analysis of Press reporting presented above must be viewed with two reservations:

(a)   On the one hand, the press reports examined were based mainly on the material prepared by the GRS and on the press conference, not on the main volume or the technical volumes of the study. For this reason, it was not to be expected that reporting would achieve the level of specialized scientific or even of popularized scientific publication. An exception was an article by Thomas von Randow (1979) in *Die Zeit*.

(b)   On the other hand, it is the task of the daily press (which provided the vast majority of documented articles) to provide and discuss down-to-earth facts and the "political" conditions for and consequences of a study of this kind.

Thus, it is scarcely surprising that notable figures (likelihood of a core meltdown, immediate deaths, and delayed damage) from the presentation generally occupied the foreground, whereas the consequences for safety technology and administration stayed in the background. The expectations of the press with regard to the usefulness and effects of the study were quite modest right from the start in comparison with the considerable effort expended on the study.

Although the press thought that the *German risk study* added nothing essential to the already high quality of safety technology of German nuclear power plants, some journalists hoped that the study would prove to be a first step toward the comparative assessment of technologies. Consequences for "administration and decision making" were seen, if at all, in the long run. This applied to licensing procedure under nuclear law, to international agreements on safety regulations and standards, and to comparative technology assessments on the basis of risk studies. Moreover, the issue of emergency plans for evacuation in catastrophes, an issue raised mainly by critics of the study, was not affected by the study and was slated for partial consideration in phase B of the study.

The greatest expectations for the study centered on its usefulness for the political controversy over nuclear energy. But many of the study's advocates were skeptical on this point. The hope that the study would make the public discussion more rational was coupled with the realization that the results of the study could be employed both by supporters and opponents of nuclear energy. Numerous editorials welcomed the widely publicized opinion of Research Minister V. Hauff that the risks of nuclear energy were no real barrier to its increased use. At the same time, a number of the study's advocates regarded its effects on the acceptance of nuclear energy with caution or pessimism. Risk studies represent only *one* possible element in the examination and evaluation by the public of risk-laden technologies.

Both perspectives have in common their individual or psychological interpretation of "residual problems." All in all, the press made almost no attempt to discuss the perceptions, interpretations, and evaluations of the figures on the extent of damage and risks in connection with *societal* opinion formation processes. Apparently the publication of the results in the press was aimed chiefly at politicians, "decision makers," and "opinion leaders" who had the responsibility for interpreting and balancing arguments, making decisions about risk, and justifying these decisions to the broad public.

It is, however, conspicuous that the press had reservations about the plan to involve professionally competent critics in phase B of the study. It is not possible here to judge whether the plan was regarded as superfluous or unrealistic. Possibly, it is merely another way of expressing the dominant press opinion that the "battle for the acceptance of nuclear energy" had to be fought on a field other than that of risk studies.

### Risk analysis and the public acceptance of nuclear energy: a concluding comment

A key aspect of all nuclear risk analyses is their effect on the public acceptance of nuclear energy. In the Federal Republic of Germany, the controversies about this technology were and still are – particularly in the wake of the Chernobyl accident – especially vehement. Here, as in the other countries treated in this volume, this phenomenon is the object of widespread social science research. How can one determine the impact of risk analyses on public acceptance? The analyses conducted for this chapter suggest two responses.

First, the social conflict about nuclear energy is too complex to be explained by a single cause. The social science literature yields a variety of different approaches that attempt to explain this phenomenon. Currently, the social-psychological line of research in the Federal Republic of Germany is represented primarily by a recent work by Renn (1981), who taps the well-known work by Fischhoff, Lichtenstein, and Slovic (Fischhoff *et al.* 1978) in the United States as well as the attitude surveys by Otway and his former group at the International Atomic Energy Agency (Otway & Fishbein 1976). The results of these researchers have received partial confirmation as well as elaboration.

Several key results are of particular interest here. For intuitive risk judgments, the statistical expressions used in scientific risk analysis are not decisive. Rather, more abstract aspects of risk and overall conceptions and views of the source of the risk assume importance. Positive and negative judgments derive from a limited number of viewpoints to which citizens usually orient themselves. Nuclear energy highlights key qualitative aspects of the attendant risk – its potential for catastrophic consequences, its unfamiliar and involuntary character, and its imperceptibility. Aspects favoring nuclear energy are that it carries benefits for all and expends extraordinary efforts to guarantee safety. In the light of these realities, it is not surprising that significant changes of opinion have not followed in the wake of the publication of major risk studies.

However, it would be wrong to conclude from this that risk studies have no effect or are redundant. Because survey results do not adequately capture the conflict about nuclear energy, the role which risk studies play cannot be fully understood by relying solely upon survey research. Opinions of individual citizens, considered in isolation from each other and as represented in surveys and psychological studies, do not determine the nature of the current conflict. Rather, those institutions and organizations that are directly or indirectly involved in the introduction of nuclear energy are the key. They come from industry, politics, and science, and include environmental protection organizations, citizen action groups, ecological institutes representing the organized part of an antinuclear movement; the Press and radio; and judicial institutions that are intermediaries in the conflict.

Sociological approaches to acceptance research (Conrad & Krebsbach-Gnath 1981, Frederichs & Loeben 1979) are more strongly concerned with the social situation within which the individual resides and forms opinions. This approach is realistic to the extent that the "normal" citizen has no direct experience of the manifold aspects of nuclear energy. Transfer of knowledge and conceptions about this technology occur via communication processes. The common features (in the judgments made by different persons) that are discovered in psychological analyses are presumably the outcome of what is actually debated in public.

For the question pursued here, it is appropriate to start from the social conflict currently accompanying the introduction of nuclear energy. It is necessary to perceive this as a complicated societal process in which the different interests, value orientations, and goals of scientific-technological and political groups, as well as of the critical public and of the public represented in the media, approach each other – or fail to do so – in an iterative process. The role of risk studies can, then, be analyzed with a view to their function and impact upon the organized actors in this conflict-laden process.

Second, in view of the broad public skepticism toward the risks of nuclear energy, the primary function of risk studies is to inform the public on what can be currently stated, on the basis of scientific methodology and according to the state of the art of science, about the potential danger. As long as nuclear energy persists as an energy-policy option and receives a great deal of public attention, the public must be kept informed about the results of scientific research. To do otherwise would probably considerably aggravate the acceptance problem, not so much because the studies themselves improve acceptance but because the failure to inform the public would be considered irresponsible.

Thus, a risk study is a datum in the public discussion which has to be reckoned with in the future course of the debate. One may criticize it or call it into question, but one cannot ignore it. Scientific experts may produce evaluations to the contrary; criticism may come from outside scientific circles; or proponents and opponents may select the findings of the study and use them as arguments for or against nuclear energy. These effects may be very indirect and very difficult to discern. An example of such an indirect impact of risk analyses on the public discussion is the common usage – and even, to some degree, proper understanding – today of terms such as "risk," "probability," "ten to the minus seventh," etc. One should not underestimate this effect, for the adoption of scientific terms also invariably entails to a certain extent the adoption of the way of thinking connected with them. If one may speak at all of a "more rational" discussion as a consequence of the publication of risk studies, such an effect would probably have its origins here. No simple answer will determine whether risk studies have an aggravating or mitigating effect on the conflict. It bears repeating that the conflict is extremely complex and empirical treatment is not sufficient.

That organizations critical of nuclear energy are increasingly asked to participate in the formulation of risk studies may possibly have a mitigating effect on conflict. In more general terms, such a process would take roughly the following course. Conceptualization and presentation of risk studies usually betray weak points that spark criticism and are subject to interpretation according to the viewpoints of the critics and commentators in the conflict about nuclear energy. Sometimes these interpretations serve to advance the strategic position of the interested parties to the conflict, either as a call for improvements or else as proof of the difficulties of making nuclear energy safer. Conflict mitigation will occur if growing numbers of critical scientists endorse the first interpretation.

Third, the function and impact of risk studies in the conflict about nuclear energy are restricted considerably if the widely held thesis that this conflict extends beyond the pure risk issue is confirmed. There can be no doubt that the nuclear controversy is open to different interpretations. One plausible hypothesis is that the controversies mark the beginning of a fundamental conflict in western industrialized societies in which the intensity and direction of overall industrial development are at stake. Without necessarily adopting such an approach, one cannot pretend not to notice that the issue of the risks of nuclear power plants apparently does not suffice to explain the conflict. Other risks should (but do not) provoke the same reactions.

On the other hand, problems of acceptance, with similar manifestations of citizens' protests, surface in other policy areas (e.g., education, town planning and housing policy, and the transport sector) that do not involve a risk such as that of nuclear energy. Such considerations call for a modification of the thesis that the widespread opposition to nuclear energy is simply a reaction of fear. Within the context of this modified thesis, risk assumes a symbolic function in the nuclear controversy. The thematic focus on risk has become the permanent issue in the course of the controversy; risk is the common topic that is the precondition for any public discussion, without, however, necessarily comprising all the dimensions that are at the root of the controversy. Such a theme does not crystallize by chance but is dependent on the extent to which it allows the articulation of opposing opinions and the definition of respective individual viewpoints. The following discussion shows how both parties in the conflict about nuclear energy enlist the risk issue to support their respective arguments.

Proponents of nuclear energy use risk considerations to point out how safe nuclear energy is, compared to other technologies. Safety research represents a field of governmental promotion to which a certain legitimizing value can be attributed. For opponents, objectives rest on the irrefutable premise that catastrophic accidents are indeed possible in nuclear facilities. Thus opponents focus on conditions that might trigger such accidents and impacts on health and the environment. Each such presentation conveys the impression of a threat which, irrespective of probability considerations, gives rise to a general feeling of concern. If probabilities are considered, the argument runs that even in cases of extremely low probability the accident might nevertheless happen tomorrow.

These arguments assume even greater weight when, in addition to the risk due to technical failure, they bring in the spectre of deliberate human actions, such as sabotage by states, terrorist organizations, or mentally deranged individuals, as possible triggers of catastrophes. The thesis that the precautionary measures necessary to protect nuclear installations and operations might even lead to police-state circumstances has met with great sympathy. The dimensions of possible accidents as well as the inconceivable time periods for which radioactive waste is left to future generations exceed normal imagination and thus lend themselves easily to arguments against the acceptability of such a technology.

The arguments concerning the risks of nuclear energy mentioned so far can indeed evoke fear and provoke a general feeling of concern. The conflict would, however, not be described adequately if the resistance against nuclear energy would be interpreted *solely* as an irrational reaction of fear. Such an explanation does not suffice to assess the political importance of the nuclear controversy, because nuclear opponents do not merely paint the dark picture of possible catastrophes but endeavor to base their arguments on detailed information, to point out the relationship of their arguments to more general political objectives, and to operationalize them for the political debate. Thus they attempt to show where nuclear energy policy contradicts other political goals, and they extend the spectrum of nuclear risks to problems of foreign policy, aid to developing countries, and to economic, environmental, and defense policies.

The arguments concerning the risk of nuclear energy put forward in the Press and in popular books, as well as in hearings and in courts of law, force experts and politicians to take a stand. Usually these arguments run up against claims that safety problems have always been solved in the past, that safety technology is highly developed, and that comparable or much higher risks exist in other fields of technology and daily life. Yet, the dialogue has witnessed no major progress in years. Both sides repeat their arguments in a more or less stereotyped manner.

This obvious talking-past-each-other confirms the above-mentioned thesis that "risk" primarily has the function of symbolizing the opposing positions in a controversy whose causes are more complex than can be perceived through the narrow perspective of safety and risk.

If this thesis proves correct, a consensus on the issue of risk will not be reached as long as the complex causes and underlying motives of the conflict continue to exist.

## Notes

1  The median is the 50-percent fractile of the probability distribution which is due to the uncertainties of the data base.
2  In 1981, the German Ministry of the Interior submitted to the Parliamentary Committee for Internal Affairs a detailed report entitled *Consequences to be drawn from the TMI-2 accident at*

*Harrisburg on 28th March 1979 with regard to radiation protection and the safety of nuclear power plants* (Bundesministerium des Innern 1981). The report concludes that no immediate consequences had been drawn from this accident because of the different conception of German nuclear power plants, compared to TMI-2, regarding technical safety systems and organizational aspects. Nevertheless, as a precautionary measure, special and thorough checkups of all German nuclear power plants were performed after the TMI-2 accident, leading to a number of improvements.

## References

Balfanz, H. P., F. W. Heuser & W. Ullrich 1974. *Nuclear Engineering and Design* **29**, 384.

Barthel, W. 1979. Das verharmloste Risiko: ein Gutachten, das die Bürger einlullen soll. *Stern*, August 20.

Bastl, W. & H. Gieseler 1970. The reliability of emergency core cooling systems of light water nuclear power plants. In *Proceedings, Specialist meeting on reliability of mechanical components and system for nuclear research safety*, Risø report no. 214.

Bastl, W., H. Hörtner & P. Kafka 1978. Influence of probabilistic safety analysis on design and operation of PWR plants. In *American nuclear society, ANS topical meeting on probabilistic analysis of nuclear safety, Los Angeles, 1978*. La Grange, Illinois: ANS.

BMFT (Bundesminister für Forschung und Technologie) (ed.) 1979a. *The German risk study: summary*. Cologne: Gesellschaft fur Reaktorsicherheit.

BMFT (Bundesministerium für Forschung und Technologie) 1979b. Pressemitteilung "Forschungsminister Hauff: 'Kernenergierisiken weder verharmlosen noch dramatisieren.'" In *Dokumentation von Aktivitäten anlässich der Präsentation der deutschen Risikostudie*, GRS. Cologne: GRS.

Borsche, L. 1979. Ein schwerer Unfall kann sich zu jeder Zeit ereignen [guest editorial]. *Stuttgarter Nachrichten*, August 24.

Bruns, K. 1979. Die Gurus und die Sicherheit. *Die Welt*, August 17.

Bubenberger, P. 1979. Reaktorsicherheit: unberechenbar. *Unsere Zeit*, August 16.

Bundesgesetz 1976. Gesetz über die friedliche Verwendung der Kernenergie und den Schutz gegen ihre Gefahren (Atomgesetz) vom 23, Dezember 1959. *Der Fassung der Neubekanntmachung*, October 31.

Bundesminister des Innern 1977. Sicherheitskriterien für Kernkraftwerke, verabschiedet im Länderausschuss für Atomkernenergie am 12. Oktober 1977. *Bundesanzeiger* **206** (November 3).

Bundesministerium des Innern 1981. *Konsequenzen für die Sicherheit von Kernkraftwerken und den Strahlenschutz aus dem Störfall im amerikanischen Kernkraftwerken TMI-2 bei Harrisburg vom 28, März 1979: Schlussbericht des BMI für den Innenausschuss des Deutschen Bundestages*. Bonn: Bundesministerium des Innern.

Bundesverband Bürgerinitiativen Umweltschutz 1979a. *Presseerklärung des BBU: Gefährdungspotential der Kernenergie statistisch nicht messbar*. Karlsruhe, August 16.

Bundesverband Bürgerinitiativen Umweltschutz 1979b. *Pressemeldung* vom 15.8.1979.

Bundesverband Bürgerinitiativen Umweltschutz 1979c. *Zweite Stellungnahme des BBU zur Deutschen Risikostudie vom 10.12.1979.*

Conrad, J. & C. Krebsbach-Gnath 1981. *Technologische Risiken und gesellschaftliche Konflikte*. Frankfurt am Main: Battelle-Institut.

Danzmann, H.-J. 1981. *Kritik der Stellungnahme zur "deutschen Risikostudie" der Gesellschaft für Reaktorsicherheit des Bremer Arbeits- und Umweltschutz-Zentrums.* GRS-36. Cologne: Gesellschaft für Reaktorsicherheit.

Deutscher Bundestag 1979. 8. Wahlperiode. Ausschuss für Forschung und Technologie, 755–2450: Kurzprotokoll der 54. Sitzung am 17.10.1979. *Protokoll* **54**, 16–24.

Deutscher Bundestag 1980. 8. Wahlperiode. Drucksache 8/4341 vom 27.6.1980: *Bericht der Enquete-Kommission* Zukünftige Kernenergie-Politik *über den Stand der Arbeit und die Ergebnisse gemäss Beschluss des Deutschen Bundestages: Drucksache 8/2628.*

Dornier System GmbH 1981. Stellungnahme zur Deutschen Risikostudie Kernkraftwerke, Phase A, und Vorschläge für weiterführende Arbeiten als Vorbereitung der Phase B. In *Auftrag des* BMFT. Bonn: Ministry for Research and Technology, unpublished manuscript.

Dressler, E. & H. Spindler 1974. Verbesserung der Verfügbarkeit von Sicherheitssystemen durch zeitlich gestaffelte Prüfungen. *Atomwirtschaft-Atomtechnik* **19**, 133.

Farmer, F. R. 1967. Reactor safety analysis as related to reactor siting. In *Containment and siting of nuclear power plants*, IAEA Proceedings series. Vienna, Austria: International Atomic Energy Agency.

Fischer, J. 1979. Milliardenspiel mit dem Risiko. *Vorwärts*, August 25.

Fischhoff, B., P, Slovic, S. Lichtenstein, S. Read & B. Combs 1978. How safe is safe enough?: a psychometric study of attitudes towards technological risks and benefits. *Policy Sciences* **8**, 127–52.

Franke, B. & B. Steinhilber-Schwab 1981. *Studie über die Folgen von Unfällen im Kernkraftwerk Grafenrheinfeld für die Bevölkerung der Stadt Schweinfurt.* Heidelberg, Institut für Energie- und Umweltforschung.

*Frankfurter Neue Presse* 1979. Die Offensive der Kernkraftbefürworter, Aug. 15.

Frederichs, G. & M. Loeben 1979. *Die Akzeptanzproblematik der Kernenergie.* KFK 2705. Karlsruhe: Kernforschungszentrum Karlsruhe.

GRS (Gesellschaft für Reaktorsicherheit) 1979a. *Dokumentation von Aktivitäten anlässich der Präsentation der deutschen Risikostudie.* Cologne: GRS.

GRS (Gesellschaft für Reaktorsicherheit) 1979b. Pressemitteilung "Deutsche Risikostudie veroffentlicht," August 8. In *Dokumentation von Aktivitäten anlässich der Präsentation der deutschen Risikostudie*, GRS Cologne: GRS.

GRS (Gesellschaft für Reaktorsicherheit) 1979c. Pressemitteilung "Die Deutsche Risikostudie fur Kernkraftwerke," August 8. In GRS, *Dokumentation von Aktivitäten anlässich der Präsentation der deutschen Risikostudie.* Cologne: GRS.

GRS (Gesellschaft für Reaktorsicherheit) 1979d. Fragen/Antworten zur Birkhofer-Studie (34 Fragen und Antworten). In GRS, *Dokumentation von Aktiväten anlässich der Präsentation der deutschen Risikostudie.* Cologne: GRS.

GRS (Gesellschaft für Reaktorsicherheit) 1980. *Deutsche Risikostudie Kernkraftwerke: eine Untersuchung zu dem durch Störfalle in Rernkraftwerken verursachten Risiko.* Cologne: Verlag TÜV Rheinland.

Hahn, L. 1981. Kritik der Deutschen Risikostudie Kernkraftwerke: Schwerpunkte der Projektgruppe Reaktorsicherheit. *Öko-Mitteilungen* **2**, 13–16.

Hauff, V. 1979. Unkorrigiertes Manuskript der Rede des BMFT für die Bundespressekonferenz am 14. August 1979. In *Dokumentation von Aktivitäten anlässich der Präsentation der deutschen Risikostudie*, GRS. Cologne: GRS.

Hofmann, G. 1979. Ist das Atom-Rennen gelaufen? *Zeit*, August 17.

Hollenstein, G. 1979a. Zahlenspielereien [editorial]. *Frankfurter Rundschau*, August 8.

Hollenstein, G. 1979b. Umweltschützer fühlen sich durch Risikostudie bestärkt: "Zahlenspielereien über Sicherheit von Reaktoren nicht viel wert." *Frankfurter Rundschau*, August 17.

Hömke, P., E. Lindauer & G. Meinlschmidt 1978. Data collection in a nuclear power plant and a pilot collection system in a lignite-power station. In American Society of Mechanical Engineers, ASME *symposium on inservice data reporting and analysis, San Francisco*. New York: ASME.

Hörtner, H., E. Nieckau & H. Spindler 1976. *Kernkraftwerk Biblis, Block A: Ergebnisse der Zuverlässigkeitsuntersuchungen für den Auslegungsstörfall "Bruch einer kalten Hauptkühlmittelleitung."* MMR 168. Munich: TU.

Jansen, P. 1979. Atomrisiko bleibt im Gespräch. *Handelsblatt*, August 16.

Kendall, H. W. 1977. *The risk of nuclear power reactors: A review of the* NRC *Reactor Safety Study, WASH-1400 (NUREG 75/014)*. Cambridge, Mass: Union of Concerned Scientists.

Kotthoff, K. & W. Otto 1976. *Vergleich von Rechenprogrammen zur Zuverlässigkeitsanalyse von Kernkraftwerken: Abschlussbericht Reaktorsicherheitsforschungsprogramm des BMFT*. RS. 172. Bonn: Bundesministerium für Forschung und Technologie.

Lindackers, K.-H. 1970. *Einflüsse des atomrechtlichen Genehmigungsverfahrens in der Bundesrepublik Deutschland auf die Auslegung und den Betrieb von Kernkraftwerken*. PhD dissertation, Rheinisch-Westfälische Technische Hochschule, Aachen.

Lindauer, E. 1981. Zuverlässigkeit und Betriebserfahrungen. In *3. GRS-Fachkonferenz München, 1980*. GRS-34. Cologne: Gesellschaft für Reaktorsicherheit.

Lukes, R. 1978. Die Verwendung von Risikoanalysen in der Rechtsordnung unter besonderer Berücksichtigung des Kernenergierechts. *Betriebs-Berater Zeitschrift für Recht und Wirtschaft*, **7**, 317–21.

Lukes, R., Fr.-J. Feldmann & H.-Chr. Knüppel 1980. Länderbericht der Bundesrepublik Deutschland: Gefahren und Gefahrenbeurteilungen in der Rechtsordnung der Bundesrepublik Deutschland. In *Gefahren und Gefahrenbeurteilungen im Recht, Part 2: Risikoforschung in der Technik: Länderberichte Bundesrepublik Deutschland und Frankreich*, R. Lukes (ed.), 71–207, espec. 166ff. Cologne: Heymanns.

*Neue Hannoversche Presse* 1979. Statistik: eher Tod im Verkehr als durch Atom. *Neue Hannovershe Presse*, August 15.

Nieckau, E. 1974. Reliability analysis of electronic modules with digital inputs. *Nuclear Engineering and Design* **30**, 117–22.

Oberverwaltungsgerichte Münster 1977. Urteil vom 20.2.1975 zum Kernkraftwerk Würgassen. *Energiewirtschaftliche Tagesfragen* 1977, 220ff.

Öko-Institut Freiburg 1981. *Vorhaben RS 482: analytische Weiterentwicklung zur Deutschen Risikostudie Kernkraftwerke*. Zwischenberichte no. 1 (February), no. 2 (May), and no. 3 (August). Freiburg: Öko-Institut.

Otway, H. J. & M. Fishbein 1976. *The determinants of attitude formation: an application to nuclear power*. RM 76–80. Laxenburg, Austria: International Institute for Applied Systems Analysis.

Piel, D. 1979. Kernkraft: neue Sachlichkeit. *Börsenzeitung*, August 18.
Pollmann, E. 1979. Vorwort. In GRS, *Dokumentation von Aktivitäten anlässlich der Präsentation der deutschen Risikostudie*. Cologne: GRS.
Probst A. 1979. Press release (Presseinformation), Garching, August 14.

Randow, T. vom 1979. Vom Fehlerbaum gefallen: die Gefahr, bei Reaktorunfällen umzukommen, ist vergleichsweise gering. *Die Zeit*, August 17.
Renn, O. 1981. *Man, technology and risk: a study on intuitive risk assessment and attitudes towards nuclear energy*. Spezielle Berichte der Kernforschungsanlage Jülich, no. 115. Jülich: Programmgruppe Kernenergie und Umwelt, Kernforschungsanlage Jülich.
Risk Assessment Review Group 1978. *Risk Assessment Review Group report to the U.S. Nuclear Regulatory Commission*. NUREG CR-0400. Washington: Nuclear Regulatory Commission, September.
Rudzinski, K. 1979. "Das Reaktorrisiko ist zumutbar": Sicherheitsanalysen mit begrentzer Aussagekraft [editorial]. *Frankfurter Allgemeine Zeitung*, August 22.

Schlösser, L. 1978. STREUSEL: *Ein Rechenprogramm zur Ermittlung der Streuung in Zuverlässigkeitskenngrössen auf Grund der Streuung der Eingaben*. GRS-A-183. Cologne: Gesellschaft für Reaktorsicherheit.
Schütz P. 1979. Wandel (Kommentar). *Stuttgarter Nachrichten*, August 17.
*Spiegel, Der* 1979. Atomenergie: still verdunsten. *Der Spiegel*, August 20.

*Tageszeitung* 1979. Neue AKW-Sicherheits-Studie: alle 40 Jahre eine Katastrophe? *Tageszeitung*, August 15.

US Atomic Energy Commission 1957. *Theoretical possibilities and consequences of major accidents in large nuclear power plants*. WASH-740. Washington, DC: Atomic Energy Commission.
US Nuclear Regulatory Commission 1975. *Reactor safety study*. WASH-1400, NUREG 75/014. Washington, DC: Nuclear Regulatory Commission.

Verwaltungsgericht (VG) Freiburg 1977. Urteil vom 14.3.1977 zum Kernkraftwerk Wyhl. In *Energiewirtschaftliche Tagesfragen*, 626ff.
Verwaltungsgericht Oldenburg 1979. Urteil vom 15.9.1978 zum Kernkraftwerk Unterweser, "Wegweiser durch das Urteil." In *Energiewirtschaftliche Tagesfragen*, 651ff.
Verwaltungsgericht Würzburg 1977. Urteil vom 25.3.1977 zum Kernkraftwerk Grafenrheinfeld. In *Energiewirtschaftliche Tagesfragen*, 444ff.

Wagner, H. 1981. Nutzen und Grenzen wissenschaftlich-technischer Risikoanalysen aus rechtlicher Sicht. In *Risiken technischer Anlagen und ihre rechtliche Bewertung*, F. Nicklisch, D. Schottelius, & H. Wagner (eds.). Karlsruhe: Kernforschungszentrum Karlsruhe.
*Wirtschaftswoche* 1979. Risikostudie: menschliche Fehler nicht ausgeschlossen [quotation of Professor von Ehrenstein]. *Wirtschaftswoche*, August 20.

# 5 Risk and the Ontario Royal Commission on Electric Power Planning in Canada

JAMES E. DOOLEY and JOHN B. ROBINSON

Unlike the other broad-scale risk assessments treated in this volume, the original impetus for the establishment of the Royal Commission on Electric Power Planning in Ontario (Canada) had nothing to do with nuclear risk issues, or a risk controversy, and was only indirectly concerned with the question of the desirability of nuclear power. In 1974, Ontario Hydro, the provincial public utility company, issued a report on long-range planning of Ontario's electric system that envisioned a doubling of electrical capacity[1] over the next ten years and again over the succeeding ten years. The capital requirements for the envisioned added capacity were enormous, causing considerable concern among rural landowners because of the land-use implications of such development. The Ontario government, which also had serious misgivings about the extensive capital requirements associated with the expansion program, established the Royal Commission on Electric Power Planning on July 17, 1975.

The primary focus of the Royal Commission was upon long-term electrical power planning in Ontario. Its mandate was:

(a)  to examine the long-range electric power planning concepts of Ontario Hydro;
(b)  to inquire comprehensively into Ontario Hydro's long-range planning program in its relation to provincial planning;
(c)  to deal primarily with the broader issues relating to electric power planning, and thus serve to alleviate the need for re-examinations of these issues at subsequent hearings of other hearing bodies on specific details such as siting, rates, etc. (Royal Commission on Electric Power Planning 1980, Vol. 1, p. 187)

Shortly after the Royal Commission was established, it became apparent that the capital requirements implied in Ontario Hydro's expansion program represented an even more serious problem than had been earlier anticipated. From 1974 to 1975 provincial government borrowings more than tripled (from $0.5 billion to $1.86 billion). 84 percent of the total, $1.56 billion, was issued on behalf of Ontario Hydro. Moreover, Ontario Hydro's capital requirements were expected to increase to $2.6 billion in 1980 (Royal Commission on

Electric Power Planning 1980, Vol. 5, p. 17). Furthermore, in 1975, partly as a result of the financial problems caused by the load of such a heavy debt, Ontario Hydro requested a 30 percent increase in bulk power rates for 1976. The response of the government was twofold. In October 1975 it established a select committee of the legislature to examine Ontario Hydro's rate proposals, and, in January of 1976, the provincial treasurer imposed limits of $1.5 billion per year on the annual borrowing of Ontario Hydro to 1982 (Smith 1982, p. 15).

Both the Royal Commission on Electric Power Planning and the select committee investigating Ontario Hydro were to have their mandates changed over their lifetimes. In December 1977 the Royal Commission was directed to examine the issue of nuclear power in Ontario and to prepare an interim report on the need for nuclear energy as a component of Ontario's future energy supply. In the context of this examination of nuclear power, the Commission took up the issue of nuclear risk management in Ontario. An interim report on nuclear power in Ontario, entitled *A race against time* (Royal Commission on Electric Power Planning 1978), reported on the Commission's findings on nuclear energy, including those relating to nuclear risk. Subsequent to the release of that report, the Three Mile Island nuclear accident in the United States sparked increased interest in Canada in nuclear risk and safety issues. The Royal Commission, therefore, allocated additional time to examining these issues and the Three Mile Island accident and commented extensively upon them in its *Final report*, issued in May 1980.

This chapter examines how the participants in the Royal Commission on Electric Power Planning and the Commission itself interpreted and treated risk and how the provincial government responded to the Commission's risk-related recommendations. The Royal Commission was chosen for study because it remains the most widespread and open examination of nuclear power in Canada. Whereas the original terms of reference of the Commission did not call for an examination of risk during the course of the Commission hearings and investigation, risk arose as a major issue and received considerable attention. The other reason for choosing the Commission relates to the importance of the nuclear industry in Ontario, as described in Chapter 2. Ontario is the province with the greatest stake in nuclear power generation; it has the greatest number of facilities and the most accumulated experience. A thorough examination of the risk questions in Ontario should be reasonably representative of a major Canadian position and, as such, provides an appropriate benchmark for an international comparative study of risk studies and their impacts.

## Data sources

The research examined documents published prior to, during, and since the Commission's work. In addition, interviews were obtained from seven key people, representing various positions and organizations, who were participants during the Commission hearings. Two faculty researchers, supported by a research assistant, conducted all the research. Both were close observers of the Commission process. One has a background in engineering and decision sciences, the other a social science background. The differing expertise of the principal investigators together with personal inclinations led to considerable debate on interpretation. The debate was a critical aspect of the research method and was particularly useful since the limited scope of resources did not permit statistical analysis of objectively measured data. As a consequence, an interpretative approach was needed.

Several documents received detailed examination. First, the documents submitted by participants who took a major role on risk issues in the hearings were scrutinized. Second, documents were chosen that were cited prominently as representing positions discussed in the interim and final reports. Third, the documents of the Commission itself were examined extensively. During the term of the Commission, the Select Committee on Ontario Hydro Affairs (a committee of the Legislative Assembly of Ontario) was also examining Ontario Hydro so its reports provided further documentation. Finally, researchers inquired into the government response to the Commission reports.

Quantitative indicators obtained from the documents included:

(a)   the number of pages of hearing transcripts devoted to questions dealing with risk;
(b)   the number of days of hearings devoted to risk issues compared to other topics;
(c)   the number of participants (large and small groups) involved in hearings on a variety of topics, including nuclear. Participants in the nuclear hearings invariably treated risk as one of their major topics.

Interviews were conducted during 1981 and 1982 with seven people who were key participants in or observers of the hearings. These retrospective interviews had the advantage that enough time had elapsed for the interviewees to put the Commission process into perspective. A set of guideline questions served to structure the interviews. Examination compared answers, across respondents, for each question. The sample size and the open-ended nature of questions did not permit statistical analysis so that, at most, observations could be made on the responses. Interviewers asked the seven respondents to respond as closely as possible on behalf of their organizations rather than to give personal opinions (although both were obtained). The respondents represented the following organizations: The Royal Commisson on Electric Power Planning (chairman); Ontario Hydro; Atomic Energy of Canada Ltd.; Ontario Coalition for Nuclear Responsibility; Atomic Energy Control Board; The Select Committee on Ontario Hydro Affairs (chairman); *Toronto Star* (reporter).

The Appendix provides the Commission's recommendations – as they appeared in their final report – relating to nuclear risks, along with a brief summary of the justifications and the government's response to each. The recommendations are one of the direct products of the Commission, although not the only one (as will be argued later). The recommendations are the clearest statement available indicating the final position of the Commission on nuclear risk issues. The responses to the recommendations suggest the impact of the Commission although they do not, of course, take account of those actions that would have occurred had the Commission not existed.

## The Ontario Royal Commission

Since the royal commission of inquiry is an institution found in only two (UK and Canada) of the five countries treated in this volume, some background on its functions and work may be useful.

In Canada the federal government or a provincial government can, by an order-in-council, call for a royal commission of inquiry into any question that needs exploration. Royal commissions serve many purposes in the Canadian political system: to delay a decision by deferring the issue "until the commission has reported," to interpret or to shape public opinion in preparation for government action, and to gain outside advice on questions of interest.

The government issues terms of reference (i.e., a mandate) to the commission. The commission may operate in a wide variety of ways, with very little predetermined procedure, allowing it to establish a *modus operandi* appropriate for its terms of reference. A commission may hold public hearings but is not required to do so. It may also initiate research studies by its own staff or others, prepare briefs and make them public if it so desires, and call witnesses (who, however, are not required to appear). The commission concludes its work with a report, usually containing recommendations, then disbands. The government may respond to or ignore the recommendations, as it sees fit.

The Royal Commission on Electric Power Planning under study in this chapter had five members:

(a)   Dr. Arthur Porter, Chairman. Professor Emeritus of Industrial Engineering, University of Toronto, formerly Dean of Engineering, University of Saskatchewan, and Professor of Electrical Engineering, University of London. He is a member (former chairman) of the Canadian Environmental Advisory Council and was chairman of Ontario's Committee of Automation and Employment. Dr. Porter was elected a Fellow of the Royal Society of Arts in 1961 and a Fellow of the Royal Society of Canada in 1970.

(b)   Robert E. E. Costello, Commissioner. Vice-President of Corporate Services, Abitibi Paper Company Limited, Mr. Costello brought to the Commission an extensive industrial background. He was a long-time resident of the north and an engineer by training. Mr. Costello resigned on May 9, 1977, due to ill health.

(c)   Solange Plourde-Gagnon, Commissioner. Journalist, a former Queen's Park correspondent for *Le Droit* and a commentator for the CBC, Madame Plourde-Gagnon represented the consumer viewpoint on the Commission.

(d)   George A. McCague, Commissioner. Aside from his own farming operation, Mr. McCague has served on the executive boards of many farm organizations, including the Ontario Federation of Agriculture, the Farm Products Marketing Board, and the Ontario Milk Commission.

(e)   Dr. William W. Stevenson, Commissioner. An economist by training, Dr. Stevenson was a member of the Ontario Energy Board and brought to the Commission an extensive background and knowledge of the electric power industry.

The Chairman's background and expertise substantially affected the Commission's approach to its mandate. The Commission saw, as one of its prime functions, the education that would result by bringing together members of the public, the nuclear industry, and government. The commissioners believed that public hearings and informative published material would be educational for the general public. They also viewed the process of education as equally important as their final recommendations. Perhaps they recognized that they would not provide definitive answers on all the issues and so set out to establish a rational basis for continuing debate and policy development.

The Commission chose to hold a series of preliminary meetings at which members of the public were encouraged to raise the issues that they believed the Commission should address. Accordingly, nine issue papers identified and summarized relevant considerations. A series of public information hearings then explored the issues, with particular emphasis on educating the public, the Commission, the scientists, and other interested parties in the electric power planning process. The proponents were exposed to the public view and, likewise, the public to the views of scientists and proponents.

Next followed the stage of hearings at which the issues were publicly debated. The commissioners acted as a review board and heard testimony from Ontario Hydro and others. Ontario Hydro representatives faced cross-examination by experts supplied by the Commission and by other interested parties. The Commission also supported financially several groups who wished to make a case but lacked sufficient resources to conduct the research. In this way, those with few funds of their own were able to make well-prepared submissions.

In addition to the public hearings the Commission had a research staff to sift and summarize the materials presented. The Commission staff, together with outside consultants, produced seven research papers as part of the final report. The Commission also produced an interim report dealing with nuclear power in Ontario (Royal Commission on Electric Power Planning 1978). Table 5.1 provides a chronology of the Commission's work as well as that of the Select Committee.

**Table 5.1**   The Commission and the Select Committee: a chronology of major events.

| Date | Commission | Select Committee |
|---|---|---|
| July 17, 1975 | established:<br>public information hearings<br>debate stage hearings | |
| November 24, 1977 | | established terms of reference:<br>cost of heavy water<br>rate increases<br>examine nuclear commitment |
| December 14, 1977 | terms of reference changed to require an interim report on nuclear power | |
| March 1978 | | report on uranium contracts |
| July 12, 1978 | terms of reference changed to include regional reports | |
| September 12, 1978 | *Interim report* | |
| October 1978 | | report on heavy-water plants |
| November 1978 | | interim report requesting extension |
| March 1979 | regional hearings start | |
| June 1979 | Southwest Ontario report | |
| July 13, 1979 | Southeast Ontario report | |
| December 1979 | | report on need for electricity |
| February 29, 1980 | *Final report* | |
| June 1980 | | report on nuclear-waste management |
| June 1980 | | report on nuclear safety |
| December 1980 | | report on uranium mining, milling, and refining |

## Major participants

The Commission encouraged individuals and groups to participate in public hearings and provided ample time at the hearings for them to do so. Some participated at their own request; others were invited to appear. Table 5.2 lists the major organizations and individuals who participated in what became known as the nuclear debate, whereas Table 5.3 provides the number of participants (groups or individuals) who made submissions as part of the commission process. The numbers recorded for various categories of issues suggest the relative importance of the nuclear debate. As Table 5.3 indicates, 50 of the 190 participants at the debate stage were concerned with nuclear issues and, for

**Table 5.2**   Major participants at the Royal Commission on Electric Power Planning.

| Category of participant | Institution or organization |
| --- | --- |
| proponent | Ontario Hydro<br>Atomic Energy Control Board<br>Atomic Energy of Canada Ltd. |
| government | Ontario Ministry of Energy<br>Ontario Ministry of the Environment<br>Atomic Energy Control Board |
| industrial and professional associations, firms | Electrical and Electronic Manufacturers Association of Canada<br>Canadian Nuclear Association |
| opponents | Ontario Coalition for Nuclear Responsibility<br>People Against Nuclear Development Anywhere<br>Sierra Club<br>Walk for Life<br>Canadian Coalition for Nuclear Responsibility<br>Energy Probe |

most of them, risk was a central concern. This is a significant number when it is recalled that the terms of reference did not specify an examination of risk. Moreover, it is also noteworthy that, of the 50 participants in the nuclear debate, 33 represented public groups and individuals who chose to participate.

The main proponents were Ontario Hydro and Atomic Energy of Canada Ltd. (AECL). Ontario Hydro is a publicly owned utility with a mandate to supply the electric power needs of the Province of Ontario. To fulfill its mandate by generation within the province, Ontario Hydro has developed a major nuclear program, whose performance has been outstanding in an international context. As a world leader in nuclear power generation, it has, of course, a large vested interest in the development of nuclear power. AECL, the Crown corporation responsible for the promotion and development of nuclear energy in Canada, was a natural proponent. The Atomic Energy Control Board (AECB) is responsible for the regulation of nuclear power in Canada. Its existence is thus dependent upon the continued development of nuclear power, although, as a regulatory agency, it officially takes no formal position on nuclear policy questions. Of the three, Ontario Hydro was the major participant in the hearings.

## The Select Committee on Ontario Hydro Affairs

On November 24, 1977, a select committee of the Legislature of Ontario received orders to:

. . . examine Ontario's nuclear commitment, taking into account the report and recommendations of the Royal Commission on Electrical Power Planning and Ontario's Energy Future, such examination to include but not be limited to:

- the performance and reliability of nuclear generating stations;
- the responsibility for, and the standards relative to the safety of, nuclear generation stations;
- environmental impact and health considerations related to nuclear power. (Select Committee on Ontario Hydro Affairs 1980b, p. A/1)

The Select Committee was empowered to demand information, to impose attendance, and to examine witnesses under oath. The Select Committee process was a quasi-judicial one in contrast to the Commission's more free-wheeling procedure. Furthermore, the Select Committee was charged specifically with examining nuclear risk.

The Select Committee produced a series of reports (Table 5.1). It is beyond the scope of this chapter to deal in depth with the work of the Select Committee, which was in many ways a complementary activity to the Commission inquiry and used a contrasting procedure. Subsequent interviews revealed that the Select Committee, using a quasi-judicial procedure, was more effective than the Commission for examining the issues in detail. Also, those interviewed generally agreed that the Commission process was effective primarily for identifying the issues. This identification subsequently assisted the Select Committee in its work. Table 5.1 suggests a substantial overlap in the activities of these two bodies.

**Table 5.3**  Numbers of particpants* in public hearings.

| Hearing | Ontario Hydro, AECL, or AECB | Government departments | Industry or professional associations, firms | Public groups or individuals | Total |
|---|---|---|---|---|---|
| A. information | 19 | 13 | 18 | 9 | 59 |
| B. debate stage demand | 1 | 2 | 3 | 13 | 19 |
| conventional and alternative generation | 1 | 3 | 9 | 17 | 30 |
| nuclear | 4 | 3 | 10 | 33 | 50 |
| transmission and land use | 1 | 1 | 4 | 5 | 12 |
| finance and economics | 1 | 2 | 4 | 5 | 12 |
| overview and total system | 2 | 5 | 15 | 19 | 41 |
| decision making | 1 | 1 | 9 | 11 | 23 |

* A "participant" might be a member or group from a department (e.g., of Ontario Hydro), a number of spokespersons acting together, or an individual (particularly in the public category).

## The risk debate

As noted earlier, the terms of reference for the Commission did not specify that risk should be examined. In fact, the word "risk" does not appear in the terms of reference. An examination of risk was not excluded, however, since the Commission was asked to deal "with the broader issues relating to electric power planning." Given the terms of reference as a starting point, the emergence of risk as a major issue is quite significant.

The early submissions by Ontario Hydro treated risk primarily as an engineering matter concerned with reliability and compliance with the AECB regulations on the design, construction, and operation of nuclear power plants. This view is limited but it should be stressed that Ontario Hydro has an excellent safety record and has experienced radioactive emission rates much lower than the regulations allow. Ontario Hydro officials with this record justified their taking a limited technical view of risk (Ontario Hydro 1976).

The early submissions of the AECB stressed its continuing review of the regulations and care in licensing for all aspects of the nuclear fuel cycle. The Board described its cooperation with the International Commission for Radiation Protection (ICRP) and noted that AECB regulations call for stricter emission limits than those allowed by ICRP standards.

AECL, pointing out that nothing is without risk, argued that nuclear plants had not resulted in any significant increase in risk to the public (AECL 1976). Officials also noted that the design limits on emissions were far lower than those allowed by AECB (Snell 1979). In general, AECL subscribed to the use of probabilistic risk analysis as used in the *Reactor safety study* (US Nuclear Regulatory Commission 1975).

The opponents took the view that nuclear weapons proliferation is a neutral extension of a nuclear industry. They argued that nuclear energy presents unique types of risk, particularly with respect to the magnitude of possible consequences of accidents, and called for a moratorium on new plants pending a solution to the waste-management problem. They disagreed with the reliability estimates provided by the industry and raised questions about possible sabotage. Finally, they challenged the argument that nuclear power is economic on the grounds that the economics are unknown until the waste-management problem is solved.

In summary, both proponents and opponents raised the issue of risk attendant on the generation nuclear power. The proponents tended to take an engineering/scientific view and to argue that the risks are "acceptably" low. The opponents enlarged the treatment of risk to include a broader spectrum of social and ethical considerations and argued in favor of energy conservation and alternative energy sources.

Risk emerged as an important issue in the preliminary public meetings. The first of nine issue papers arising from the public meetings specifically addressed nuclear power (Royal Commission on Electric Power Planning 1976, p. 4). The main issues set forth in this paper illustrate the broadening of the scope of risk debate.

(a)  The safety and reliability of CANDU nuclear reactors:

    (i)    unique characteristics of the CANDU reactor;
    (ii)   types of accidents which might occur;
    (iii)  the supervision, monitoring, and control of nuclear reactor operation;
    (iv)  the role of international and federal regulatory bodies;
    (v)   sabotage and acts of terrorism.

(b)  Environmental impact and health aspects related to nuclear power:

    (i)    the siting of nuclear power stations and heavy-water plants;
    (ii)   radiation from routine nuclear reactor operation;
    (iii)  the relationship between radiation dose and health (including radiation protection standards);
    (iv)  the management of spent nuclear fuel, transportation and disposal of spent fuels and radioactive wastes, including the decommissioning of nuclear reactors;
    (v)   the ethical issues.

(c)  The economics of nuclear power:

    (i)    availability of capital;
    (ii)   capital and operating costs;
    (iii)  security of fuel supplies;
    (iv)  recycling of nuclear fuel;
    (v)   future developments in nuclear power;
    (vi)  nuclear power generation capacity.

The next stage of the Commission process was the Debate Stage Hearings (May 1976–May 1979) in which formal examination of industry witnesses occurred. In this stage, 335 exhibits were filed, of which 160 dealt with aspects of nuclear power. Risk was typically part of each submission on nuclear power and included such issues as risks in nuclear waste management, operator preparedness, low-level emissions from routine operations, and decommissioning of nuclear power plants.

The entire public hearings of the Commission generated about 36,000 pages of transcripts, dealing with a wide range of planning topics, of which about 2,250 pages (6 percent) treated aspects of nuclear risk. This provides a gross measure of the relative amount of attention in the Commission process to risk issues.

## Issues and positions

To some extent the positions of the participants changed over the life of the Commission. Although it is not possible to pinpoint the causes of these changes, some speculations are offered toward the end of the chapter.

## ONTARIO HYDRO

Ontario Hydro was the first to make submissions to the Commission, perhaps because it would be affected directly by the Commission's conclusions (Ontario Hydro 1976). The early submissions, as already noted, conceived nuclear risk in narrow terms, largely relating to plant design and operations. Risk, in this view, had been considered and dealt with most satisfactorily in the technical design, construction, and operation of the plants. Technical devices were stressed much more than the human element in plant operation; the only mention of the latter was that the employees were well trained and had primary responsibility for their own job safety. Ontario Hydro also stressed its strict adherence to AECB's conservatively safe standards and criteria. The utility also emphasized that the public had never been at risk in Ontario from events resulting from the operation of a nuclear power plant.

By the time of its second submission, when safety issues had become more prominent, Ontario Hydro gave much greater emphasis to safety matters. Whereas the basic arguments remained the same, it went into much more detail in the evidence for support. New comments appeared regarding decommissioning, environmental impacts, and security from sabotage. Reliance on the *Reactor safety study* (US Nuclear Regulatory Commission 1975) seems to have disappeared by the later submission.

In subsequent interviews, Ontario Hydro officials pointed out that many instances arise for which there are no historical data upon which to base probability estimates. In such cases, they use technological means (e.g., computer simulation), similar to those used in commissioning new aircraft, to estimate risk. The interviews also revealed that by 1981 (when the interviews were conducted) Ontario Hydro officials had a heightened awareness of the broader social issues, fears, and concerns associated with nuclear risks. They claim to have been moved by the sincere emotions of the concerned public. They felt that risk emerged as an issue as a result of the submissions made to the public hearing stage of the Commission process.

Comparing the Commission to the Select Committee, Ontario Hydro officials pointed out that the structure of the Select Committee lent itself to a more thorough examination of the issues for the following reasons:

(a)  the Select Committee required sworn testimony;
(b)  the audience (members of the Select Committee) remained to hear all of the testimony, compared to the "floating" public who heard testimony before the Commission;
(c)  there was time for thorough cross-examination;
(d)  the Select Committee could order witnesses and documents.

On the other hand, the Commission paved the way for the Select Committee by setting the issues before the public.

ATOMIC ENERGY OF CANADA LIMITED (AECL)

Throughout the Commission's work, AECL maintained that nuclear power generation is safe. It insisted that safety had always been a primary concern, and that safety features had been incorporated at every stage of the generation process. The "defense-in-depth" approach in all fuel processing systems and in the safety system itself was cited as particularly important. AECL officials also pointed to their strict adherence to AECB limits on accident frequencies and on radiation release doses, and emphasized that radiation exposure from their generating stations was much less than the natural background exposure. Early submissions gave the impression that all safety risks were well contained and posed no public danger. Officials cited particularly the *Reactor safety study* as providing realistic estimates to support their position.

Later comments became more defensive, although their position did not change (Robertson 1978). AECL officials argued that the risk of using nuclear energy must be compared quantitatively with the risks of other energy sources and that all human activities involve risk. They stressed AECB's rules and the adherence of AECL to them while at the same time defending AECB's analyses. Even sabotage prevention was claimed to be accomplished as well as is possible. AECL officials also claimed that antinuclear groups exaggerated the significance of the sabotage and radioactive waste problems.

The only problem the AECL members acknowledged was the success of antinuclear groups in swaying public opinion. They felt that the public could be persuaded by the facts, if it only had them, rather than by the "irrational" appeals of the antinuclear groups. Thus, AECL officials repeatedly argued that the public would remove its objections to nuclear power if it knew the risks as compared to other risks. Furthermore, the public would want some funds diverted from nuclear to other risks to obtain much greater overall societal risk reduction for the same expenditure (Siddall 1979). AECL officials also touted scientific objectivity as the only means of providing the public and political decision makers with information. Finally, one AECL interviewee, commenting on the low level of public participation at the hearings, opined that, except for a few who are deeply concerned, the public did not care about nuclear risks.

ATOMIC ENERGY CONTROL BOARD (AECB)

The first submission of the AECB for the Public Information Hearings, in 1976, was more of a presentation of duties and responsibilities than any sort of argument for nuclear energy. It also noted its role in setting exposure standards; defining requirements for security of substances, facilities, and information; advising on uranium extraction and regulating mine safety; and setting design standards for fuel fabrication, heavy-water production, and transportation systems.

In the AECB's later submission, the tone was still descriptive but related almost entirely to research on risk issues, to the regulation of radioactive wastes, and to the results of the Inhaber report (Inhaber 1979a, b), which purported to quantify the safety of various energy sources. AECB officials also noted financial and personnel limitations, especially as they affected the AECB's participation in the Commission. Like the AECL, they did not provide any interpretation of risk.

## CANADIAN COALITION FOR NUCLEAR RESPONSIBILITY (CCNR)

The CCNR was quite active throughout the Commission hearings. Arguments put forth at the symposium on November 10, 1976 focused on the decision to "go" nuclear, the risks of foreclosing a nonnuclear future, the dangers of nuclear proliferation, and the technical integrity of the CANDU design and its associated costs. This group was the first to recommend a nuclear moratorium at the symposium. Finally, the CCNR presented a rebuttal to claims of Ontario Hydro, AECL, and AECB, particularly with respect to the security of the plutonium contained in spent fuel and the safety issues in waste disposal.

Much of the summary argument of the CCNR consisted of a metaphorical discussion of nuclear technology as machine. Particular concerns concentrated on the possibility of a core meltdown, arguing that Ontario Hydro, AECL, and AECB had not provided adequate guarantees against that possibility, AECB's licensing practice (was it a rubber stamp?), and the adequacy of insurance and liability arrangements.

## ONTARIO COALITION FOR NUCLEAR RESPONSIBILITY (OCNR)

OCNR's submission (Torrie et al. 1977, Torrie 1981) offered the most extensive criticism of nuclear energy presented at the hearings. Drawing extensively on the hearings and the wider literature on the nuclear debate, it recounted all of the popular and semi-technical antinuclear positions. It also included a critique of CANDU standards and Ontario Hydro and AECL figures on, and justifications of, nuclear safety. Although the industry conception of risk was never explicitly questioned, concern over risk issues predominated.

## PEOPLE AGAINST NUCLEAR POWER DEVELOPMENT ANYWHERE (PANDA)

This antinuclear group also enunciated the familiar arguments against nuclear safety, listing all the reactor accidents that had occurred and questioning whether waste disposal would ever prove feasible. PANDA depicted Ontario Hydro, AECL, and AECB as conspiring vested interests and insisted that no safety shortcoming in nuclear power could be tolerated.

## ONTARIO PEOPLE'S ENERGY NETWORK (OPEN)

OPEN, apparently a one-person organization, presented risk arguments that were phrased in popular terms. The arguments addressed uranium mining, reactor accidents and their costs, the feasibility of reprocessing, and the threat of nuclear proliferation. The representative proposed a five-year moratorium on waste-disposal "development" projects, with the stipulation that no new reactor development should take place until the waste-disposal problem was solved.

## The Commission's response

In its *Interim report*, published in 1978, the Commission provided a general overview of the arguments for and against nuclear power, including the arguments related to risk, that had been presented at the hearings. Though the report reached some general conclusions regarding nuclear power, it did not include any specific recommendations regarding nuclear risk issues. Following a further set of hearings in 1978 and 1979 – which included an examination of the implications of the Three Mile Island accident for the Canadian nuclear program – the Commission presented its recommendations in its *Final report*, issued in February 1980 (Table 5.4).

The recommendations in the *Final report* relating to nuclear risk issues (see Table 5.4 and the Appendix) were only a small part of the 88 recommendations, covering such broad topics as energy demand, technology, alternative energy sources, economic issues, environmental impacts, land use, and decision making.

In discussing the bases for these recommendations, as described in the Commission's two main reports, it is useful to divide the recommendations into three major categories:

(a)   energy risks and society (the social dimension);
(b)   risk estimation and safety (the technical dimension);
(c)   public participation and decision making (the political dimension).

## Energy risks and society

The Commission accepted the view that energy is necessary to sustain the lifestyle that has evolved in many parts of the world and recognized that the relationship between energy and gross national product (GNP) is complex. But it rejected the notion of a "direct causal relationship between energy consumption and the quality of life" (*Interim report*[2], p. 6). It notes, nevertheless, that "abundant energy is clearly the cornerstone of any modern society" and that "the risk of not having sufficient energy at some point in the future is very real" (*Interim report*, p. 153).

The Commission cited the technological view presented by industrial concerns and individuals (e.g., Maxey 1977) as well as the "small is beautiful" concept (Schumacher 1973). One major influence was Ralph Torrie's notion of "worldview," which the Commission quotes (*Interim report*, p. 153):

It is impossible to understand the nuclear debate without understanding the different world views which underlie the two sides of the debate. . . . Different world views correspond to different visions of reality. . . . The world-wide debate on nuclear power has evolved into a debate about the most fundamental values of society.

The scope of the nuclear debate became an important issue. Earlier we noted

**Table 5.4** Summary of Commission recommendations relating to risk (Royal Commission on Electric Power Planning, 1980, Vol. 1).

| | |
|---|---|
| 5.1 | Ontario Hydro should publish a report as soon as possible on the expected exposure levels resulting from any reactor retubing operation. |
| 5.2 | A new division devoted exclusively to nuclear power safety, reporting directly to the Executive Vice-President (Operations) of Ontario Hydro, should be established. |
| 5.3 | The new safety division recommended for Ontario Hydro should establish a small emergency task force . . . that could be transported expeditiously . . . to any nuclear generating station in the province. |
| 5.4 | A systematic attempt should be made by Ontario Hydro to look for patterns in operating and accident experience available from both CANDU and other reactor systems. These patterns should be fed back into the process of setting design, operating, and safety criteria. |
| 5.5 | Operational procedures and especially the reporting systems at CANDU stations should be critically assessed to improve communication. |
| 5.6 | The current CANDU control room and indicator design should be reviewed and assessed from a human factors perspective to ensure that the equipment will display clear signals on reactor status to the operator under both normal and accident conditions. |
| 5.7 | The educational requirements and training programs for all nuclear supervisory, operational, and maintenance personnel should be critically reviewed. |
| 5.8 | Provision should be made for the continuous updating and monitoring of the performance of all reactor operators and maintenance personnel; there should be much more imaginative use of simulators. . . . |
| 5.9 | The AECB should establish a human factors group to ensure that human factors concepts and engineering become central elements in safe design, construction, operation, and maintenance. . . . |
| 5.10 | All aspects of contingency planning should be assessed in the light of the experience at Three Mile Island, and a comprehensive plan for each nuclear facility should be made publicly available. . . . |
| 5.11 | Continuing epidemiologic evaluation of Elliot Lake miners and uranium mill workers should be undertaken. . . . |
| 5.18 | No further development of the 1,250 MW CANDU reactor . . . should be undertaken by Ontario Hydro. . . . |
| 5.19 | . . . R&D priorities in the nuclear field should be focused primarily on the human factor in reactor safety, on the management and disposal of wastes . . ., and on the decommissioning of nuclear facilities. |
| 5.24 | The role of the AECB on-site resident inspector should be strengthened and the reports of the inspector should be made public. |

that one group felt that the nuclear debate should be restricted to technical issues whereas others argued for a broader view that would encompass social, ethical, and environmental issues. In the *Interim report* the Commission appears to subscribe to the latter view: ". . . we have not only to weigh the risks and benefits of energy technology to present generations but also to consider the risks and benefits to future generations" (p. 7). The Commission recognized that "In the view of many concerned citizens, the use of nuclear energy raises new social, political, and ethical issues of a profound nature" (*Interim report*, pp. 153–4).

The Commission accepted that "All currently available conventional energy systems . . . have social, ethical, economic, environmental or political costs associated with their deployment" (*Interim report*, p. 6). It also accepted nuclear weapons proliferation as a possible by-product of nuclear power generation. It maintained, however, that countries could create weapons without having nuclear power reactors. Thus, it did not view nuclear power generation as encouraging nuclear proliferation and cited such sources as Rose & Lester (1978), the Windscale report (Parker 1978), and the Nuclear Power Policy Study Group (1977) in support.

In Ontario, nuclear electricity generation plants are concentrated at a few large sites. The Commission noted that the associated centralization of society could result in a loss of diversity (*Interim report*, p. 64). Thus, it expressed concern that large-scale centralization and a creation of technical elites might be associated with nuclear power development. How can civil liberties be protected, it queried, while at the same time achieving adequate power plant security (*Interim report*, p. 155)? It was felt, in this period prior to the accidents at Bhopal and Mexico City, that the consequence of a breach of security could be greater at a nuclear facility than at other kinds of industrial concentration. Elsewhere it argued (*Interim report*, p. 160), however, that many large industrial complexes could pose a risk to public safety from malicious actions. The Commission viewed these matters as serious because of "the growing acts of terrorism in the world."

In the *Final report* (p. 55), the Commission returned to the broader societal questions surrounding nuclear risk management, noting that

Society is faced with three basic questions. First, how can risk be assessed? Second, how much risk is acceptable? And third, how can risk be regulated? These questions have physical, psychological, and social dimensions.

It concluded that a direct comparison of voluntary and involuntary risks was not meaningful, because such comparisons failed to take into account psychological factors (*Final report*, p. 55). It surmised that any nuclear risk–benefit assessment must include a broad assessment of the social, ethical, and political implications of nuclear development (*Final report*, p. 75).

## Risk estimation, health, and safety

This volume makes clear that risk estimation has been a controversial issue in the nuclear debate in a wide variety of countries. One reason for this controversy is the lack of accumulated empirical experience to support risk estimates. In simple cases, such as the life expectancy of light bulbs, one can record the observed lifetime of a large number of light bulbs and, for the same kind of bulbs, have some faith that the average lifetime is fairly predictable. In the case of nuclear power, by comparison, estimates that a nuclear plant will experience a specified kind of disaster once in 10,000 years of reactor operation (or some such figure) are made despite the fact that such an event has never occurred. All estimates, therefore, are extrapolations from analogous devices or are based upon component reliability (fault-tree analysis). In either case, a great deal of judgment is needed, and such judgments are always open to debate, an issue taken up in Chapter 8, which addresses the future of large-scale probabilistic risk analysis.

The Commission cited the *Reactor safety study* (us Nuclear Regulatory Commission 1975) as the most comprehensive existing study and appeared to endorse the approach (but not necessarily the absolute numerical values). It went on to discuss Ontario Hydro estimates of risk (*Interim report*, p. 78) but recognized that some people have criticized the validity of the probability estimates (and particularly the probability of dual failure of the cooling system).

The Commission wisely avoided taking a position on failure probabilities. It did, however, conclude that "nuclear power . . . represents a risk to society which is vanishingly small, particularly when compared to the risks to which we are already, often voluntarily, subjected" (*Interim report*, p. 63). Instead of debating numerical values, it turned its attention to questions of the adequacy of existing safety measures. As in Britain (see Ch. 7), the Commission accepted the philosophy that "the main emphasis, to ensure a high level of safety, should be on improving the reliability of specific components, processes, and assemblies" (*Interim report*, p. 79).

The Commission, much impressed by expert testimony and by the Three Mile Island accident, came to regard human factors as a major concern. Actually, it took this position prior to the Three Mile Island accident; that event, however, reinforced the judgment on the importance of human factors in reactor safety. In the *Final report*, several recommendations appear concerning human factors (see recommendations 5.6–5.9 in Table 5.4 and in the Appendix).

Waste-handling and disposal issues arose in the hearings and the Commission considered them at length. In the *Interim report* (p. xiii), the Commission recommended that:

An independent review committee should be established to report to the Atomic Energy Control Board (aecb) on progress on waste disposal research and demonstration. If the committee is not satisfied with progress by 1985, a moratorium on additional nuclear power stations would be justified.

To support this position, it cited two Canadian studies on waste-handling and disposal (Aikin *et al.* 1977, Uffen 1978), the Swedish KBS (1977) report (Ch. 3), a British study (Gray *et al.* 1976), and a US report (Carter 1978). The Commission still had concern for waste disposal at the time of its *Final report* but its recommendation for a moratorium extended the date of "satisfactory demonstration" from 1985 to 1990, on the basis of progress achieved in the interim between the two reports.

The Commission's primary health concern centered on the potential amount of public or occupational exposure to high- or low-level radiation. While recognizing that "exposure of people to radiation should be kept as low as practicable," the Commission endorsed the ICRP limits and AECB's acceptance of them. It did note, however, the continuing scientific conflict over long-term consequences to low-level exposures, which it placed in the context of the much higher exposure from natural sources.

Several recommendations addressed the safety of workers in mining, milling, and plant operations. Recommendation 5.1 dealt with worker safety in a forthcoming reactor retubing operation. Recommendation 5.11 called for continuing epidemiologic evaluation of possible health effects on Elliot Lake miners and uranium mill workers.

The Commission recognized that, regardless of the degree of safety precautions, accidents can and do occur and emergency planning should be part of the protection from such events. Recommendation 5.2 calls for a safety division devoted to nuclear power safety, and recommendation 5.3 calls for the establishment of an emergency task force. The Commission recommended that the emergency-response procedures should be examined in the light of the Three Mile Island incident (recommendation 5.10). Finally, safety was a dominant consideration in the Commission's recommendation (5.18) to cease further development of the 1,250MW CANDU reactor.

## Public participation, decision making, and regulation

Through its inquiry process, the Commission implicitly accepted a role for the public in decisions on nuclear issues. It recognized that many of the issues, such as health and safety, are highly technical and difficult to discuss even with well-informed members of the public. It praised AECL's contribution to the technical literature but viewed it as unintelligible to the general public. The Commission also noted the educational work of several public-interest groups but still viewed most of the public as uninformed (*Interim report*, p. 8).

The systemic (or holistic) view of decision making states that all important aspects of a decision problem should be considered in making a choice. The Commission noted, with some disappointment, that the debate had been sporadic and had focused on only a few of the many relevant issues (*Interim report*, p. 61). Sources contributing to the Commission's view of a narrow debate included several inquiries and studies in Canada (Aikin *et al.* 1977, Bayda 1978). The Commission concluded that "Clearly, the 'nuclear debate' must accommodate and cope with discussion of both highly technical and scientific matters as well as emotional concerns and fundamental anxieties," and later that ". . . the debate over the future role of nuclear power is ultimately a political debate – in the broadcast sense of the word" (*Interim report*, p. 62).

Thus, in spite of the technological complexities, the Commission had recognized as early as the *Interim report* that nuclear power decisions are political and that the public has a role in these decisions. This conclusion constitutes a landmark in its recognition that the decisions cannot be left to the technocrats alone. Questions still remain, however, as to how best to involve the public and whose values should prevail. The Commission's general position is well articulated in the *Interim report* (p. 65):

Two things therefore seem clear to us. First, we must find new and imaginative ways to inform and involve the public in these important issues and decisions. To do otherwise risks unexpected and time-consuming resistance to future projects when the local implications become obvious to affected communities that may perceive a different relationship between the risks incurred and the benefits to be derived than the planners did.

Secondly, we have concluded that if an informed and reasonably sophisticated public involvement in the energy debate is to be achieved, then greater and freer public access to information is essential. This is particularly important in the case of nuclear power where, perhaps because of the historical links of civilian nuclear energy to military weapons programmes, an aura of secrecy still shrouds the contemporary nuclear industry. This aura, together with the quite natural tendency of any industry to promote its products, has often led to public suspicion that unfavourable data are withheld and that the information which is made available by the nuclear industry, which often intimidates laymen because of its technical complexity, is not always objective. If these suspicions are to be allayed and if public trust and acceptance of nuclear power are to be maintained, then the nuclear industry must continue to become more open to public scrutiny.

In its *Final report* the Commission returned to the question of public involvement and nuclear risk management. In particular, it had strong things to say about the question of scientific literacy and the contribution of scientific expertise to the nuclear debate. After concluding that a higher level of scientific literacy among the public is not a prerequisite for public participation in decisions relating to nuclear power, the Commission notes (*Final report*, p. 76):

If, as some claim, the nuclear power controversy is more quasi-religious than technical, then, in the words of R. L. Mechan: "Exposure and examination of the ideological aspects of the issue, using both traditional liberal arts and contemporary social science techniques, might do more to restore rationality than widespread improvement of scientific literacy."

The Commission also restated its observation in the *Interim report* that risk decisions cannot be left to the experts since inescapable value judgments and political, social, and ethical issues are involved (pp. 165–6). It also stressed the need for full public disclosure ". . . we have concluded that full disclosure of technical, economic, environmental, health, and all other information in understandable form that relates to future energy policies would enhance trust and broaden the base of public understanding" (*Final report*, p. 166).

The Commission made several recommendations pertaining to decision making. Recommendation 5.14 suggests that the public should have a say in the future expansion of the Ontario nuclear program. Other recommendations dealing with aspects of decision making called for a nuclear waste social advisory committee (5.16); for safeguards for professional dissent (5.22); for public participation in standards setting (5.23); and for inspection reports to be made public (5.24).

## Conclusions

### DIFFERING CONCEPTS OF RISK

The divergent views among various participants on nuclear safety in Canada prior to the Ontario Royal Commission appeared to stem, in large part, from quite different concepts of the meaning of "risk." Two views of nuclear risk dominated the submissions to and activities of the Commission. The first concept defined risk in quantitative technical terms usually as the expected consequence (sum of consequences weighted by their probabilities) of a hazardous event. In this view, the management of nuclear risk is primarily an engineering issue related to plant safety, whereas nuclear risk acceptability is primarily a matter of judging the results of quantitative risk assessment calculations, often according to some explicit risk–benefit calculation.

The other view saw nuclear risks as part of a broad social assessment of the relative desirability of nuclear power, including environmental, social, political, and ethical considerations. Taking the quantitative risk of nuclear accidents as an important component of risk assessment, proponents of this view would place such risks in a broader context of social issues, including some that are intangible or nonquantifiable. Further, they view individual

perceptions or risk, as well as scientific calculations of probabilities and consequences, as directly relevant to risk management goals.

These different concepts of risk are necessarily somewhat idealized. Nevertheless, something akin to these two broad concepts appeared to underlie,
respectively, the initial submissions of Ontario Hydro, AECL, and the AECB on
the one hand and the several public-interest groups attending the Commission
hearings on the other. As noted above, the early submissions of the nuclear
industry, to the degree that they addressed nuclear risk questions, tended to
focus largely upon engineering safety issues. Environmental groups, meanwhile, focused upon reactor safety, high-level waste disposal, and low-level
radiation risks, often cast in terms of a broad environmental perspective and
critique of modern technological society.

These different concepts of risk influenced the types of risks considered
important by participants and their opinions about how to evaluate risks. The
more technical concept of risk is susceptible, in principle, to precise specification, but not necessarily to measurement. This not only permits a comparative analysis of energy risks but suggests that a scientifically sound risk
assessment (or at least a risk-estimation method) can reasonably guide risk
management decisions. Risk assessment, then, is primarily a scientific process,
with the focus upon the scientist as expert advisor to policy makers.

The competing, broader, concept of risk calls for a different approach to risk
assessment and management. Since important trans-scientific issues enter into
evaluating and measuring risks, risk assessment, it is argued, cannot be a
purely scientific process. One must take into account important questions
relating to values, ethics, and individual perceptions, and quantitative models
are poorly equipped to do this. Risk assessment, in short, is viewed as inherently value-laden and judgmental. The proper model for risk assessment and
management, therefore, is a political rather than a scientific one. Accordingly,
the focus should be upon the political balancing of perceived risks and benefits
conducted in a pluralistic or adversarial process.

In the light of these different viewpoints, the approach of the Commission is
particularly noteworthy. While not neglecting technical risk questions, the
Commission emphasized strongly the social, political, and ethical dimensions
of risk assessment. In so doing, it came close to endorsing a social conception of
nuclear risk. Indeed, one major contribution of the Commission, according to
virtually all those interviewed, was that it broadened the nuclear debate in
Ontario to include the social, political, and environmental dimensions of
nuclear power.

Part of the reason for this broadening of risk lies in the wide mandate of the
Commission, wherein nuclear risk issues were only part of a more general
concern with electric power planning. Moreover, the explicit focus on planning
and decision making in the Commission's work meant that nuclear risk assessment was explicitly put into a planning and decision-making framework. This
suggests, as argued in the Swedish case (Ch. 3), that the mandate of a major
risk study will influence strongly the treatment of risk that emerges.

THE ROLE OF PROBABILISTIC RISK ANALYSIS

Although a broad perspective on risk needs not be incompatible with a careful scientific analysis, the Commission's conclusions on the desirability of a generic reactor risk study (such as the *Reactor safety study*) bear repeating. Such studies, as is apparent in the *German risk study* (Ch. 4), are extremely resource-demanding, expensive, and time consuming. This issue receives further treatment in Chapter 8. In its *Interim report*, the Commission concluded that the CANDU reactor was "safe within reasonable limits." With respect to the assessment of risk, the Commission noted the controversy over the *Reactor safety study* but concluded that it represented an important approach to assessing nuclear safety. The Commission, however, also concluded that no equivalent study was necessary in Canada, in part because of doubts about the possibility of incorporating human behavior in quantitative models.

After the Three Mile Island accident, the Commission instituted a further review of this position, taking into account the preliminary findings of the presidential commission appointed to investigate the accident (Ch. 6). The review concluded that the Three Mile Island accident reinforced earlier concerns about the importance of "human factors" and that human errors, in combination with equipment malfunction, could possibly lead to equally severe accidents in Canada.

Despite these conclusions, the Commission still maintained that no large-scale probabilistic risk analysis of reactor safety was necessary in Canada. Three reasons were offered in support of this position. First, the Commission felt that it would be virtually impossible for such a study to reach a definitive result. It is interesting to see the findings of the Lewis report (US Risk Assessment Review Group 1978) cited as evidence for this view, suggesting that the Lewis report, ironically, might have discouraged similar major risk studies in Canada. Second, the Commission suggested that Canada lacked sufficient scientific expertise to undertake such a study. Finally, it observed that, since the results of such a study would likely be controversial even among scientists, they could actually increase confusion about nuclear risk issues. This conclusion, it is worth noting, may have been influenced by the extremely critical reception accorded to the Inhaber report (Inhaber 1979a, b, 1982)[3] in the United States and Canada. (The lack of any reference to that report in the Royal Commission's *Final report* supports this supposition.) Despite these reservations, Ontario Hydro has, as noted in Chapter 1, undertaken a major probabilistic risk analysis of the CANDU reactor.

Insofar as the Royal Commission can be said to have examined the role and function of scientific risk assessment in nuclear risk management, its view appears to be that risk assessment can perform a valuable, albeit limited, role in providing information to policy makers. As a technique, probabilistic risk analysis appears incapable, however, of addressing the broader, social, political, and ethical issues stressed by the Commission. As a result, whereas the

Commission emphasized the importance of undertaking risk assessments of specific issues, it recommended against an overall risk assessment of nuclear safety, suggesting instead that individual risk studies be assessed in the context of a socially oriented concept of risk. This is quite a different position from that taken in Germany and the United States but is in greater accord with national responses in Sweden and the United Kingdom.

IMPACTS ON NUCLEAR RISK MANAGEMENT

Any assessment of the impact of the Royal Commission on nuclear risk management in Canada runs into the complication of dual jurisdiction (see Ch. 2). Since both the provincial and the federal governments have jurisdiction over nuclear power issues in Canada, both have some say in nuclear risk management. Moreover, though the relative jurisdictions of each level of government are fairly clear in general terms, considerable overlap exists with respect to any specific issue, such as the management of nuclear risk. The regulatory policy of the AECB, for example, makes the nuclear industry the "front line" agency with respect to nuclear risk and safety. That is, the onus is on industry to demonstrate that safety requirements have been met. This means that decisions on risk management and risk policy making occur at both the federal and the provincial levels. One effect of this overlap is that it is easy for provincial participants to argue that the jurisdiction or the ability, or both, to make or implement policy lies at the federal level and vice versa.

Despite this problem, it is possible to draw some general conclusions about the impact of the Commission on risk management in Canada, based on the interviews and the formal response of the Ontario government to the Commission's recommendations. Although the Commission strongly endorsed a social context for risk, it made no recommendations in this area. Perhaps this is because such questions lend themselves more to conclusions than to recommendations. It did, however, make recommendations with respect to technical matters and to decision making and policy issues. In general, the technical recommendations addressed the analysis of safety issues and the training and monitoring of nuclear personnel. These recommendations tended to be readily accepted by the government, and often the measures necessary to implement them were already under way when the Commission's report was published (as occurred with the report of the Kemeny Commission in the United States). It is difficult to determine, however, whether to attribute these changes to the Commission or to such events as the Three Mile Island accident (see Ch. 6 for further discussion of this attribution, or causality).

Concerning decision making on nuclear safety, the Commission made a number of recommendations that generally reflected its broad social perspective on risk. First, the Commission stressed the need for more explicit attention to matters of nuclear safety, largely by improving institutional mechanisms (e.g., upgrading Ontario Hydro's nuclear safety group from a section in the Design and Development Division to a new Safety Division). Second, the

Commission recommended much more attention to "social science" issues and to public participation in nuclear safety decision making. It specifically recommended that the AECB establish social science advisory committees and that the Ontario government establish a "nuclear waste social advisory committee."

The response of the Ontario government to these decision-making recommendations tended to be negative to those issues that were within provincial jurisdiction and noncommittal to those addressed to the AECB (which were referred to the federal government "for consideration"). No commitments were made to enact or support these recommendations.

The Commission made fewer recommendations on nuclear policy issues. The gist of its recommendations was that the bulk of nuclear R&D funding, which the Commission felt should no longer dominate the government's total energy R&D funding, should be devoted to safety and waste-disposal issues and that the expansion of the Ontario nuclear power program should be contingent on satisfactory progress in the management of both spent fuel and uranium mill tailings. The Ontario government rejected these recommendations.

Overall, whereas the more technical recommendations of the Commission were adopted, the broader policy-oriented recommendations related to nuclear risk management were either largely rejected, accepted in only a noncommittal manner, or referred to the federal government. Unfortunately, perhaps because the Commission was provincially appointed, the federal government never released any formal response to the Commission's recommendations. Despite this lack of government reaction, the recommendations have had a significant impact on industry (cf. Chs. 3, 4, & 6). Ontario Hydro has implemented, to some degree, most of the recommendations. The Appendix provides the 1986 status of response to the risk-related recommendations of the Commission.

The lack of enthusiastic federal and provincial governmental response to the Commission's recommendations suggests that the Commission's greatest impact on the public dimension of nuclear risks in Canada, namely its role in stimulating and broadening the nuclear debate in Canada, may have been indirect. Although it is impossible to measure its impact in this area, all of those interviewed agreed that the Commission had widened and increased the level of sophistication of the debate. Further, it is clear that the Commission significantly influenced the Select Committee on Ontario Hydro which, in turn, educated certain Members of Parliament on nuclear risk issues. Given the Commission's strong emphasis upon public education and decision making, it is entirely fitting that its most enduring legacy may have been as an educational process.

The Royal Commission provides a model of how technical and nontechnical submissions may be presented and debated. The Commission was a vehicle for presenting information to as wide an audience as possible. Further, the Commission's interim and final reports synthesized all the material presented, both technical and nontechnical, into a series of conclusions and recommendations. Whatever the direct substantive effect of those recommendations, the

Commission process was perceived to have been a significant contribution to the nuclear debate. All this implies that it might be appropriate to conceive of the Commission as a risk assessment in the broadest sense of that term, with the emphasis upon sociopolitical judgments about technical issues.

This is not to say that the Commission was a flawless model. Nor is it clear that such a model, rooted as it is in the particular characteristics of the Canadian political culture, is transferable to other nations. A royal commission, of the type represented by this case, provides one effective means for placing technical issues – in this case, nuclear risks – into a broader sociopolitical context and for clarifying the major public policy choices which are involved.

This conclusion puts into sharper relief the lack of a mechanism for implementation in Canada. The findings of a royal commission are only advisory – they do not bind the government that requests them. Indeed, the lack of response by the provincial government in the case at hand underlines the ability of government to ignore part or all of any such recommendations. Moreover, the commission process itself runs parallel to a policy formation process within the relevant government departments and agencies, none of which is bound by, or necessarily even involved in, the commission's actions. With respect to nuclear risk management (as with all areas of public policy), the final policy decisions take place at the Cabinet level, on the basis of advice from both the relevant government departments and from public inquiries. Since the policy process is not open to public scrutiny, it is difficult to assess the relative influence of departmental or external advice, or of technical or nontechnical information. Thus one final contribution of the Royal Commission on Electric Power Planning is to illustrate how few formal mechanisms exist in Canada for the explicit integration of technical issues into the policy-making process.

*Appendix: Commission recommendations and government and industry responses (as of February 1986)*

RECOMMENDATION 5.1[4]

Ontario Hydro should publish a report as soon as possible on the expected exposure levels resulting from any reactor retubing operation, addressing, in particular, the following questions:

(a) How many workers (Ontario Hydro employees and others) will be subjected to the 5 rem annual dose limit in connection with the retubing of a single reactor?

(b) Will workers be subject to high dose levels on a continuing basis when the retubing of the Pickering A and Bruce A reactors begins on a sequential basis?

(c)    A worker could receive an aggregated dose of 50 rem over, say, a 15-year period. Is this medically acceptable? Should these exposures be age-dependent?

(d)    What is the total number of workers required, on a continuing basis, to undertake retubing operations? Are that many adequately skilled workers at present available?

(e)    To what extent can the retubing operation be undertaken by "remote control," thereby minimizing the aggregated exposures of workers?

(f)    Will workers who may be subjected to higher-than-normal radiation doses, and their unions, be fully informed of the nature of the risk?

*Commission justification*   Workers in nuclear power stations are generally exposed to higher doses of radiation than the public, even when they are well within established dose limits. A "retubing" operation at Pickering A and Bruce A nuclear stations may become necessary and would expose workers to higher-than-normal radiation doses. In no case should the established dose limits be exceeded.

*Government response and justification*   Accept: Ontario Hydro is already preparing a similar report. It anticipates no overexposure of employees to radiation.

*Implementation*   In 1984, Ontario Hydro retubed Pickering Units 1 and 2, lowering the radiation level in the work locations to a few millirem. New tubes will soon be installed. No overexposures have occurred.

### RECOMMENDATION 5.2

A new division devoted exclusively to nuclear power safety, reporting directly to the Executive Vice-President (Operations) of Ontario Hydro, should be established.

*Commission justification*   Nuclear power safety is overseen by a section in Ontario Hydro's Design and Development Division. It ought not to compete with other sections in the Division and should be seen as having greater importance than at least some of them.

*Government response and justification*   Further study by Ontario Hydro is required. Independent groups within Ontario Hydro already review nuclear safety, and an interdisciplinary Nuclear Integrity Review Panel has been set up.

*Implementation*   Ontario Hydro established a new safety division reporting directly to the Executive Vice-President.

RECOMMENDATION 5.3

The new safety division recommended that Ontario Hydro should establish a small emergency task force, available 24 hours a day on an "on call" basis. This force should be one that could be transported expeditiously in an emergency, by road or helicopter, or both, to any nuclear generating station in the province.

*Commission justification* The implication (unstated) is that such an emergency force does not exist.

*Government response and justification* Further study by Ontario Hydro is required. Senior station personnel are already formally on call. A task force could at best be advisory. The operators are best equipped to respond.

*Implementation* Ontario Hydro, viewing its existing Preparedness Committee as adequate, chose not to establish an emergency task force.

RECOMMENDATION 5.4

A systematic attempt should be made by Ontario Hydro to look for patterns in operating and accident experience available from both CANDU and other reactor systems. These patterns should be fed back into the process of setting design, operating, and safety criteria.

*Commission justification* Significant Event Reports from Bruce generating station indicate that inadequate attention is paid to these reports. They do not always appear sufficiently thorough nor have they been used to correct recurring problems.

*Government response and justification* Accept: the analysis of operating and accident experience is already an ongoing process at Ontario Hydro.

*Implementation* Ontario Hydro improved feedback and significant event review procedures. The Nuclear Integrity Review Panel ensures that necessary changes are implemented.

RECOMMENDATION 5.5

Operational procedures and especially the reporting systems at CANDU stations should be critically assessed to improve communication.

*Commission justification* At least one of the reports that the Commission reviewed cited a communications breakdown between important actors, and another pinpointed a failure in communication to the next work-shift of actions that had been taken.

*Government response and justification* Accept: the review of operational and reporting procedures is already an ongoing process at Ontario Hydro.

*Implementation* An Operational Information Feedback Task Force reviewed communications and reporting and thereby improved "interface" communications.

## RECOMMENDATION 5.6

The current CANDU control room and indicator design should be reviewed and assessed from a human factors perspective to ensure that the equipment will display clear signals on reactor status to the operator under both normal and accident conditions.

*Commission justification* The operation of a nuclear power station depends on immediate and appropriate responses, on the parts of operators and supervisors, to the information provided by their extensive instrumentation. Many of the Significant Event Reports indicate errors by the operators or supervisors. In addition, unclear instrumentation failure can be considered a human error.

*Government response and justification* Accept: government endorses RCEPP emphasis on "human factors." Human factors have been considered in all control room designs; these have been built into simulators and tested.

*Implementation* Increased emphasis has been placed on displaying clear signals and information and on improved person–machine interactions.

## RECOMMENDATION 5.7

The educational requirements and training programs for all nuclear supervisory, operational, and maintenance personnel should be critically reviewed.

*Commission justification* Any staff member who assumes a senior position on a shift should have a university degree in engineering, the appropriate training program, and at least two years' operating experience. Emphasis should be placed on the ability to assess and respond to unexpected events.

*Government response and justification* Accept in principle. Refer to the federal government. Ontario Hydro's training programs are already subject to review by AECB.

*Implementation* Consultants to Ontario Hydro conducted an extensive review of its training program. Although some changes were enacted, the consultants judged the program as basically sound.

RECOMMENDATION 5.8

Provision should be made for the continuous updating and monitoring of the performance of all reactor operators and maintenance personnel; there should be much more imaginative use of simulators in this regard.

*Commission justification*  Operating and maintenance personnel should be required to attend frequent seminars and workshops on subjects directly related to their jobs. These subjects might also be of interest to safety personnel and academic people.

*Government response and justification*  Accept: evaluation procedures and performance-record review procedures are already established at Ontario Hydro. Refresher and update training are already ongoing practices.

*Implementation*  Full-scope simulators are in place for each of the operating nuclear stations and a training simulator for the Darlington station is under design.

RECOMMENDATION 5.9

The Atomic Energy Control Board should establish a human factors group to ensure that human factors concepts and engineering become central elements in the safe design, construction, operation, and maintenance of Ontario's nuclear stations. Further, human factors concepts should be reflected in the licensing requirements for both nuclear stations and key operating personnel.

*Commission justification*  Human factors research recognizes a wide variety of factors that might prove significant in a specific case of human error and that it might be possible to prevent or reduce the influence of these factors.

*Government response and justification*  Accept in principle. Refer to the federal government. Government endorses RCEPP emphasis on "human factors."

*Implementation*  The AECB has increased its expertise on human factors.

RECOMMENDATION 5.10

All aspects of contingency planning should be assessed in the light of the experience at Three Mile Island, and a comprehensive plan for each nuclear facility should be publicly available. The public must be aware of these plans, which must be rehearsed regularly if they are to be credible. Special attention should be paid to preparing in advance for the sensitive and accurate handling of information during an accident.

*Commission justification*  Contingency planning can help to minimize the effects of a nuclear accident. A contingency plan is an effective way to ensure the safety of a nuclear power station and should be a condition of plant licensing.

*Government response and justification*  Accept: Ontario government reviewed and rearranged contingency plans following the Three Mile Island accident. Rehearsals have been conducted but will not involve actual evacuation. Two communication centers are being established.

*Implementation*  A Provincial Nuclear Emergency Plan has been implemented. In 1985, a rehearsal of the plan, involving a simulated accident at Pickering, was performed.

RECOMMENDATION 5.11

Continuing epidemiologic evaluation of Elliot Lake miners and uranium mill workers should be undertaken. The public should be informed of the progress of these studies.

*Commission justification*  Mining and milling conditions have improved, but not all of the implications of the conditions that existed are yet understood with certainty. In addition, it is not yet certain to what degree those conditions have been or can be eliminated.

*Government response and justification*  Accept: a large study of causes of mortality in 50,000 miners (of whom 18,000 mine uranium) in Ontario is being conducted by the Ministry of Labour and the Workmen's Compensation Board.

*Implementation*  Results were published and sent to the unions concerned.

RECOMMENDATION 5.12

Ontario should contribute its share to any national research program on uranium mining and milling wastes.

*Commission justification*  Understanding of both the nature and the capacity of the pathways followed by radionuclides from mine and mill tailings to humans must be improved. This problem is national in scope.

*Government response and justification*  Accept in principle. The National Technical Planning Group on Uranium Mine Waste Research has been investigating present activities with the goal of making them more effective.

*Implementation*　Findings of this National Technical Planning Group have been made available.

RECOMMENDATION 5.14

The future expansion of the nuclear power program in Ontario, and in particular the uranium mining and milling portion of the fuel cycle, should be contingent on demonstrated progress in research and development with respect to both the short- and the long-term aspects of the low-level uranium tailings waste-disposal problem, as judged by the provincial and federal regulatory agencies and the people of Ontario, especially those who would be most directly affected by uranium mining operations. It would be unacceptable to continue to generate these wastes in the absence of clear progress to minimize their impact on future generations.

*Commission justification*　There is at present insufficient understanding of, and research available on, the effects of uranium tailings. In addition, great quantities of such tailings have already accumulated. Even present dumping sites are not leakproof.

*Government response and justification*　Accept: government agrees but is confident that research and regulations will provide for the appropriate progress.

*Implementation*　The government concluded that work was progressing satisfactorily.

RECOMMENDATION 5.15

All existing and planned Ontario Hydro nuclear stations should be retrofitted or designed for the interim storage on site of their spent fuel for the next 30 years, by which time a disposal facility should be available.

*Commission justification*　Spent fuel reprocessing or storage will not be operating until after 2000. The interim storage sites currently used are safe and effective but must have capacity to hold the next 20–30 years' wastes. Interim storage in on-site concrete silos also appears satisfactory.

*Government response and justification*　Accept: an Ontario Hydro study has reached the same conclusions, and a plan is under way.

*Implementation*　Fuels continue to be stored on site in water-filled bays constructed of double-walled reinforced concrete.

RECOMMENDATION 5.16

An independent "nuclear waste social advisory committee" should be established to ensure that broad social, political, and ethical issues are addressed. This committee should be chaired by an eminent Canadian social scientist.

*Commission justification* Research progress toward, or demonstration of, a nuclear waste disposal facility cannot ensure the public acceptance of the project. AECL has a technical advisory committee reviewing its R&D programs, so that this social advisory committee could operate in parallel with it on matters of nuclear waste disposal.

*Government response and justification* Accept in principle for the site-selection/acquisition phase of the nuclear fuel waste-management program. Refer to the federal government. The government recognizes that the issues implied here will not arise until site selection is called for, which is several years away at least.

*Implementation* The advisory committee was not created.

RECOMMENDATION 5.17

If progress in high-level nuclear waste disposal R&D, in both the technical sense and the social sense, is not satisfactory by at least 1990, as judged by the technical and social advisory committees, the provincial and federal regulatory agencies, and the people of Ontario – especially in those communites that would be directly affected by a nuclear waste-disposal facility – a moratorium should be declared on additional nuclear power stations.

*Commission justification* The research and development of waste-disposal methods should not be rushed, especially since on-site interim disposal is considered to be safe and effective.

*Government response and justification* Accept in part. Government agrees that a sound and accepted method must be developed. Current research progress and interim storage are satisfactory; therefore, there is no time pressure.

*Implementation* AECL is proceeding with R&D. Expert review and public views will be sought. It is anticipated that hearings before the Regulatory Board will occur at the end of the 1980s to seek approval for high-level nuclear waste disposal in hard rock.

RECOMMENDATION 5.18

Ontario Hydro should not undertake further development of the 1,250MW CANDU reactor, even in the concept stage. Any additional nuclear base-load power stations in the post-Darlington period should be based on 850MW CANDU reactors. We believe that such standardization will facilitate reactor safety as well as optimizing the average capacity factors of these stations.

*Commission justification*   No justification given for the comment on safety.

*Government response and justification*   Accept: Ontario Hydro has ceased developing the 1,250MW reactor. No further work is expected.

*Implementation*   The plan for a 1,250MW reactor was abandoned.


RECOMMENDATION 5.21

Nuclear power should no longer receive the lion's share of energy R&D funding, and R&D priorities in the nuclear field should focus primarily on the human factor in reactor safety, on the management and disposal of wastes at the front and back ends of the fuel cycle, and on the decommissioning of nuclear facilities.

*Commission justification*   The development of the present CANDU fuel cycle has been adequately demonstrated. Research and development of any advance fuel cycles will not be needed until after 2010, and should not receive priority over health and safety matters.

*Government response and justification*   Refer to the federal government. Government remains strongly convinced of the importance of nuclear power. Funding should not decrease and should be based on need and potential for each energy source. Decommissioning research is not yet necessary. Human factors research merits no special priority.

*Implementation*   The federal government has reduced by 50 percent AECL's budget for nuclear R&D over the five-year period 1986 to 1990.


RECOMMENDATION 5.22

Procedures should be established to ensure fair handling of bona fide cases of professional dissent. Procedures should include the following concepts:
   Concerns should be expressed in writing and considered by a special review group consisting of representatives of management, professional engineering staff, and at least one outside expert.
   The review group should obtain evidence from the dissenting staff member's colleagues.

The review group should assess management's response to the concerns.

*Commission justification*   Dissent, with respect to the safe operation of nuclear facilities in Ontario, has been recorded but not heeded. Further, such dissent can be a credible feedback operation by which improvements can be achieved.

*Government response and justification*   Accept in part. Provision for dissent and response exists in Ontario Hydro.

*Implementation*   Ontario Hydro has officially encouraged employees to bring dissenting views to proper authorities and has established new procedures to ensure fair consideration. Unresolved matters may be referred to the Nuclear Integrity Review Panel (see 5.2).


RECOMMENDATION 5.23

Standard-setting for the nuclear fuel cycle should proceed in an open manner, including opportunities for public participation in the process.

*Commission justification*   The main goal of standard-setting for the nuclear fuel cycle is safety. Public participation, which should increase public knowledge of the concerns in addition to giving the public a say in the decisions, should be sought as early in the process as possible.

*Government response and justification*   Accept in principle. Refer to the federal government. AECB is responsible for setting standards. Current practice is to allow 60 days for comment on all proposed regulations.

*Implementation*   Some minor institutional changes have been made to encourage public participation.


RECOMMENDATION 5.24

The role of the Atomic Energy Control Board on-site resident inspector should be strengthened and the reports of the inspector should be made public.

*Commission justification*   Assurance of compliance and attention to monitoring are important ways of ensuring the safety of a nuclear power station and of nuclear generating in general. These two tasks, already assigned in part to the resident inspector, must be upgraded. Publicizing the inspector's reports will satisfy the public's right to know what has occurred.

*Government response and justification*   Accept in principle. Refer to the federal government. AECB is responsible for the duties and performance of the on-site resident inspectors. AECB's current policies require that significant hazard and event reports and licensee reports be made public.

*Implementation*    The AECB on-site inspection system continues to recognize a low "public profile."

## Notes

1    In 1974 the dependable peak December capacity was approximately 18,000 MW.
2    The remainder of this chapter uses the abbreviated references *Interim report* and *Final report* to refer to the two main reports of the Royal Commission on Electric Power Planning (1978, 1980). Unless otherwise stated, *Final report* refers to Volume 1 of that report.
3    As noted in Chapter 1, the Inhaber Report, published initially by the AECB, attempted to evaluate the comparative risks of nuclear and other energy systems. Its methods and conclusions have been strongly challenged (Holdren *et al.* 1979); the AECB withdrew the report from circulation, but it has subsequently been published by Gordon & Breach (Inhaber 1982).
4    The recommendation numbers are the same as those used in the *Final report*. Only the recommendations dealing with nuclear risk are contained in this Appendix.

## References

AECL (Atomic Energy of Canada Ltd.) 1976. *Nuclear power in Canada: the Canadian issues*. Ottawa (exhibit 158). Mississauga, Ontario: AECL.
Aikin, A., F. K. Hare & J. M. Harrison 1977. *The management of Canada's nuclear wastes*. Report EP 77-G. Ottawa: Energy, Mines and Resources Canada.

Bayda, Justice E. D. 1978. *Cluff Lake Board of Inquiry, report*. Regina, Saskatchewan: The Board.

Carter, L. J. 1978. Nuclear wastes: the science of geologic disposal seen as weak. *Science* **200**, 1135–7.

Gray, D. A. *et al.* 1976. *Disposal of highly active solid radioactive wastes into geologic formations*. Institute of Geologic Sciences, report no. 76/12. London: HMSO.

Holdren, J. P., K. Anderson, P. Gleick, I. Mintzer, G. Morris & K. Smith 1979. *Risks of renewable energy resources: a critique of the Inhaber report*. Report ERG 79-3. Berkeley: Energy and Resources Group, University of California.

Inhaber, H. 1979a. Risk with energy from conventional and nonconventional sources. *Science* **203**, 718–23.
Inhaber, H. 1979b. *The risk of energy production*, 4th edn. AECB 1119. Ottawa: Atomic Energy Control Board.
Inhaber, H. 1982. *Energy risk assessment*. New York: Gordon & Breach.

KBS (Kärn–Bränsle–Säkerhet) 1977. *Handling of spent nuclear fuel and final storage of vitrified high level waste*. Stockholm: KBS.

Maxey, M. 1977. Public ethics and radioactive wastes: criteria for environmental criteria in United States Environmental Protection Agency. *Proceedings of the workshop on issues pertinent to the development of environmental protection criteria for radioactive wastes*. Washington: The Agency.

Nuclear Power Policy Study Group 1977. *Nuclear power: issues and choices*. Cambridge, Mass.: Ballinger.

Ontario Hydro 1976. *Generation – Technical*. Submission to Information Hearings (Exhibit 2).

Parker, R. J. 1978. *The Windscale inquiry*. Presented to the Secretary of State for the Environment on January 26, 1978, 3 vols. London: HMSO.

Robertson, J. A. L. 1978. AECL's *final argument relating to nuclear energy before the RCEPP*. Chalk River, Ontario: Atomic Energy of Canada Ltd.
Rose, D. J. & R. K. Lester 1978. Nuclear power, nuclear weapons and international stability. *Scientific American* **283** (4), 45–57.
Royal Commission on Electric Power Planning 1976. *Nuclear power in Ontario*, Issue paper No. 1. Toronto: The Commission.
Royal Commission on Electric Power Planning 1978. *A race against time: interim report on nuclear power in Ontario*. Toronto: The Commission.
Royal Commission on Electric Power Planning 1980. *Final report*. Volume 1: *Concepts, conclusions, and recommendations*. Volume 2: *The electric power system in Ontario*. Volume 3: *Factors affecting the demand for electricity in Ontario*. Volume 4: *Energy supply and technology for Ontario*. Volume 5: *Economic considerations in the planning of electric power in Ontario*. Volume 6: *Environmental and health implications of electric energy in Ontario*. Volume 7: *The socio-economic and land-use impacts of electric power in Ontario*. Volume 8: *Decision-making, regulation, and public participation: a framework for electric power planning in Ontario for the 1980's*. Volume 9: *A bibliography to the report*. Toronto: The Commission.

Schumacher, E. F. 1973. *Small is beautiful*. New York: Harper & Row.
Select Committee on Ontario Hydro Affairs 1980a. *The management of nuclear fuel waste*. 4th session, 31st parliament, 29 Elizabeth II.
Select Committee on Ontario Hydro Affairs 1980b. *The safety of Ontario's nuclear reactors*. 4th session, 31st parliament, 29 Elizabeth II.
Siddall, E. 1979. *Nuclear safety in perspective*. Presentation to the 19th annual conference of the Canadian Nuclear Association, Toronto.
Smith, G. 1982. *Electric power planning in Ontario: public participation at the normative level*. Paper presented to the Canadian Association of Geographers, annual general meeting, special session on energy policy. Ottawa, June 9–12, 1981.
Snell, V. G. 1979. *Safety of CANDU nuclear power stations*. Report AECL-6329. Ottawa: Atomic Energy of Canada Ltd.

Torrie, R. D. 1981. *Half life: nuclear power and future society*, rev. edn. Ottawa: INFOEARTH.
Torrie, R. D., T. McQuail & G. Wood 1977. *Half life: nuclear power and future society*. Seaforth, Ontario: Ontario Coalition for Nuclear Responsibility.

Uffen, R. J. 1978. *The disposal of Ontario's used nuclear fuel.* Kingston: Queen's University.

US Nuclear Regulatory Commission 1975. *Reactor safety study* WASH-1400, NUREG 75-014. Washington, DC: The Commission.

US Risk Assessment Review Group 1978. *Report to the Nuclear Regulatory Commission.* NUREG CR-0400. Washington, DC: The Commission.

# 6 The Kemeny Commission and the accident at Three Mile Island

ROGER E. KASPERSON

The accident at Three Mile Island nuclear power plant on March 28, 1979 was by consensus the worst to occur in the history of commercial nuclear power generation in the United States. Prominent among the post-mortems on the event was the report of the President's Commission on the Accident at Three Mile Island, popularly known as the Kemeny Commission.

Appointed two weeks after the accident, the 12-member commission was carefully balanced to reflect a diversity of viewpoints. The Chairman was John Kemeny, President of Dartmouth College and a one-time Manhattan Project researcher. Only two commission members – Thomas Pigford and Theodore Taylor – could qualify as nuclear power experts. The remaining eight members included representatives from industry, labor unions, and universities, the President of the National Audubon Society, a former Deputy Secretary of the Army, and a mother of six who lived across the river from the nuclear plant at Three Mile Island. The charge to the Commission was:

. . . to conduct a comprehensive study and investigation of the recent accident involving the nuclear power facility on Three Mile Island in Pennsylvania. The Commission's study and investigation shall include:

(a)  a technical assessment of the events and their causes; this assessment shall include, but shall not be limited to, an evaluation of the actual and potential impact of the events on the public health and safety and on the health and safety of workers;

(b)  an analysis of the role of the managing utility;

(c)  an assessment of the emergency preparedness and response of the Nuclear Regulatory Commission and other federal, state, and local authorities;

(d)  an evaluation of the Nuclear Regulatory Commission's licensing, inspections, operation, and enforcement procedures as applied to this facility;

(e)  an assessment of how the public's right to information concerning the events at TMI was served and of the steps which should be taken during similar emergencies to provide the public with accurate, comprehensible, and timely information; and

(f)    appropriate recommendations based upon the Commission's findings.

The Commission labored for six months, eventually taking some 150 formal depositions, interviewing hundreds of individuals, hearing testimony under oath from numerous witnesses, and collecting sufficient material to fill 90 meters of shelf space. In its work, the Commission was supported by a budget of $1 million and a substantial staff. Its final report, issued in October of 1979, received more immediate media coverage and congressional attention than any other document on nuclear power safety (U.S. President's Commission on the Accident at Three Mile Island 1979).

The report is one of a genre of risk assessments. Unlike most of the assessments treated in this volume, and particularly the *German risk study* (Ch. 4) which relied heavily upon expert assessment dealing with the quantitative probabilistic assessment of risk, the Kemeny Commission inquired into the larger issues of nuclear safety as indicated by a particular accident. Because of the significance of the crisis event and the direct responsibility of the Commission to the President, the report had a unique opportunity to contribute to the shaping of nuclear safety policy and national response in the United States.

This chapter inquires into the nature and extent of the societal impacts of this assessment. Specific objectives are:

(a)    to characterize the presentation of the report by the media to scientists, activist publics, and general publics, identifying any major problems that may have occurred;

(b)    to assess major impacts of the report (and the accident) upon the management of nuclear safety in the United States;

(c)    to evaluate the effects, if any, of the accident and the report upon the nuclear debate and upon public attitudes.


*A methodological note*

Evaluating the impacts of the Kemeny Commission report on nuclear safety policy and other societal responses requires the isolation of the report from the numerous other risk assessments conducted after the accident, from the accident itself, and from the deliberations of ten congressional subcommittees that had conducted hearings on the subject by the first anniversary of the Three Mile Island accident. This cannot be done. In fact, the U.S. Nuclear Regulatory Commission quite explicitly and systematically integrated the various report findings, in order to fashion a coordinated response. In addition, a number of safety problems were evident in the accident itself, and it is quite futile to determine which source stimulated a particular response.

Within these constraints, however, there are some opportunities. A substantial part of the industry and governmental response occurred well in advance of the issuance of the Kemeny report some seven months after the accident, most of which would have presumably occurred even in the absence of the Commission. Also, several post-accident evaluations and congressional inquiries appeared prior to the Kemeny report and thus provide a benchmark from which to assess the particular contributions of the Kemeny report. Finally, there is not a complete overlap in these reports so that some of the individual findings and recommendations of the Kemeny report can be distinguished and assessed as to impacts.

## Presentation of the report and the performance of the media

Much of what policy makers, scientists, and various publics learned about the Kemeny report came not from the report itself but from its presentation by the various media – key scientific journals, newspapers, television, and the media of industry and environmentalists. To evaluate how and why society responded as it did, it is first necessary to understand how the report was characterized. A report of such length and complexity will necessarily be simplified by the media. How this distillation occurred may hold some clues to why different elements of society responded as they did.

### COVERAGE BY THE SCIENTIFIC PRESS

To assess the presentation of the Kemeny report, the author undertook a review of all articles appearing in *Science* and *Nature*, the two prestigious scientific journals with broad coverage and scientific readerships. Presentation of the Kemeny report in the sources, it turned out, differed in several important respects.

*Science* carried three articles on the Kemeny Commission before the report's release, treating the makeup of the committee and its budget and constraints, the ending of the licensing moratorium, and the iodine-131 problems. *Nature* mentioned the Kemeny Commission only twice prior to the report and referred to completely different issues, namely the California study of Three Mile Island and a news brief on the dissolution of the citizens' advisory panel.

*Science* and *Nature* both published only one article to cover the report's findings and recommendations. Both provided extensive coverage of the report, with *Science* somewhat more specific and comprehensive. Neither journal, however, included a verbatim listing of either the findings or the recommendations. The *Science* article (Marshall 1979b), under the somewhat misleading headling "Kemeny Report: Abolish the NRC," referred to 23 specific findings, nine recommendations, and two criticisms of omitted recommendations. The report drew fire because it did not "[go] the extra step and [demand] the 'fundamental changes' in nuclear power production" (Marshall 1979b, p. 797) and also for failing to ask for a licensing moratorium.

The reporting in *Nature*, treating eight findings, five recommendations, plus a section on the happenings of the accident, was less complete than that in

*Science. Nature* did, however, discuss immediate reaction to the report by pronuclear and antinuclear groups: critics charged that the report's "bark may . . . turn out worse than its bite," and the nuclear industry interpreted the Kemeny report's message as "proceed with caution" (*Nature* 1979, p. 121). *Nature* (1980b) later followed with an article that challenged the latter view.

In terms of post-Kemeny report coverage, the two journals presented only one major article (Marshall 1979a) specifically addressing responses to the report. Briefer treatments, however, did appear as well. On February 8, 1980, for example, *Science* dealt with the Rogovin report (Rogovin *et al.* 1980), noting the agreement of the two reports on the need to reorganize the NRC (Carter 1980).

*Nature* carried three post-Kemeny articles. The first covered congressional debate over the moratorium issue, noting that the Kemeny report did not recommend a licensing moratorium (*Nature* 1979). The second included a discussion of nuclear safety, with attacks authored by Russell Peterson (a former Kemeny Commissioner) and an alternate view presented by Nobel prize winner Rosalyn Yalow (*Nature* 1980a). Finally, in an article (June 19) entitled "What (if any) future for nuclear power?" *Nature* (1980b) criticizes the Kemeny report for its lack of criticism and its minimal impacts.

Overall, the scientific press, as indicated by coverage in *Nature* and *Science*, was reasonably balanced and analytical in its treatment of the report. On the other hand, the follow-up coverage of responses was insufficient to provide the reader with an informed treatment of what the report eventually wrought for nuclear power.

COVERAGE BY THE POPULAR PRESS

To assess presentation by the popular Press, coverage of the report by the *New York Times* was examined. The *New York Times* is not representative of the popular press, of course, and one would expect a much more detailed and scientific coverage because of the newspaper's resources and readership. In this sense, the pattern of coverage is probably a best-case analysis, with greater problems likely in other newspapers.

In regard to coverage by the popular media, it bears emphasizing that the Kemeny Commission report represents a special case among nuclear risk assesments. First, it came in the wake of the accident at Three Mile Island, the top news story of the year. Consequently, the Commission operated under a spotlight of media attention from the time it was created by President Carter until it published its report some seven months later. Second, unlike most other risk assessments covered in this volume, the Kemeny report was intended to investigate the problems that led to an *actual* event and then to make recommendations on how best to *avoid* any similar occurrences in the future.

Interest in the Kemeny Commission by the *New York Times* was intense well before the report actually appeared. The paper published 31 articles and three editorials on the Commission's activity prior to the report's release. This coverage exceeded the number of articles that appeared in a corresponding period after the release (Fig. 6.1). Since there are further references to the Kemeny Commission report included in articles on related topics (e.g., the Rogovin Commission) after the report, and coverage tended to switch to specific report issues, our column-inch count suggests that pre- and post-Kemeny coverage was probably roughly about equal.

The *New York Times* first reported the creation of the Kemeny Commission on April 6, 1979 (Burnham 1979), after President Carter's announcement that a presidential commission of experts would be convened in order to "investigate the causes of this accident and . . . make recommendations on how we can improve the safety of nuclear power plants." The first article on the Kemeny Commission that sought to "paint a picture" of the Three Mile Island accident, and nuclear power in general, appeared on May 20 (Ayres 1979). The Commission had just completed its first day of hearing testimony from residents of Middletown, and the article captured the emotionalism of the session: "Citing estimates that a few additional cases of cancer might develop as a result of the accident . . . [a resident] asked, his voice rising with emotion: 'Who'll be the ones? Myself? My son? My wife?'" (Ayres 1979, p. 21). As the testimony mounted, first with the control-room operators, then with NRC officials, Babcock and Wilcox executives, and Pennsylvania state officials, an image of mismanagement, carelessness, ineptitude, and complacency unfolded in the pages of the *New York Times*. The reader of these articles could not easily come away with anything but a generally pessimistic view of nuclear power in America, but one that was probably consistent with the record of testimony.

With the evidence in and the jury in deliberation, the Press was left to wait for the verdict. Following up on rumors and strategically placed leaks, the *New York Times* focused its attention upon an anticipated moratorium of some form. Apart from this issue, the preliminary findings alluded to in the *New York Times* did, for the most part, show up in the Kemeny report. Key among them were:

(a) The NRC had a major attitudinal problem and was preoccupied with licensing. It would be recommended that the NRC be reorganized as an executive agency.
(b) There must be an approved licensing plan.
(c) There should be periodic relicensing of nuclear power plants.
(d) Operator training should be upgraded with increased government regulation and better (possibly standardized) design for control rooms.

These findings and recommendations, however, received much less attention than the moratorium issue.

The Kemeny report ultimately included 81 specific findings and 44 recommendations. Of the 81 findings, the *New York Times* (1979) reported on only 13 (see Table 6.1). Of the 44 recommendations, the newspaper covered only eight (*New York Times* 1979). The treatment, in short, was highly selective,

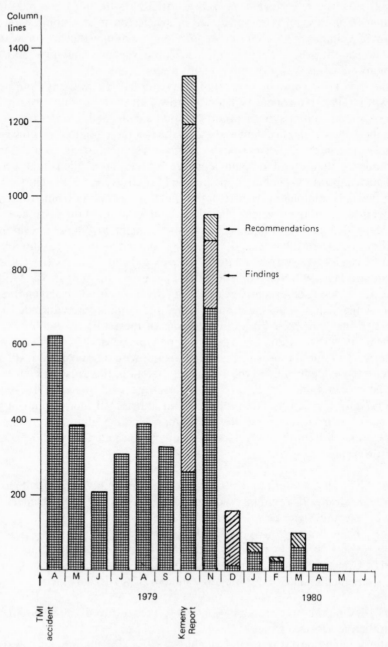

**Figure 6.1** Column lines of Kemeny Commission general coverage, findings, and recommendations in the *New York Times*.

emphasizing what the *New York Times* found important. At the same time, however, those selected findings and recommendations received extensive coverage. The finding "that fundamental changes are necessary if those risks are to be kept within tolerable limits," *the* central finding according to the *New York Times*, elicited no fewer than nine articles during the post-report period.

Two recommendations, the reorganization of the NRC and the upgrading of licensing procedures, dominated the overall coverage. Interestingly, the recommendation – the proposal to reorganize the NRC – which overwhelmingly dominated coverage, was the one not ultimately adopted. Even the recommended upgrading of licensing procedures was discussed primarily in terms of the moratorium issue.

Coverage of the report fell rapidly off the *Times*' reporting agenda, although, as noted above, analysis of the coverage is difficult because attention shifted to specific issues rather than the overall report. A gleaning of the *New York Times Index* suggests that specific issues pursued by the *Times* were

**Table 6.1** Recommendations and findings from the Kemeny Commission report as reported in the *New York Times* (1979), excerpts from Presidential Commission's report on the Three Mile nuclear accident (in print lines).

| | 1979 Oct. | Nov. | Dec. | 1980 Jan. | Feb. | Mar. | Apr. | Total | Total no. of articles |
|---|---|---|---|---|---|---|---|---|---|
| *Recommendations* | | | | | | | | | |
| Reorganize NRC | 70 | 30 | 119 | 9 | — | — | — | 228 | 13 |
| Establish executive oversight committee | 6 | — | 8 | — | 7 | — | — | 21 | 3 |
| Broaden utility responsibility in emergency | — | 3 | — | — | — | — | — | 3 | 1 |
| Upgrade licensing procedure | 50 | 30 | 21 | — | — | — | — | 101 | 9 |
| Improve operator and operating procedure | 22 | — | — | — | — | — | — | 22 | 3 |
| *Findings* | | | | | | | | | |
| Overall conclusion | 136 | 24 | 15 | — | — | — | — | 175 | 9 |
| Assessment of significant events | 249 | — | — | — | — | 35 | — | 284 | 7 |
| Public right to know | 159 | 104 | — | — | — | — | — | 263 | 6 |
| NRC | 117 | 12 | 3 | — | — | 4 | — | 136 | 9 |
| Utility and supplier | 107 | 20 | 3 | — | — | — | — | 130 | 7 |
| Public health and health effects | 54 | 14 | — | — | — | — | — | 68 | 5 |
| Operators and operating personnel | 38 | — | — | — | — | — | — | 38 | 3 |
| Attitudes: personal and institutional | 78 | — | — | — | — | — | — | 78 | 3 |

safety conditions at various nuclear plants, problems surrounding Indian Point, economic problems (including fines, cost overruns, delays) of the nuclear industry, and the political struggles between pronuclear and antinuclear forces. By contrast, the *Times* neglected the important but less conspicuous reponses, within both industry and government, that dealt with the generic safety issues raised by Three Mile Island and the report. Throughout 1980, in the year following the accident, no substantial discussion of the NRC's *Action plan* (US Nuclear Regulatory Commission 1980), the single most important governmental response to emerge from the accident and the Kemeny Commission report, appeared in the pages of the *New York Times*.

## COVERAGE BY TELEVISION

To assess how television presented the Kemeny report, the author used the *Television Index* of the Vanderbilt University Television Archives to identify all network news programs dealing with the report. Acquisition and viewing of videotapes of each of the news programs revealed a number of characteristics of television coverage and presentation.

At the time the Commission was formed, the network nightly news broadcasts devoted only a few lines to the announcement. Unlike coverage in the *New York Times*, the television network largely ignored the record of testimony as it unfolded in the hearings of the Kemeny Commission. The first television treatment of the report occurred approximately one week prior to its formal release (October 22 and 23, 1979), at which time major findings were known. These findings, however, were not lead stories for the news broadcasts.

As with the *New York Times*, the networks focused strongly on the decision not to include a moratorium on new nuclear plants. The American Broadcasting Company (ABC) and the Columbia Broadcasting System (CBS) each covered four to five other recommendations, but the National Broadcasting Company (NBC) treated only the proposed reconstitution of the Nuclear Regulatory Commission. Visual imagery was largely confined to file footage of Three Mile Island. The language used by broadcasters was attention-getting in places: ABC reported that the Commission "blasts" the NRC, CBS picked up on a reference to the NRC as a "headless monster," and NBC underscored that the moratorium decision occurred after "a lot of angry arguing." On the whole, however, the presentations were factual, if highly selective in coverage.

The release of the Kemeny report on October 30 was the evening's lead story and each of the networks carried major stories. The coverage by CBS was most informative, treating 13 findings and recommendations (as compared to 11 for ABC and 9 for NBC). In terms of balance in presentation, there were differences among the networks. ABC included interviews with three commissioners (Babbitt, Lewis, and Taylor), but chose three more critical of nuclear power. It also included interviews with three residents of Three Mile Island, and these were well balanced in viewpoint. CBS interviewed the Commission Chairman, Kemeny, and added interviews with two representatives (Commissioner

Dieckamp and Floyd Lewis) from industry (but no environmentalists). NBC included two interviews (Babbitt and Dieckamp), thereby balancing Commission viewpoints.

By one day after the appearance of the Report, television coverage was essentially over. CBS carried no further stories on the Kemeny Commission, and ABC only one brief follow-up story on October 31. NBC, however, provided an interesting commentary by David Brinkley on what the Commission accomplished, ending with the prophetic observation:

On the broad question "should any more plants be built?" the Commission did not agree. It said there is risk. If the country wants to take the risk, then changes would [be] needed to keep the danger down to an acceptable level. If not, it said the industry and government will totally destroy the public's confidence and *they* will be responsible for the elimination of nuclear power in this country.

COVERAGE BY THE ADVERSARIAL PRESS

Finally, the author inquired into the coverage by pronuclear and antinuclear information sources for their portrayal of the report. Three key pronuclear journals, *Nuclear News, Nuclear Industry*, and *Public Utilities Fortnightly*, and three antinuclear journals, *Critical Mass, Nucleus*, and *Not Man Apart*, were selected for analysis. The author also surveyed all articles treating the Kemeny report for a one-year period following issuance of the report.

Table 6.2 summarizes the results of this review. Among the pronuclear journals, *Nuclear News* and *Nuclear Industry* provided detailed, factual, and fairly comprehensive coverage of the findings and recommendations. By comparison, coverage in *Public Utilities Fortnightly* was more general and cursory.

Among the antinuclear journals, with considerably more limited space, of course, only *Critical Mass* provided coverage equivalent to that of *Nuclear News* and *Nuclear Industry*. *Nucleus* provided no substantial coverage of the report, whereas *Not Man Apart* had only one article summarizing the report, and that was quite cursory.

In conclusion, both pro- and antinuclear readers had access to reasonably broad and factual coverage of the report, but the coverage in the pronuclear journals was both broader and more detailed.

COMPARATIVE CONCLUSIONS

Comparing the presentations in the different media, several conclusions emerge:

(a)  Each of the media provided reasonably factual and objective coverage of the report, although each was more limited in scope than news space

**Table 6.2**  Coverage of Kemeny Commission recommendations in pronuclear and antinuclear journals.

|  | Journal | Coverage of recommendations |
|---|---|---|
| pronuclear | *Nuclear News* (monthly) | Of the 16 articles on the report, 5 covered recommendations, and 1 was a verbatim reprint of all the recommendations. Coverage of the recommendations constituted nearly one-half of all coverage of the report. Proposal to restructure NRC described as ineffective. |
|  | *Nuclear Industry* (monthly) | Of the seven articles on the report, two covered recommendations. One was a comprehensive summary of the report; the other a detailed summary of Part A (institutional) recommendations. Coverage of recommendations nearly one-third of total coverage. |
|  | *Public Utilities Fortnightly* (fortnightly) | Of the six articles on the report, two covered recommendations but only in a broad and cursory manner. No comprehensive survey of recommendations provided. Coverage of recommendations only approximately 10 percent of total coverage of report. One article rates restructuring of NRC as the most important recommendation. |
| antinuclear | *Critical Mass* (monthly) | Of the nine articles on the report, five covered recommendations, one of which covered all the recommendations in a thorough and comprehensive manner. Coverage of recommendations: approximately 20 percent of total coverage. Particular emphasis to safety emphasis in licensing. |
|  | Union of Concerned Scientists' *Nucleus* (six times yearly) | In its three articles on the report, *Nucleus* had no coverage of recommendations. |
|  | Friends of the Earth, *Not Man Apart* (monthly) | Of the three articles on the report, only one covered recommendations and then only in cursory manner. Coverage of the recommendations comprised only approximately 10 percent of the total coverage. Safety emphasis in licensing acted as Commission's strongest recommendation. Recommendation on restructuring NRC seen as ineffective and inappropriate. |

restrictions would require and each, with perhaps the exception of the adversarial press, failed to provide sustained treatment of longer-term effects.

(b)  Whereas the *New York Times* had far and away the most extensive coverage, it skewed its treatment heavily to pre-report stories, to the moratorium issue, and to political aspects of the Commission's work.

(c)  The scientific media's factual coverage of the report's findings and

recommendations, although more technical in treatment, was not substantially fuller in scope than that of the *New York Times.*
(d)  Television networks, unlike newspapers, largely ignored the pre-report stories, concentrated on the report itself, and within broadcast time constraints, performed as well as the other media in achieving a factual and balanced treatment of the report's findings and recommendations.
(e)  The adversarial press and the pronuclear and antinuclear journals presented reasonably objective coverage of the report, although the treatment by pronuclear journals was more comprehensive and detailed.

## *Impacts of the report upon nuclear safety*

The most far-reaching question for the Kemeny report is whether, and to what degree, it stimulated a higher level of safety for nuclear power plants. To address this question, the author identified 12 key areas from among the 43 specific recommendations of the Commission. For each key area, public documents were searched, speeches reviewed, and interviews taken to define major societal responses and unsolved issues. An overall assessment was then provided for the degree and effectiveness of the response. Table 6.3 provides a summary of results. The discussion below reviews impacts upon institutions, risk assessment and management, emergency preparedness, and the formulation of an overall safety goal for nuclear power.

### INSTITUTIONAL CHANGES

The Kemeny Commission made a number of biting judgments concerning the primary institutions responsible for the assurance of nuclear safety. The most notable of these were:

(a)  *The Nuclear Regulatory Commission:* "With its present organization, staff, and attitudes, the NRC is unable to fulfill its responsibility for providing an acceptable level of safety for nuclear power plants" (p. 56).
(b)  *The Advisory Committee on Reactor Safeguards* (ACRS): The Committee is the only body independent of the NRC staff which regularly reviews safety questions, but the Committee "has established no firm guidelines or procedures," its members are "part-time and have a very small staff," and it relies heavily upon the NRC staff for follow-up of concerns.

**Table 6.3**  Societal response to key Kemeny Commission recommendations.

| Recommendation | Response |
| --- | --- |
| Restructure/Improve NRC (A1) | President does not accept Kemeny reorganization recommendations. Congress retains collegial structure with strengthened powers of chairman. Chairman designated as spokesman in emergencies. |
| | *Assessment:* basic problems of the Commission referred to in report remain unresolved, restructuring is not achieved, but improvements in emergency response and regulation of operating reactor capabilities are apparent. Long-term improvement in mind-set problems remains unclear. |
| Improve ACRS (A3) | NRC opposes any mandatory response to recommendations of the Advisory Committee on Reactor Safeguards (ACRS). On Feb. 11, 1980, ACRS charges NRC "largely ignores" its input on Kemeny Commission responses. |
| | *Assessment:* no substantial action undertaken to improve ACRS. It remains unlikely that the ACRS can and/or will greatly influence changes within the NRC. |
| Establish new oversight committee (A2) | Executive Order establishes Nuclear Safety Oversight Committee on March 18, 1980. Committee issues three letter reports to the President on NRC action plan, radiological consequences of nuclear accidents, and emergency response planning. President Reagan does not renew committee mandate and it goes out of existence. |
| | *Assessment:* Committee provided a limited but useful function during its short duration. |
| Upgrade reactor operator and supervisor training (A4, C1, C4) | Nuclear Safety Analysis Center establishes computerized communication system connected to all utilities on operating incidents. Utilities improve training in emergency events. New training program inaugurated in cooperation with utilities. Severity of licensing exams increased, with failure rate rises. Institute for Nuclear Power Operations has established a training accreditation program. |
| | *Assessment:* substantial upgrading is evident though adequacy remains a question. |
| Increase safety emphasis in licensing (A10) | NRC reorganizes licensing staff to correct weaknesses in licensing process. Increased attention to operator training, utility management, emergency planning, reactor design features, and evaluation of plant operating experience; NRC decides against Office of Hearing Counsel. |
| | *Assessment:* actions taken fill a number of gaps in safety coverage, but the degree of substantial improvement unclear. NRC licensing of Sequoyah plant questions commitment to safety. Reduced role of intervenors and effort to speed up licensing may weaken safety focus. |

**Table 6.3** *(continued)*    Societal response to key Kemeny Commission recommendations.

| Recommendation | Response |
| --- | --- |
| Improve safety inspection and enforcement (A11) | NRC establishes resident inspectors at power plants, requires annual evaluation of licensees, improves reporting requirements. A new NRC Office for Analysis and Evaluation of Operational Data established (prior to Kemeny report). Fines for utilities increased. |
| | *Assessment:* potential substantial improvement in inspection and regulation of operating reactors only partially realized. Resident inspector program has, however, been implemented. 1985 Office of Technology Assessment study concludes that current system for fining utilities does not work. In 1986, NRC inspection program remains fragmented and unfocused. |
| Improve technical assessment and equipment (D1–D3) | Utilities initiate widespread improvements in control room design and instrumentation. |
| | *Assessment:* substantial improvements implemented or ongoing in improved instrumentation, equipment, and monitoring. |
| Initiate new reactor risk assessments (D4–5, D7, E1) | NRC reorients risk assessment research program with new attention to higher probability events, accident mitigation, and human factors. Retrospective iodine-release study of TMI accident suggests possible past overestimate of consequences by factor of 10 but a 1985 American Physical Society report concludes more research needed on source terms. Utilities establish improved monitoring and dissemination system of operating incidents. NRC establishes Division of Human Factors and attempts to define levels of acceptable risk. Epidemiologic studies of effects of low-level radiation initiated. 15–20 major plant specific probabilistic risk assessments initiated by utilities' power plants. Radiation Policy Council established in Executive Branch, but is abolished by the Reagan Administration. |
| | *Assessment:* significant changes instituted to give new priority to TMI-like events, to human factors, and accident mitigation. Individual plant risk assessments should improve safety performance and enlarge accident response capability. Effort on human factor and on operator error still inadequate. |

**Table 6.3**  *(continued)*   Societal response to key Kemeny Commission recommendations.

| Recommendation | Response |
| --- | --- |
| Improve industry attitudes and performance (B1–B3, B5) | Industry establishes two new institutions: Institute for Nuclear Power Operations (INPO) with power plant evaluation and training as primary functions and Nuclear Safety Analysis Center (NSAC) with analysis of operating experience and other technical assessment its primary activities. International cooperation with NSAC makes world experience data base a possibility. |
| | *Assessment:* substantial industry response: new institutions and particularly INPO, are important safety vehicles. INPO plant assessments now broad and still evolving, searching for root causes of safety management problems. Still unresolved are prevailing attitudes and assurance of high level of overall technical competence in individual utility management structure. Continued problems in management by some utilities a continuing issue, as suggested by shutdown of all TVA reactors. |
| More remote siting of nuclear power plants (A6) | NRC proposes (NUREG 0625) upper limits on population densities around plants and making siting criteria distinct from engineered safeguards. Estimates suggest 49 of 84 currently operating plants would fail to meet criteria. Strong industry opposition. |
| | *Assessment:* proposal fails due to controversy but new plants not ordered in any event. Since no retrospective application of criteria, limited safety impact on 100–150 GWE nuclear system. |
| Improve emergency response and mitigation (A7–8, E3–5, F1–3) | NRC issues new rule on emergency-response plans, extending 5-mile zone to 10-mile zone and 50-mile radii. All operating reactors have formulated and tested emergency plans. NRC installs a crisis management communications link of all power plants to NRC headquarters. New rule mandates that state be able to notify every person within 10 miles of a nuclear power plant of accident and to shelter or evacuate population. Proposal to distribute potassium iodide pills fails. Drills and exercises indicate numerous problems in implementation of plans. |
| | *Assessment:* utilities and the NRC have improved substantially their emergency-response capabilities. The overall capacity of society to respond adequately to a major accident will become clear only in future crisis events but should be improved. |
| Educate the public (F4, G5) | NRC planned to investigate need for literature, but no broad-based program instituted. A tendency to use propaganda rather than education. |
| | *Assessment:* no substantive response despite widespread scientific belief as to need. The Atomic Industrial Forum and the Committee for Energy Awareness implement well-funded propaganda campaigns. |

(c)  *The utility:* The utility (Met. Ed.) failed in a number of important cases "to acquire enough information about safety problems, failed to analyze adequately what information they did require, or failed to act on that information" (p. 43). "It did not have sufficient knowledge, expertise, and personnel to operate the plant or maintain it adequately" (p. 44).

To deal with these institutional deficiencies, the Commission recommended a broad set of changes involving the NRC, the ACRS, and industry.

*The Nuclear Regulatory Commission*  The Kemeny Commission found that the Nuclear Regulatory Commission lacked sufficient organizational and management capability to ensure safety, a judgment supported by the Rogovin report (Rogovin *et al*. 1980). Unfortunately, the Commission recommended the rather shop-worn suggestion of agency reorganization – in this case a change from an independent regulatory commission to an executive branch agency with an administrator as the most prominent means of redress. The Kemeny Commission was the first accident post-mortem to call for this change, which subsequently also found favor in the Rogovin report. The recommendation was unpopular from the start: the NRC staff opposed it, all but one of the NRC Commissioners also opposed it, Congress was lukewarm to the idea, and President Carter, sniffing congressional opposition, never supported the recommendation. Instead, he called for, and Congress eventually approved, a strengthening of the Chairman's role.

Three years after the accident, one NRC Commissioner judged top leadership in the Commission as an outstanding problem, "analogous to hitching four horses at different points around a sled" (Bradford 1980). A lack of policy direction from the Commission to the staff also tended to result in confused research priorities and schedules (Reactor Safety Research Review Group 1981, p. vi-2). The general weakening of regulatory agencies in the Reagan Administration also eroded coherent, effective leadership committed to safeguarding public health and the environment. Indeed, although the Reagan appointments to the Commission have afforded greater consensus, they have (arguably) led the Commission *away* from rather than toward the vigorous regulator sought by the Kemeny Commission.

Within four months of the accident (and thus well in advance of the Kemeny report), the NRC established a new office for analysis and evaluation of operational data aimed at rectifying serious deficiencies, apparent from the Three Mile Island accident, in learning from past reactor incidents and malfunctions. The Commission also initiated a program of resident inspectors. The Commission first committed itself to placing two resident inspectors at every operating reactor site, but even by 1981 scaled down its commitment to one resident inspector at sites with a single reactor and two at sites with two or more reactors. By 1985, the program had largely been implemented.

Underlying these institutional changes is the more basic problem of attitudes and orientations throughout the professional staff of the Commission. The Kemeny Commission was quite specific about these problems:

> . . . we have seen evidence that some of the old promotional philosophy still influences the regulatory practices of the NRC. (p. 19)
>
> . . . the evidence suggests that the NRC has sometimes erred on the side of the industry's convenience rather than carrying out its primary mission of assuring safety. (p. 19)
>
> There seems to be a persistent assumption that plants can be made sufficiently safe to be "people-proof." (p. 20)
>
> We do not see evidence of effective managerial guidance from the top, and we do see evidence of some of the old AEC promotional philosophy in key officers below the top. (p. 21)

The Kemeny Commission was hopeful that the reorganization of the NRC would begin a change in attitudes top down. A coherent plan for dealing with these difficult behavioral problems never emerged, yet obviously substantial changes are critical to a strengthened regulatory performance. The behavior of the Commission in the seven years since the accident suggests, unsurprisingly, that the pre-accident attitudes are difficult to extirpate.

Meanwhile, the US Office of Technology Assessment (OTA 1984, p. 165–6) report on nuclear power found continuing management problems within the Commission, including

(a) a tendency to react to immediate, pressing problems, thereby giving small problems more attention than warranted;
(b) a regulatory process which remains too cumbersome and legalistic;
(c) inconsistency in reviews;
(d) serious problems in the rule-making process.

The response of the NRC to the Kemeny report (and other post-mortems), in summary, has improved regulatory performance in a number of areas, specifically in crisis–response capability and the regulation of operating reactors. Yet the NRC's response betrays an overall preoccupation with formal, specific regulations aimed at individual problems, a tendency that led one pronuclear member of the Kemeny Commission to conclude early that ". . . the NRC shows little recognition of the fundamental flaws in its approach to reactor safety" (Pigford 1981, p. 48). More basic problems are evident in 1987: the need for more effective top leadership, continuing management problems impeding more effective regulation, and ingrained attitudes inimical to safety in the professional staff. The antiregulatory efforts of the Reagan Administration and its expressed intent (if not behavior) to develop nuclear power have undoubtedly exacerbated these problems, particularly those that are behavioral in nature.

*The Advisory Committee on Reactor Safeguards*  The Kemeny Commission called for a strengthening of the staff of the ACRS on the elimination of the requirement that it review each license application, the provision of a statutory right of the Committee to intervene in hearings, and provision of the right of the Committee to initiate rule-making on generic safety issues. Significant actions have not been forthcoming to increase the capabilities of the staff, to enlarge the role of the Committee in generic safety issues, and to improve communications with the NRC itself. There is evidence that the Committee's difficulties in making its views heard at the NRC have not been completely resolved. Less than one year after the Three Mile Island accident, the Committee officially complained that the NRC had largely ignored its input on matters relating to NRC's post-Three Mile Island responses and the requirements for near-term operating licenses (*Nuclear News* 1980). In 1987, efforts to revise the Committee's role in licensing decisions were still in process, with debate over the most desirable course.

The Kemeny Commission also recommended the institution of a new independent committee whose purpose would be "to examine, on a continuing basis, the performance of the agency [NRC] and of the nuclear industry in addressing and resolving important public safety issues associated with the construction and operation of nuclear power plants, and in exploring the overall risks of nuclear power" (US President's Commission on the Accident at Three Mile Island 1979, p. 62). President Carter established the Nuclear Safety Oversight Committee in March, 1980 under the chairmanship of Governor Bruce Babbitt of Arizona. During its brief existence, the Committee concentrated on post-Three Mile Island responses, issuing three letter reports on the NRC's *Action Plan*, iodine release in nuclear accidents, and emergency planning and response, and commissioning an independent technical review of the national program of reactor safety research (Reactor Safety Research Review Group 1981). The Committee played a useful oversight function but its mandate was not renewed by the Reagan Administration.

*Industry*  Of equal or greater significance to the public institutions has been the impact of the Kemeny Commission Report on industry itself, especially the utilities that manage the operation of nuclear power plants. The Commission found far-reaching problems in the role of the utilities, warning that "the nuclear industry must dramatically change its attitudes toward safety and regulations" and that it must also "set and police its own standards of excellence to ensure the effective management and safe operation of nuclear power plants" (US President's Commission on the Accident at Three Mile Island 1979, p. 58).

In fact, the major elements of industry response were set in motion well before even the appointment of the Kemeny Commission. Figure 6.2 shows the structure of this response. Within two weeks of the accident, the four major industry groups, the American Public Power Association, the Atomic Industrial Forum, the Edison Electric Institute, and the National Rural Elec-

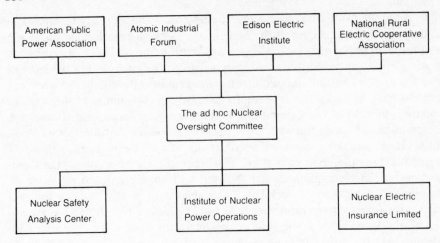

**Figure 6.2**   Response effort to the Three Mile Island accident by the nuclear industry.

tric Cooperative Association, joined to create a policy task force (the Three Mile Island *ad hoc* Nuclear Oversight Committee) to address the safety issues presented by the accident. The seven subcommittees formed to develop policy recommendations indicated by the concerns immediately identified were: emergency response planning, operations, systems and equipment, post-accident recovery, safety analysis considerations, control room design, and unresolved generic safety issues. Most committees reported their findings in September of 1979; these findings also formed the industry's contribution to the NRC's Lessons Learned Task Force (Office of Chief Counsel of the NRC 1979). In a statement issued some three months after the accident, Floyd Lewis, Chairman of the Industry *ad hoc* Committee, could point to three new institutions already begun or planned, as well as a wide range of other utility responses (US Congress 1979, pp. 130–5).

Approximately one month after the accident, the Nuclear Safety Analysis Center (NSAC) was established to conduct technical analyses of the accident, to interpret the lessons to be learned, to develop strategies to prevent future such accidents, and to address generic safety issues. Financed by the utilities and possessing a professional staff of 50, the Center had by 1986 performed a detailed technical analysis of the Three Mile Island accident, developed a priority system for needed safety changes, initiated a program on the testing of relief valves, conducted studies of a computerized data base of 22,000 reactor operating failures (licensee event reports), instituted a computerized communication system linking 60 utilities for rapid dissemination of, and requests for, information, conducted case studies of specific safety problems (e.g., the loss of electrical power to non-nuclear instrumentation at the Crystal River Nuclear Plant), and examined the problem of degraded cores.

To deal with the "people problems" apparent in the Three Mile Island accident, the industry announced in June, 1979 its intent to establish the Institute of Nuclear Power Operations (INPO). Chauncey Starr, with an advisory group drawn from the Navy's nuclear program, the National Aeronautics and Space Administration, and airline safety, developed the mandate and structure of the Institute. With the participation of all US utilities with nuclear power plants and utilities in some 13 other nations, the Institute has developed benchmarks for excellence in nuclear operations, conducted evaluations of operating experience and management at all member utilities, formulated educational and training requirements for operating personnel, and accredited training organizations. It has also developed the Significant Events Evaluation and Information Network (SEE-IN) to process information on an industry-wide basis. The utilities have also cooperated to create a mutual insurance plan to apply to the extraordinary costs accruing to a utility experiencing a major nuclear accident. INPO has evident growing influence and has achieved success in obtaining voluntary utility compliance with its recommendations.

Taken together, these new industry institutions appear to represent a significant upgrading in industry's capacity and effort to manage nuclear power plant safety. And it is noteworthy that the institutions emerged from industry's response to the accident and preceded the recommendations of the Kemeny Commission. Yet, as with the Nuclear Regulatory Commission, significant questions remain as to the overall impact on the management of nuclear safety. By 1983 approximately $60 million had been spent on each reactor for upgraded safety (Phung 1984, p. 139), yet unambiguous evidence translating these upgradings into better reliability, fewer safety-related incidents, and improved overall safety performance is unavailable. It may well be that an industry with such diverse interests and actors will have difficulty in achieving overall substantial gains (US General Accounting Office 1985, p. 134).

And as with the Nuclear Regulatory Commission, perhaps the most important question is whether change has occurred in basic attitudes among the rank-and-file of industry. Even eight years after the accident, it is difficult to assess this issue, although a tendency is apparent within industry to regard the problems at Three Mile Island as a thing of the past. The institutionalization of response to Three Mile Island seems to encourage some propensity to declare nuclear power as safe rather than to work to make it safe. The recent accident at Chernobyl may, of course, change this complacency.

*The mass media*    In its assessment of how the public's right to information was served in regard to Three Mile Island, the Kemeny Commission found that reporters frequently had difficulty communicating to the public in an understandable form, that the news media presented a balance between "alarmist" and "reassuring" views, and that the vast majority of newspapers covered the accident in much the same way as the major suppliers of news (e.g., the wire services, the broadcast networks, *The New York Times*, and *The Washington Post*).

The Commission's advice to the mass media, to improve their performance in future nuclear crisis events, includes three major recommendations:

(a)   All major media outlets (wire services, broadcast networks, news maga-zines, and metropolitan daily newspapers) should hire and train specialists who have more than a passing familiarity with reactors and the language of radiation. All other news media, regardless of their size, located near nuclear power plants should attempt to acquire similar knowledge or make plans to secure it during an emergency.

(b)   Reporters should discipline themselves to place complex information in a context that is understandable to the public and that allows members of the public to make decisions regarding their health and safety.

(c)   Reporters should educate themselves to understand the pitfalls in inter-preting answers to "what if" questions. Those covering an accident should have the ability to understand uncertainties expressed by sources of information and probabilities assigned to various possible dangers.

The primary information on the initial response of the media to these recommendations comes from a mail survey by the Media Institute (1980) of some 59 news directors of radio stations, two energy reporters for wire services, 27 energy reporters and editors of newspapers, 127 news directors of television network affiliate stations, 54 news directors at independent television stations, 50 national television network news executives, correspondents, and bureau assignment desks, and 10 energy reporters for national news magazines. The results are difficult to interpret because the survey was superficial and because of the overall low rate of return (37 percent) and the low rates of participation by some groups (1 of 50 for major news networks; 0 of 10 for national news magazines). Those results that are available are somewhat encouraging. For example, within a year of the Three Mile Island accident:

(a)   of the television network affiliate stations responding, some 55 percent has assigned a staff member to cover nuclear power issues, 83 percent of those assignees had sought to improve their understanding, and 49 per-cent of respondents had actually read the section of the Kemeny report dealing with the "Public's Right to Information";

(b)   over 90 percent of all newspapers responding had designated a person to cover nuclear power issues, nearly all the designated individuals had sought to increase their understanding, and nearly half of all respondents had read the "Public's Right to Information" section;

(c)   even radio stations, with smaller staffs and resources, have been responsive to the recommendations: one-third of stations had designated an individual as specialist, all of those designees had taken action to improve their understanding, and a third had read the "Public's Right to Information" section (Media Institute 1980, pp. 21–9).

The degree to which these early survey responses reflect actual longer-term improvements in the mass media's capabilities must await future crisis events, but there are indications that the media recognize a problem and that many have undertaken at least minimal efforts to respond.

## RISK ASSESSMENT AND MANAGEMENT

An important impact of the Three Mile Island accident and the subsequent post-mortems was a reorientation in the overall risk assessment program of both government and industry. Three key changes involve new attention to a broader spectrum of reactor accidents, to human–machine interactions in risk, and to accident consequence mitigation.

Since the publication of the *Reactor safety study* (US Nuclear Regulatory Commission 1975), it has been clear that most postulated accidents come from small reactor leaks, such as occurred at Three Mile Island, and not from large pipe breaks leading to catastrophes. Yet the *Reactor safety study* concluded that the greatest public risk is due to comparatively rare events in which a postulated melted core released a large fraction of its contents to the atmosphere. Only a minor portion of the public risk by contrast was assessed to result from the more frequent melts leading to smaller releases.

The Nuclear Regulatory Commission has reoriented its programs to this assessed structure of reactor risks. Thus, its risk assessment program and its criteria for design analysis prior to Three Mile Island focused heavily upon large pipe breaks leading to major loss-of-coolant accidents. Since the Three Mile Island accident, the NRC's light-water reactor safety research program has shifted substantial resources away from big pipe breaks and transients toward higher probability/lower consequence events. This received further impetus from the report of the Reactor Safety Research Review Group (1981) which called for a de-emphasis of large loss-of-coolant accidents and more attention to smaller accidents (pp. v–vi). A similar change has also occurred in the light-water reactor safety research program of the Electric Power Research Institute's Nuclear Power Division.

A second major change is the allocation of significant new attention to human error as an ingredient in reactor accidents. The *Reactor safety study* was quite inadequate in its attention to this issue, largely assuming human error rates taken from industries judged to be similar to nuclear power plants. In fact, numerous analyses, several of which were available before Three Mile Island, have demonstrated the importance of human error in reactor risks:

(a)  NRC official Merrill Taylor informed the Lewis Commission in 1978 that 50–85 percent of the hypothetical safety system failures he had examined in detail would be caused by humans (Sugarman 1979, p. 62).

(b)  The 1978 *German reactor risk study* found that human failure was responsible for two-thirds of all risks (Ch. 4, this volume).

(c)  About 20–50 percent of all Licensee Event Reports are due to human error (Sugarman 1979, p. 63).

(d)  The NRC reports that in about 1 percent of all Licensee Event Reports (about 35 incidents per year), there are indications that a safety feature has been seriously compromised or made unavailable by human error (Sugarman 1979, p. 63).

(e)  Analyses of accident precursors since the Three Mile Island accident have demonstrated that human errors are involved in a significant percentage of major precursors and that operator errors of commission are not modeled well in PRAS (US Nuclear Regulatory Commission 1984, p. B–36).

Despite this evident need to conceptualize reactor operations as a human–machine system, the NRC's approach to reactor risks remains as unduly equipment-centered. Also, the NRC preoccupation with large-break accidents ensured a neglect of human factors (since such accidents require extremely fast reaction), thereby accentuating the role of automatic control through equipment. It is not surprising, then, that a post-accident detailed review of the NRC's regulatory guides and standard review plan found "no examples of criteria written with a clear intent to include human engineering considerations in the licensing and regulatory system" (Rogovin *et al.* 1980, vol. 2, pt. 2, p. 345).

The Kemeny Commission, along with the other accident post-mortems, was quite direct as to the significance of human behavior:

. . . as the evidence accumulated, it became clear that the fundamental problems are people-related problems and not equipment problems. (p. 8)
. . . wherever we looked, we found problems with the human beings who operate the plant, with the management that runs the key organization, and with the agency that is charged with assuring the safety of nuclear power plants. (p. 8)
The most serious "mindset" is the preoccupation of everyone with the safety of equipment, resulting in the down-playing of the importance of the human element in the nuclear power generation. We are tempted to say that . . . what the NRC and industry have failed to recognize sufficiently is that the human beings who manage and operate the plants constitute an important safety system. (p.10)

Since the accidents and the assessments, a number of efforts have been made to internalize human factors into nuclear risk assessment and management. The NRC has established a new Division of Human Factors and has restructured its risk assessment program to give greater emphasis to human error. The Institute for Nuclear Power Operations has undertaken a major effort to improve the training of reactor operators, the single issue that most worried the Kemeny Commission. All 2,200 licensed reactor operators in the US have gone through the Three Mile Island accident sequence on training simulators and had other retraining. The Nuclear Safety Analysis Center also evaluated human response in recommending design and instrumentation changes in reactor control rooms. Again, most of these issues were apparent and the response under way prior to the Kemeny Commission report.

Despite these encouraging changes, questions remain as to the adequacy of response, particularly in the Nuclear Regulatory Commission. In 1980 testimony before the Nuclear Safety Oversight Committee, Saul Levine (1980), the former director of NRC risk evaluation studies, complained that ". . . the Agency is still grappling with equipment problems. Equipment is the be-all and end-all" and that the NRC continues to give insufficient attention to research on human factors. The Reactor Safety Research Review Group (1981) found similar cause for complaint:

> Since TMI, both NRC and the industry have launched substantial human factors research programs, but the present knowledge base is inadequate and more research is required. (p. v–1)
> . . . the accomplishment of many of the objectives would appear to require more resources than are currently assigned to the work. In many cases, the deliverable results of the research are not well defined. (p. v–2)

In addition, assessments performed in the PRA studies since the Three Mile Island accident suggest that human error remains relatively poorly understood and data bases underdeveloped, and human interactions have been only weakly integrated into probabilistic risk assessment (US Nuclear Regulatory Commission 1984, p. A–19).

Unlike, for example, the Federal Aviation Administration's example with the training of pilots, the NRC had decided against taking a lead role in the training of operators. It is questionable whether human behavior will ever become fully internalized into nuclear safety regulation without the direct role of the Commission in such issues and a staff capability to enable in-depth analyses.

The third change in risk assessment involves a new focus on accident mitigation. Traditionally, this has also been an area badly neglected both by industry and the NRC. In no small measure, this is due to the widespread assumption that a serious reactor accident simply would not happen and to the possible expenses involved in requirements for retrofitting. The imbalance in NRC hazard control has been apparent for some time; a 1976 analysis by the present author of regulatory guides issued through 1975 (Fig. 6.3) revealed a general lack of attention to both the "upstream" and "downstream" control of reactor risks. The Kemeny Commission dealt primarily with emergency response, and the changes resulting from those recommendations will be considered below. Suffice it to note here that accident mitigation options are present and may have considerable potential for overall risk reduction. Consider, for example, that

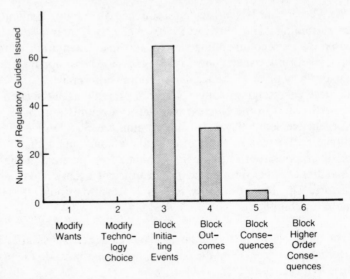

**Figure 6.3** Number of regulatory guides by hazard stage issued by the Nuclear Regulatory Commission (data through 1975). Note the paucity of guides under stages 5 and 6.

(a)   better designs of containment buildings, with filtered release systems to prevent containment failure due to internal overpressure, could reduce the probability of a major release;

(b)   means are available for interdicting the flow of contaminated water in the event of a meltdown from beneath reactor containment buildings to nearby water bodies, but the NRC has made no appropriate preparations;

(c)   underground or more remote siting could substantially lower the consequences of a major accident;

(d)   thyroid blocking by use of potassium iodide pills could reduce thyroid tumor cases by as much as 100,000 over an area extending 200 miles [320 km] downwind from the release source (von Hippel 1979, p. 79).

Belatedly, the NRC is giving new emphasis to accident mitigation in its risk assessment program, as in research on alternative containment designs. Most attention has focused, however, on emergency planning. The post-Three Mile Island findings that a reactor accident might release substantially less volatile iodine than previously assumed may detract from the effort on accident mitigation but the source-term issue persists as a matter for active debate (American Physical Society 1985).

### EMERGENCY PREPAREDNESS

The Three Mile Island accident elevated emergency preparedness into a primary area of nuclear safety concern. The incident demonstrated quite conclusively that none of the responsible parties was prepared for a major nuclear accident. The utility was unprepared to deal with the radiological aspects of the accident, the response by the NRC was disorganized and confused, and the local governments in the power plant region had no emergency plans that provided adequately for protective action. The neglect within the NRC is evident in that only three full-time professionals and one secretary out of 2,500 NRC employees worked on emergency-preparedness issues prior to the Three Mile Island accident (*Nucleonics Week* 1979, p. 10). The Kemeny Commission found few grounds for optimism (p. 17):

> The response to the emergency was dominated by an atmosphere of almost total confusion. There was lack of communication at all levels. Many key recommendations were made by individuals who were not in possession of accurate information, and those who managed the accident were slow to realize the significance and implications of the events that had taken place.

But although the Commission noted a number of problem areas, it made no clear recommendations. Much of the response to and outpouring of documents on the accident and the various post-mortems, including the Kemeny report, have centered nonetheless upon improving emergency response. By the time the Kemeny report appeared, the Atomic Industrial Forum had developed a model plan for emergency response by the nuclear industry. The plan calls for four well-coordinated but independent emergency centers near the site, inter-connected with reliable communication. The Institute for Nuclear Power Operations has also recommended, and evaluated, upgraded training of reactor operators in effective emergency response.

The Nuclear Regulatory Commission has instituted a series of changes to improve its capabilities in this area, the more important of which are as follows.

(a)   The establishment of six teams to assess the emergency planning and preparation of every operating nuclear power plant. In addition, resident inspectors, located at each plant, have well defined duties during an accident.

(b)   Provision to the Chairman of the NRC of clear lead responsibility during emergencies and of an emergency management coordinator to work with him.

(c)   NRC, in cooperation with the Federal Emergency Management Agency, has developed guidance for emergency response plans (US Nuclear Regulatory Commission 1980).

(d)   Upgrading of the NRC's Operations Center in Bethesda, which now includes dedicated reactor operations telephone lines to each facility, with extensions in each control room. The NRC has also instituted a data link between the plant's control room and a technical support center located on site as well as to NRC's Bethesda center.

(e)   The licensing of new plants has been made conditional on the development of acceptable emergency plans, and plants must complete a full-scale exercise testing of these plans each year (amendments to 10 CFR Part 50).

Substantial improvement has occurred in short, in the emergency-response capability of industry and the NRC alike.

More problematic is the role of the states and local governments. The US Federal Emergency Management Agency (1980) has lead responsibility in this area and has mandated that a state be able to notify every person within a 10 mile (16 km) radius of a nuclear power plant that a nuclear accident has occurred and indicate what actions the person must take for personal safety. State governors hold the authority, unless delegated to local governments, for ordering evacuations. Eight years after the Three Mile Island accident, despite widespread improvement, it is also apparent that not all problems have been solved: the ability of officials to notify all portions of the population within the 10 mile (16 km) region is doubtful, failures in the warning systems have been common in drills and exercises, police and other local officials frequently lack equipment and training needed to carry out the plans, sheltering has been relatively neglected as a protection strategy, and drills and exercises have lacked realism as a searching test of preparedness. Further, the emergency plans remain heavily dependent upon human factors under stress, and uncertainty exists as to whether behavior in an actual crisis will be in accord with expert predictions.

## A SAFETY GOAL FOR NUCLEAR POWER

An important issue not addressed by the Kemeny report is the level of safety to which the NRC and the industry should aspire. This issue, however, has received considerable attention from the industry and was accorded high priority in the Rogovin report (Rogovin et al. 1980) and the NRC Lessons Learned report (US TMI-2 Lessons Learned Task Force 1979). The US Office of Technology Assessment (OTA 1984) argued in 1981 that in the absence of a safety goal agreed upon by society, the adequacy of the NRC response to the Three Mile Island accident was impossible to assess and created a large uncertainty in the licensing process (*Nucleonics Week* 1981, p. 4). Congress eventually passed the Bingham Amendment which required a proposed safety goal for nuclear reactor regulation by June 30, 1981.

The Commission sponsored several thoughtful studies of the issues in defining "acceptable risk" levels (Fischhoff et al. 1980, Salem et al. 1980). In February 1982 the Commission proposed its goal, the essential features of which were:

(a)  The risk, to an individual or to the population in the vicinity of a nuclear power plant site, of prompt fatalities that might result from reactor accidents should not exceed one-tenth of 1 percent (0.1 percent) of the sum of prompt fatality risks resulting from other accidents to which members of the US population are generally exposed.

(b)  The risk, to an individual or to the population in the area near a nuclear power plant site, of cancer fatalities that might result from reactor accidents should not exceed one-tenth of 1 percent (0.1 percent) of the sum of cancer fatality risks resulting from all other causes.

(c) A guideline of $1,000 of expenditure per man–rem averted should be adopted so that risks will be "as low as reasonably achievable."

(d) The likelihood of a nuclear reactor accident that results in a large-scale core melt should normally be less than one in 10,000 ($10^{-4}$) per year of reactor operation.

The cost-effectiveness requirement ($1,000 per person–rem [0.01 Sv] averted) was subsequently deleted, seriously weakening the level of safety afforded by the policy (US Nuclear Regulatory Commission 1982b).

In issuing the safety goal policy statement, the NRC stipulated that it be used on an experimental basis. The safety goal is quite consistent with current reactor operation and would appear to require no additional stringency. It is unlikely, in this regard, that it will produce any greater consensus on nuclear power. The implicit consequence of the goal, as pointed out by then NRC Commissioner Bradford (US Nuclear Regulatory Commission 1982a, p. 7), is the acceptance of 13,000 deaths over the lifetime of the 150 reactors now operating or under licensing review, a figure unlikely to win the approval of a risk-averse public. Similarly, the high level of risk aversion to major catastrophes would suggest the need for a safety margin provided in a $10^{-5}$ rather than a $10^{-4}$ probability for a major core melt. Finally, as then NRC Commissioner Gilinsky noted, the safety goal is so remote from nitty-gritty safety decisions that "it is . . . so hard to tell what the implications of the proposed safety goals are that one doesn't know whether to agree or disagree with them, quite apart from knowing whether they are workable or not" (US Nuclear Regulatory Commission 1982a, pp. 7–8). Interestingly, the safety goal approach enhances the importance of large-scale probabilistic risk analysis since it would appear to represent the primary means for confirming attainment of the goal. This is a controversial issue, however, for proponents and opponents alike; one dealt with at further length in the next chapter.

## Other societal impacts

The Kemeny report, as a presidential commission effort and as a major accident post-mortem, could reasonably be expected to have impacts beyond the industry and regulatory agencies. Two such impacts – that on the ongoing nuclear debate and that influencing public attitudes – appear critical.

### THE NUCLEAR DEBATE

One function of a major risk assessment, particularly one by a group as balanced and prestigious as the Kemeny Commission, could be to narrow the nuclear debate, to settle some areas of contention, while clarifying the major areas of actual dispute.

**Table 6.4**  Conclusions drawn from the Kemeny Commission Report.

| Group or journal | Vindication of industry | Balanced judgment | Indictment of industry |
|---|---|---|---|
| Pronuclear<br>  *Nuclear News* | No conclusion that nuclear power too dangerous. Accident caused by operating error. Apart from the control room, NRC primary cause of accident. | | |
|   *Nuclear Industry* | Plants are safe; it is people who are not. Nuclear power is safe if managed well. | | |
|   *Public Utilities Fortnightly* | | Mechanical malfunctions were exacerbated by human error. Deficiencies in equipment, training, and attitudes pervaded the industry, NRC changes required if nuclear power not to be eliminated by public opinion. | |
| antinuclear<br>  *Critical Mass Energy Project* | | | A serious indictment of the nuclear industry and a clear vindication for the nuclear critics. Nuclear power is shown to be unsafe. |
| Union of Concerned Scientists, *Nucleus* | | | A far-reaching indictment of practices of NRC and industry. Report fails to address problems of safety deficiencies. |
| Friends of the Earth, *Not Man Apart* | | | Commission did not go far enough in implicating the risks of nuclear power. |

    To assess whether the report made such contributions, the author conducted two experiments. The first involved an exercise with the three pronuclear and three antinuclear journals (reported on above) to determine what message each derived from the report. Presumably similar assessments of the overall meaning of the

Commission's findings might well help focus the debate on a more common ground.

Not surprisingly, as with press coverage of risk assessments in Sweden (Ch. 3), each journal tended to find what it wanted in the report (Table 6.4). The pronuclear journals tended to see the report as a vindication of the inherent safety of nuclear power plants and safety approaches, whereas antinuclear journals saw the report as an indictment of both industry and the NRC. And, in fact, both messages can be found in the substance of the Kemeny report (and other post-mortems). Nor are these positions simply posturing by the two sides, for similar views were apparent in the several years following the accident in speeches, congressional testimony, and assessments of post-accident responses.

The second exercise focused on the debate agenda, contrasting some 12 major issues which dominated a key pronuclear and antinuclear journal 12 months *before* the Three Mile Island accident, 17 months *after* the issuance of the Kemeny report, or both. The assumption is, of course, that the important elements of the nuclear debate tend to occupy the reporting space of the key journals. A survey of all articles (but not news blurbs) appearing during those time periods then grouped the subjects by major topics (Table 6.5).

**Table 6.5** Agenda structure of the nuclear debate: before and after the Kemeny report (as indicated by a content analysis of *Nuclear News* and *Critical Mass*).

| | Attention (in number of articles and rate per month) | | | |
| --- | --- | --- | --- | --- |
| | *Nuclear News* | | *Critical Mass* | |
| Issue | Before (12 months) | After (17 months) | Before (7 issues over 12 months) | After (17 months) |
| development of nuclear power | 31 (2.6)* | 43 (2.5) | 10 (1.4) | 23 (1.4) |
| economics | 32 (2.7) | 32 (1.9) | 23 (3.2) | 21 (1.2) |
| emergency planning | 4 (0.3) | 11 (0.6) | 3 (0.4) | 12 (0.71) |
| human factors | 1 (0.1) | 6 (0.4) | 1 (0.1) | 2 (0.12) |
| industry performance | 12 (1.0) | 14 (0.8) | 6 (0.9) | 27 (1.6) |
| institutional issues | 15 (1.3) | 38 (2.2) | 17 (2.4) | 34 (2.0) |
| licensing | 20 (1.7) | 30 (1.8) | 2 (0.3) | 8 (0.5) |
| NRC performance | 8 (0.7) | 34 (2.0) | 0 | 16 (0.89) |
| proliferation | 16 (1.3) | 17 (1.0) | 9 (1.3) | 5 (0.28) |
| reactor safety | 33 (2.8) | 50 (2.9) | 8 (1.1) | 19 (1.1) |
| siting | 5 (0.4) | 6 (0.4) | 1 (0.1) | 3 (0.18) |
| waste management | 39 (3.3) | 52 (3.0) | 15 (2.1) | 29 (1.7) |

* Figure in parentheses shows number of articles per month (in monthly journals).

The results do suggest some changes. Attention increased to a set of issues, specifically emergency planning, human factors, the performance of the NRC, and, of course, Three Mile Island itself, apparent in the accident and treated at length in the Kemeny report. But the perennial issues of nuclear power – proliferation, radiation health effects, economics, waste management – did not disappear. And, although not indicated by these data, it is more generally apparent that reactor safety has re-emerged as a central issue of contention.

From these exercises and our more general following of the debate, one may conclude that the report has neither narrowed nor diminished the nuclear debate. Rather, it has provided more data and evidence for the claims of disputants and added several new areas of contention.


PUBLIC ATTITUDES

The Three Mile Island accident, as the worst accident in the history of the US light-water reactor program, was certainly a major event in the public's perception of nuclear power. Media coverage of the accident was enormous, even in the context of the continuing heavy media coverage of nuclear power, suggesting that the accident was a traumatic technological event in the United States. In comparison, the work and report of the Kemeny Commission received scant and short-lived attention. Although survey information is not available, it is highly likely that only a tiny minority of the public has any real knowledge of, or attitude toward, the Kemeny report. As a result, it is undoubtedly the accident itself that had the dominant effects on public attitudes.

As Figure 6.4 suggests, even the effects of the accident are not entirely unambiguous. There is, in fact, the suggestion in the trend of Cambridge Reports (1974–86) national surveys that attitudes to nuclear power had begun to shift prior to the accident at Three Mile Island. The effects of the accident bore out the author and colleagues' pre-Three Mile Island anticipation that ". . . a major reactor accident could well do for the nuclear conflict what the Tet offensive did for the Vietnam debate – cast doubt on the longstanding convictions of the expert proponents, introduce substantial doubt among public supporters, and redouble the efforts of the opposition" (Kasperson et al. 1979, p. 23). The most visible effect of the accident has been, after several years of closely divided opinion, to move the majority of the public into opposition to nuclear power. Increasingly, the accident appears to have constituted a critical event in fashioning public attitudes toward the technology.

Within this general picture, the Kemeny report itself would appear to have had only minor effects (if any at all), but it may have added to the current lack of confidence in nuclear (and other) management institutions.

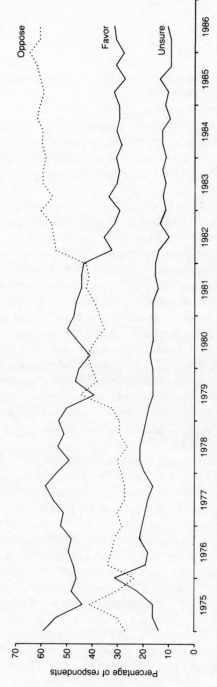

**Figure 6.4** Trends in public opinion on nuclear power. Note that the "unsure/don't know" category is neither verbalized nor offered to respondents – they offer it on their own.
*Source*: Cambridge Reports 1974–86; reproduced with permission.

## Conclusions

Over the eight years since the publication of the Kemeny report, its major impacts are relatively clear. The most notable are:

(a)   The various media provided reasonably accurate and objective information to their readers of the findings and recommendations of the Kemeny report, although each was more limited in scope and particularly in sustained coverage than limitations in space and resources required.

(b)   Television coverage largely ignored pre-report stories, concentrated on the report itself, and within broadcast-time constraints performed as well as other media in achieving a factual and balanced treatment of findings and recommendations.

(c)   The major elements of societal response were apparent several months after the accident and well in advance of the Kemeny report. As a presidential commission, the Kemeny Commission wielded considerable symbolic value and doubtlessly contributed to the momentum for change, but it identified few issues not treated in other accident post-mortems.

(d)   Many of the problems that emerged during the accident had previously been identified, by managers or critics, but lacked sufficient priority to command the attention of those responsible for nuclear safety. The Three Mile Island crisis sufficiently restructured the nuclear agenda and the balance of forces to overcome for a finite time the normal range of obstacles and political resistance to produce safety innovation.

(e)   The response by those managers responsible for nuclear power had addressed the range of concerns noted in the Kemeny Report and other assessments, but uncertainty remains as to whether the deeper problems, especially those more fundamental to institutions and established processes, have been resolved.

(f)   The response by industry was most timely and effective; the mass media generally responded affirmatively, whereas regulatory responses were more delayed and uneven. The overall regulatory response was heavily dependent upon the role of industry. The long-term effect of the accident may, ironically, have furthered self-regulation in nuclear power.

(g)   The changes instituted by industry and government tended to address the obvious gaps and specific problems apparent in the accident. The more fundamental and integrative problems of capability and attitudes which formed the primary concern of the Kemeny Commission and the need for new initiatives and ideas were unevenly addressed in the Three Mile Island response.

(h)   Although the record since the Kemeny Commission report reveals an unprecedented imposition of new requirements on operating reactors, a comprehensive rationale for "back-fitting" requirements was not instituted. In fact, various new rules and regulations were implemented in advance of a safety goal, which presumably should shape such decisions.

(i)   The failure to resolve the basic institutional problems of the NRC points toward a continuing vacuum in societal leadership for nuclear safety in the United States.

(j)   The Kemeny report had few impacts on the broader nuclear debate, but those impacts that did occur largely rekindled the reactor safety controversy and added new issues to the debate agenda.

(k)   Although reliable evidence is unavailable, the Kemeny report apparently had few (if any) impacts upon public attitudes, unlike the accident itself which contributed to the growth of majority opposition to nuclear power.

## References

American Physical Society 1985. Report to the APS of the Study Group on radionuclide release from severe accidents at nuclear power plants. *Reviews of Modern Physics* **57** (3), pt. 2 (July).
Ayres, B. D. Jr. 1979. A-plant neighbors voice frustrations. *New York Times* (May 20), 21.

Bradford, P. A. 1980. *Reasonable assurance, regulation, and reality*. Speech before the ALI–ABA Course of Study on Atomic Energy Licensing and Regulation (September 24).
Burnham, D. 1979. President establishing commission to study nuclear reactor mishap. *New York Times* (April 6), A1 and A17.

Cambridge Reports 1974–86. *Cambridge Report program of national public opinion research*. Cambridge, Mass.: Cambridge Reports, Inc.
Carter, L. 1980. A new call for abolishing the NRC. *Science* **207**, 624, 626.

Fischhoff, B., S. Lichtenstein, P. Slovic, R. Keeney & S. Derby 1980. *Approaches to acceptable risks: a critical guide*. NUREG/CR-1614. Oak Ridge, Tenn.: Oak Ridge National Laboratory.

Kasperson, J. X., R. E. Kasperson, C. Hohenemser & R. W. Kates 1979. Institutional responses to Three Mile Island, *Bulletin of the Atomic Scientists* **35** 20–4.

Levine, S. 1980. As quoted in *Inside N.R.C.* 2 (Dec. 1), 13.

Marshall, E. 1979a. Carter backs "spirit" of Kemeny report. *Science* **206**, 1380.
Marshall, E. 1979b. Kemeny report: abolish the NRC. *Science* **206**, 796–8.
Media Institute 1980. *The public's right to know: communicators' response to the Kemeny Commission Report*. Washington: The Institute.

*Nature* 1979. End nuclear complacency – 3 Mile Island report. *Nature* **282**, 120–1.
*Nature* 1980a. Nuclear accident casts a long shadow. *Nature* **283**, 235.
*Nature* 1980b. What (if any) future for nuclear power? *Nature* **285**, 521–2.
*New York Times* 1979. Excerpts from Presidential panel's report on the Three Mile nuclear accident. *New York Times* (October 31), A22.
*Nuclear News* 1980. The ACRS says the NRC has "largely ignored" its input. *Nuclear News* **23**(4), 14.
*Nucleonics Week* 1979. Major emergency plan changes to affect 911 US reactors. *Nucleonic Week* **20** no. 45, 9–10.

*Nucleonics Week* 1981. Special Issue (March 12), 4.

Office of Chief Counsel of the NRC 1979. *Staff report to the President's Commission on the Accident at Three Mile Island*. Washington, DC: The Commission.
OTA (Office of Technology Assessment) 1984. *Nuclear power in an age of uncertainty*. Washington, DC: Government Printing Office.

Phung, Doan L. 1984. *Assessment of light water reactor safety since the Three Mile Island accident*. ORAU/EA-84-3(M). Oak Ridge, Tenn.: Institute for Energy Analysis.
Pigford, T. H. 1981. The management of nuclear safety: A review of TMI after two years. *Nuclear News* **24**(3), 41–8.

Reactor Safety Research Review Group 1981. *Report to the President's Nuclear Safety Oversight Committee*. Washington, DC: Government Printing Office.
Rogovin, M., G. T. Frampton Jr. & the Special Inquiry Group 1980. *Three Mile Island: a report to the Commissioners and to the public*, 3 vols. Washington, DC: Special Inquiry Group, the Nuclear Regulatory Commission.

Salem, S. L., K. A. Solomon & M. Yesley 1980. *Issues and problems in inferring a level of acceptable risk*. Santa Monica, Calif.: Rand Corporation.
Sugarman, R. 1979. Nuclear power and the public risk. *IEEE Spectrum* 16(1), 59–79.

US Congress 1979. Senate Committee on Interior and Insular Affairs, Subcommittee on Energy and the Environment. *Oversight hearings on industry's response to the accident at Three Mile Island*. 96th Congress, 1st Session. Washington, DC: Government Printing Office.
US Federal Emergency Management Agency 1980. *Report to the President: state radiological emergency planning and preparedness in support of commercial nuclear power plants*. Washington, DC: The Agency.
US General Accounting Office 1985. *Probabilistic risk assessment: an emerging aid to nuclear power plant safety regulation*. GAO/RCED-85-11. Washington, DC: USGPO.
US Nuclear Regulatory Commission 1975. *Reactor safety study*. WASH-1400, NUREG-75/014. Washington, DC: The Commission.
US Nuclear Regulatory Commission 1980. *NRC action plan developed as a result of the TMI-2 accident*. NUREG-0610. Washington, DC: The Commission.
US Nuclear Regulatory Commission 1982a. Safety goals for nuclear power plants: a proposed policy statement. *News Releases* **2**, 1–9.
US Nuclear Regulatory Commission 1982b. *Toward a safety goal: discussion of preliminary policy considerations*. Washington, DC: The Commission.
US Nuclear Regulatory Commission 1984. *Probabilistic risk assessment (PRA) reference document*. Washington, DC: The Commission.
US President's Commission on the Accident at Three Mile Island 1979. *The need for change: the legacy of TMI*. Washington, DC: Government Printing office.
US TMI-2 Lessons Learned Task Force. 1979. *TMI-2 Lessons Learned Task Force final report*. NUREG 0585. Washington, DC: Office of Nuclear Reactor Regulation, Nuclear Regulatory Commission.

von Hippel, F. 1979. Physicist suggests way to mitigate effects of nuclear accident, *IEEE Spectrum* **16**, 79.

# 7 *Assessing and managing nuclear risk in the United Kingdom*

TIMOTHY O'RIORDAN

This chapter analyzes the United Kingdom's approach to the control of possible dangers to the general public associated with the operation or malfunctioning of nuclear reactors. Its point of departure is a review of existing nuclear energy supply and possible future capacity in the light of a highly contentious discussion over the composition of all aspects of energy supply in the UK over the next 40 years (Ince 1982). The central aim of the chapter is to look at how far regulatory authorities and the electricity generating boards responsible for nuclear plant safety rely upon the methodologies and assumptions contained in the major generic risk assessment studies produced in the mid-1970s. In this respect, the treatment adopts a broad approach (as in the chapter on Sweden) rather than (as in the other country studies) addressing a single risk assessment.

This chapter also seeks to assess whether, if at all, such studies have influenced scientific opinion over nuclear-related risks, and whether the debate that the nuclear safety issue engendered generally has narrowed or widened the gap between "public opinion" and "scientific judgment." These are vague terms. What is really meant here is whether the public mood regarding all safety aspects of the nuclear fuel cycle is more or less trusting of the scientific judgments of those who have a responsibility to manage health and safety and those whose duty it is to supervise the management of nuclear plant design and operation.

As noted in Chapter 2, in the UK all aspects of nuclear plant safety are the statutory responsibility of the two electricity generating boards, or licensees. The licensee establishes all conditions applied to plant design, quality assurance of component parts, plant construction, operation, emergency arrangements, waste disposal, and decommissioning. The official regulatory authority, the Nuclear Installations Inspectorate (NII), sets guidelines for safety and reviews the safety proposals of the licensee. The process of licensing is, therefore, a prolonged negotiation between client and regulator, each of whom sees the other as professionally competent, able to draw upon independent expert advice, and, in general, capable of resolving differences without recourse to public analysis. So in the UK, the actual mechanics of nuclear plant safety design, execution, and regulation is largely a secretive and closed business into which "the public" has not in the past been allowed to stray.

Licensee responsibility and the confidentiality of the licensing process have two important repercussions for this study. First the criteria and judgments through which safety matters are conceived and assessed are normally opaque to the general public. It is therefore all but impossible for the informed outside analyst to discover how far, if at all, particular risk assessments influence the management of nuclear plant safety. The other consequence is that the whole process operates on the expectation that politicians and the public alike have confidence in the people and the organizations charged with the statutory responsibility of licensing and operating a nuclear plant reliably.

This expectation breeds in the people and in the organizations in which they work a self-assurance, at times bordering on arrogance and conceit, about their skills and abilities. Moreover, statutory provisions that grant absolute discretion to the Nuclear Installations Inspectorate to license every nuclear facility, be it a reactor or a waste-disposal repository, bolster this self-confidence, at times close to the point of complacency. In effect, neither politicians nor "public concern" have demonstrable control over the final decision that determines the public safety of nuclear operations.

The collegiate approach to the management of nuclear safety, however, jars with the trend, now observable in all western societies, for the public to want to be more informed and involved in all matters nuclear and to have a say in judgments about health and safety. A number of factors encourage this mood. Evidence indicates that the nuclear industry is at times fallible. Accidents do occur, near-accidents are ineffectively hushed up, insiders sometimes blow a very discomforting whistle. Also, nobody can claim a premium on truth; nuclear safety is a matter of growing controversy among scientific experts. Insofar as nuclear plants are proving tremendously expensive to construct and operate, their proclaimed cost advantages over other energy options are diminishing. Finally the problems associated with the "back end" of the fuel cycle, notably waste transport and disposal and decommissioning, are becoming so politically intractable that the once self-assured regulators are becoming bemused as to how to cope and genuinely alarmed about the level of political interference (as they see it) over the management of nuclear facilities. It is this last point, above all others, that is having the greatest effect on the management of nuclear risk in the UK.

The consequence of all this is that in the UK, as elsewhere in the western world, all aspects of nuclear safety are now expected to be open to independent scrutiny. Above all, both the judgments and the assumptions that lie behind judgments as to appropriate levels of safety and plant reliability must be shown to have approval from qualified independent analysts with international reputations. Nuclear risk management in the UK, therefore, is both an open and a closed process. The openness is only partial but coping with it is proving agonizing for the clients and regulators. But the closedness of the actual operation of the licensing process remains. The major difference is that various advisory bodies are being brought in to observe and comment on what was once a very secretive operation. Public concern is thus partly assuaged by the exposition of the licensing process to a degree of outsider examination and by the knowledge that relatively independent appraisal is being applied at all points of the design–operation–disposal–decommissioning process.

The event that allows the exploration of these points and upon which much of the argument in this chapter turns is the Sizewell B Public Inquiry (O'Riordan 1984, Kemp et al. 1984). The public inquiry is a peculiarly British phenomenon. Its antecedents lie in parliamentary procedures to ensure that those whose property was being taken for a greater common good, could have their case heard before an independent adjudicator. Its purpose was to ensure that both private interest and public benefit could be properly balanced, based on principles of natural justice. Public inquiries have evolved over the years into a peculiar mix of the quasi-judicial and an administrative mechanism that seeks to assist a minister faced with a decision involving a mixture of private interest and public good (for a detailed discussion see Kemp et al. 1984).

The Secretary of State for Energy convened the Sizewell B Inquiry to enable him to judge the merits of the case advanced by the Central Electricity Generating Board (CEGB) to construct Britain's first pressurized-water reactor (PWR) at the Sizewell B site on the coast of Suffolk in eastern England. Because of all the factors outlined earlier, the Energy Secretary requested the Inspector to pay, among other matters, particular regard to the health and safety considerations associated with the reactor and to satisfy himself that the procedures for licensing the plant were satisfactory (see O'Riordan 1984). So the Sizewell B Inquiry became the first major public examination of how nuclear reactor safety is managed and regulated in the UK, and as such it provided a window on the process of risk assessment and licensing judgment – a window that permitted much illumination. This is an especially important matter, since the CEGB members clearly regard Sizewell B as the first of a "family" of 5 or 7 PWRs which they hope to construct over the next 15–20 years. Each member of this "family" is to be cloned on the Sizewell B design. The CEGB hopes that, assuming the Sizewell B decision goes in its favor, any future PWR inquiry will be short and confined to site-specific environmental and planning considerations. Hence the critical significance of the Inquiry in reviewing and adjudging the criteria and procedures for the management of safety in nuclear reactors.

## Electricity use in the UK and the development of nuclear power

In 1980, the total demand for energy use in the UK was 321.8 million tonnes of coal equivalent: 29 percent of this was consumed by the domestic sector, 32 percent by industry, 26 percent by transport, and 13 percent by other consumers. In terms of primary fuel input, coal provides 60 percent, oil and gas 27 percent, and nuclear 6 percent. Electricity provided only 13.4 percent of all delivered energy, but it plays a vital role in the UK economy. Necessary for running certain kinds of machinery, for lighting, and for some heating, electricity is an essential ingredient in both the domestic and industrial sectors. It is hardly surprising that in 1979 electricity investment and expenditure accounted for £6.2 billion of the total of £21.2 billion spent on energy in the UK, or about 45 percent of all expenditure, if the transportation sector (where virtually no electricity is used at present) is excluded. In terms of electricity production, in 1984 coal provided 60 percent of fuel, oil and gas 26 percent, and nuclear 9 percent. Official energy projections to the year 2000 suggest an increase in the nuclear-supplied component from between 25 to 50 percent, depending upon the assumptions made (DOE 1982). An important part of the CEGB case was to diversify fuel sources. The miners' strike of 1984–5 and the general unease within the coal industry place a political question mark over the future availability and cost of UK coal. A major nuclear program would, in the government's view, reduce that dependency (DOE 1981).

In 1984, of a total installed electricity generating capacity of 62.3 GW ($10^9$ watt = GW), approximately 5.6 GW was supplied by nuclear plants (Table 7.1). The history of the development of civilian nuclear power in the UK is a highly complicated one characterized by indecision, investment overruns, delays in plant commissioning, and the absence of a clear-cut policy either on reactor type or even reactor design within a given reactor type. The most comprehensive history is written by Williams (1980), though more recent accounts appear in Bending & Eden (1984) and Patterson (1985).

The first generation of nuclear reactors in the UK was the magnox, a British-designed reactor based upon graphite fuel, magnesium oxide alloy cladding (hence the name magnox), and carbon dioxide coolant. Between 1962 and 1971, nine commercial magnox stations were constructed throughout Britain, each on a prototype and each designed and built by a different consortium, with a total generating capacity of some 3.8 GW. In 1966, the government followed this with a program of five advanced graphite-cored and $CO_2$-cooled reactors that used enriched fuel and had a much higher power density. Dogged by construction delays and cost overruns (adding up to 21 years of lost power and £224 million of additional expenditure), the program is not yet complete. In 1978, the government, under pressure to maintain the troubled nuclear construction industry, ordered two additional advanced gas-cooled reactors (AGRs) with a combined output of 2.5 GW.

Table 7.1 Generating capacity in the UK, 1980 (million tonnes of coal equivalent).

| Fuel | Capacity | % |
|---|---|---|
| coal | 89.7 | 76.8 |
| oil | 11.2 | 9.6 |
| nuclear | 15.3 | 13.1 |
| renewables | 0.6 | 0.5 |
| | 116.8 | 100.0 |

Source: annual reports of UK generating boards.

Throughout the 1970s, considerable debate surrounded the choice of the next generation of reactors following the AGR series. Some wanted to continue with the AGR, a plant that was only beginning to prove its reliability; others preferred another British-designed plant, the steam-generated heavy-water reactor (SGHWR). Still others wished to adopt the Canadian version (CANDU) of the SGHWR. The more powerful influences behind the scenes, however, wanted Britain to adopt a PWR, partly because it was believed to be a proved design with a reliable safety record (prior to the Three Mile Island incident which took place after this debate was concluded) and partly because it was regarded as a major export order winner (again these thoughts were active in the early 1970s when the debate over nuclear proliferation and international safeguards was still in its infancy).

In 1979, the Conservative administration went further than its Labour predecessor had in 1978 by stating that a PWR should not only be retained as an option but that it should be the basis of the third generation of UK nuclear reactors (O'Riordan 1984). In 1981, the CEGB announced its proposal to build Britain's first PWR at Sizewell B in Suffolk. Should the PWR be accepted, then the CEGB's aim is to construct "a nuclear family" of six more PWRs before the end of the century. Nuclear power could provide some 25 percent (cf. 14 percent at present) of total installed electricity generating capacity in England and Wales.

There are a number of points to be made about the brief history of the British nuclear program in the context of this study.

(a)   In the 1950s and 1960s, civilian nuclear power enjoyed wide support throughout all sections of society. It was seen as part of the technological revolution regarded as essential for Britain's economy. Little public discussion of safety considerations and virtually no publicly expressed anxiety over nuclear development occurred in the United Kingdom.

(b)   The safety aspects of both the magnox and the AGR stations were never properly standardized because the stations were all unique. Safety, based largely upon design safeguards and engineering excellence, developed plant-by-plant.

(c)   The early to mid-1970s, when the nuclear world was deeply concerned about generic societal risk, saw no orders for new reactors. This meant that British nuclear engineers and safety experts had time, without public scrutiny, to consider more carefully how nuclear safety was to be achieved and to prepare designs and engineering standards in advance of public opinion (insofar as this could be judged).

(d)   Just at the time when a new reactor type was receiving serious consideration, electricity demand fell sharply in the UK. Since 1980, average cold-spell demand had dropped by 15 percent (due mainly to industrial recession, but partly to more efficient electricity use). Also at this time, it became apparent that local management (by shifting the nature and timing of the peak and injecting electricity from France) could further reduce peak demand by at least the equivalent of one nuclear station. This, plus the general concern over the future of the coal industry, promising developments in combined heat and power, and intense debate over the job creation prospects of different electricity supply and conservation possibilities, led to a growing protest over the "need" for additional nuclear stations at this time and the relative economic advantages of nuclear over other electricity management options. All this argument has fueled doubts as to whether a truly safety-conscious nuclear industry can be cost effective.

Table 7.2 lists current nuclear power plants in the United Kingdom.

## Nuclear power safety criteria in the UK

In his study of nuclear plant safety, Chicken (1982, pp. 45–58) notes that when the first reactors were built (in the 1950s), there were no quantitative reactor safety criteria and the only guidance for designers came from engineers in the chemical industry and from the International Commission for Radiological Protection (ICRP). The standards that were arrived at were based on vaguely worded guidelines, really exhortations rather than regulations. This created problems for plant manufacturers and designers who were unsure of what requirements their plant had to satisfy. Often it took several years of discussion.

The criteria against which the first British nuclear reactor sites were judged were: "in any 10°-sector around the reactor there should be less than 500 people within 1½ miles, less than 10,000 people within 5 miles, or less than 100,000 people within 10 miles" (Farmer 1977, pp. xi–xxi). The principal agent of hazard was regarded as release of iodine-131 and so the original criteria applied to $^{131}$I and $^{90}$Sr release and gave rise to considerable public alarm and increased attention to safety. In some aspects Britain was fortunate to experience a serious but not catastrophic nuclear accident early in its reactor-construction program. The Windscale fire of 1957 scattered a number of radionuclides over the surrounding countryside and prompted the precautionary destruction of large quantities of local milk. The rather crude approach to safety assessment, based only on chance, was subsequently refined by applying a weighting factor according to distance on the basis that radioactive doses would decline with distance. The outcome was a site rating, graded 1–3, in which grade 1 sites were chosen. These early calculations dealt merely with potential consequences, not with probability.

In 1967, F. R. Farmer, then Head of the Safety and Reliability Directorate of the UK Atomic Energy Authority (UKAEA), proposed a new set of safety criteria based upon statistical techniques of reliability analysis as already used by aerospace engineers (see Green & Bourne 1977, Watt Committee 1984, p. 53). This was in response to a felt need to link probabilities to accident sequences and to avoid dependence on calculations of failures in engineering systems.

**Table 7.2** Nuclear power stations in the UK.

| Station | MW | Commission date |
|---|---|---|
| *magnox series* | | |
| Calder Hall* | 200 | 1956 |
| Chapeleress* | 200 | 1959 |
| Berkeley | 276 | 1962 |
| Bradwell | 245 | 1962 |
| Hunterston A | 300 | 1964 |
| Dungeness A | 410 | 1965 |
| Hinkley Point A | 430 | 1965 |
| Trawsfynydd | 390 | 1965 |
| Sizewell A | 420 | 1966 |
| Oldbury | 434 | 1967 |
| Wylfa | 840 | 1971 |
| *SGHWE* | | |
| Winfrith* | 93 | 1968 |
| *FBR* | | |
| Dounreay* | 250 | 1976 |
| *AGR series* | | |
| Hinkley Point B | 1,150 | 1976 |
| Hunterston B | 1,150 | 1976 |
| Dungeness B | 1,100 | 1984 |
| Hartlepool | 1,100 | 1984 |
| Heysham I | 1,100 | 1984 |
| Torness | 1,240 | 1987 |
| Heysham II | 1,255 | 1988 |
| *possible PWRS* | | |
| Sizewell B | 1,155 | 1994 |
| Hinkley Point C | 1,155 | 1997 |
| Winfrith | 2,200 | ? |
| Dungeness C | 2,200 | ? |
| Sizewell C | 1,100 | ? |
| Druridge Bay | 2,200 | ? |

* Denotes a research or military reactor which occasionally supplies the national grid.
*Source*: Bending & Eden (1984), and the CEGB; copyright © 1984 Cambridge University Press, reproduced with permission.

The heart of the process is the use of network analysis to establish the spectrum of accidents and their probabilities. These networks are now referred to as fault trees. For a reactor complex, the overall accident probabilities are synthesized from the characteristics of individual systems, which in turn are synthesized from the design and performance characteristics of individual components, ranging from values to pipes and pumps to pressure vessels.

This is the basis of the UK approach to probabilistic risk assessment (PRA) which in turn formed the methodological foundation for the *Reactor safety study* (US Nuclear Regulatory Commission 1975). Once a PRA has been completed for a system as a whole, for any accident sequence, or for an individual component, it can be compared to both the Nuclear Installations Inspectorate (NII) safety principles and to criteria set by governments for acceptable levels of risk. *PRA is still only a guide*, however, in UK regulatory practice. The final safety assessment is based on wider considerations, including what is regarded as technically and economically practicable.

These criteria have now been translated by the generating boards into fairly precise quantitative standards that are acceptable to the National Nuclear Corporation (NNC) and the NII. In summary, the present standards are as follows:

(a) The predicted accident frequency for doses up to 1 Emergency Reference Level (ERL) should not exceed $10^{-4}$ per reactor year. Accidents resulting in lower doses are acceptable with higher frequencies. The standard established by the NRPB (1981) is 1 ERL, and refers to the lower level of dose equivalent at which consideration should be given to plant evaluation. The accepted guide is 100 MSv (10 rem) dose equivalent to the whole body or 300 MSv (30 rem) dose equivalent to the thyroid. For the general public living around a nuclear plant, the radiation dose from normal operation is designed not to exceed 50 MSv (5 millirem) or $\frac{1}{30}$th of the ICRP recommended limit (Matthews 1982, p. 5).

   In a subsequent analysis, the NII (1984) looked at what these levels mean to societal risk. It concluded that there were many assumptions and uncertainties that required clarification, but that the chance of 10 cancer deaths should not exceed $5 \times 10^{-5}$ per year, 100 cancer deaths $\leqslant 5 \times 10^{6}$ per year, and 1,000 cancer deaths $\leqslant 5 \times 10^{-7}$ per year. These are based on an assumption of a linear dose–response relationship with no threshold. All of these conclusions will undergo further refinement.

(b) For any single accident which could give rise to a large uncontrolled release of radioactivity to the environment resulting from the protection systems and barriers having failed then the overall design should ensure that the fault frequency is less than $10^{-7}$ per reactor year. This is interpreted as follows: the product of the initiating fault frequency and the probability of failure to control the incident should be less than $10^{-7}$ per reactor year.

(c) The total frequency of all incidents leading to such uncontrolled releases should be less than $10^{-6}$ per reactor year. If these targets cannot be achieved in all circumstances, then some variation may be acceptable, but only with the agreement of the CEGB and the NII.

It is worth noting that these criteria go well beyond the concept of maximum credible accident, a concept that is not used in the UK because it is regarded as both misleading and far too narrow in application. The British approach is to focus on accident sequences, upon externally caused common-mode problems (especially airplane crashes, earthquakes, and terrorist attacks), and upon component reliability. Within this mix are numerous "credible accidents"; hence the guideline probabilities. Also, the British believe that too much emphasis on the maximum credible accident concept implies that less attention is given to more probable, albeit smaller-scale, accidents.

These criteria also go beyond what is expected in US practice but form the basis of the post-Rasmussen approach to nuclear reactor safety (and indeed for system reliability for over 80 other industries). The UKAEA does not confine its safety advice to the nuclear industry. Nevertheless, design engineers are at pains to stress that these PRAS are targets only because they must always be hypothetical and seek to avoid any interpretation of numerical determinancy. As the Director of Health and Safety for the CEGB puts it (Matthews 1980, p. 45):

The assessors (NII inspectors) will judge that a reactor has an acceptably low risk on the basis of qualitative assessment, supported by numerical analysis, and taking into account factors not readily amenable to numerical analysis, such as safety administrative procedures, operator recovery and damage control arrangements. Overall acceptance of a design is not based on a particular numerical standard.

Because of the public examination of the Sizewell B safety case, the CEGB and Westinghouse provided very detailed statements of how they approached and carried out PRAS. It is clear from their evidence (see especially Harrison 1982, 1983, Gittus 1982a, Farmer 1982) that the *Reactor safety study* provided the basic methodology and impetus, but in the intervening eight years, an enormous improvement in the computer codes and statistical techniques has occurred. For the Sizewell B application, both event- and fault-tree analysis were produced for 12 and 11 categories of fault, respectively (see Table 7.3).

To illustrate the development of the Sizewell B safety assessment methodology and its differences from the *Reactor safety study*, it is useful to examine the genesis of the degraded core analysis. Degraded core analysis is a PRA of conditions leading up to loss-of-coolant, where there is insufficient coolant to remove the heat from the nuclear fuel core. The genesis of the PRA was done in the US by Westinghouse (Westinghouse Electric Corporation 1982) and in the UK by the UKAEA (Gittus 1982b). These analyses were subject to two independent reviews, one by the NNC (1982) and one by the NRPB (Kelly *et al.* 1982). The latter was concerned more with consequence than with probability, but that is in part what the PRA covers. Of interest here is the fact that in accord with CEGB guidelines, the NNC gave to Westinghouse design parameters from the original study. (One will note the control of PRAS by the licensee, not the regulatory authority.) The NII, of course, was examined before the Inquiry to justify its own assessment of these PRAS. So, in addition to the three separate studies of the Westinghouse PRA, the NII conducted a fourth. It is this "tiered independence" of

**Table 7.3**  Faults subject to PRA in the Sizewell B Safety Study.

---

inadvertent trip

steam line break inside containment

steam line break downstream of main stream isolation valve

loss of main feed

inadvertent closure of main stream isolation valve

loss of all electricity supplies

small loss of coolant accident

large loss of coolant accident

steam generator tube rupture

loss of all component cooling water

loss of main cooling water supply

---

*Source*: Harrison (1982).

assessment that is such a striking feature of risk assessment in the UK. The NII, however, points out that, although valuable for clarification and elucidation, the PRA is not a formal part of the safety case (NII 1983a, p. 19; see also below).

The Westinghouse study drew upon the *Reactor safety study*, but it was developed further by the Zion Probabilistic Study, prepared for Westinghouse by the Brookhaven Laboratories. In the Sizewell B evidence (Transcript Days 211–12), Dr. Gittus pointed out that every aspect of the Zion study was critically reassessed by the three independent UK studies and a number of changes were made. These included adopting a lower frequency for small break accidents, use of different data bases to reflect differences in component reliability, and the significant fact that the Zion study operated on an expected frequency of uncontrolled release of $10^{-4}$, whereas the Sizewell B study had to meet the CEGB criteria of $10^{-6}$. The *Reactor safety study*, however, was based on a probability of $10^{-2}$.

Here was an interesting departure from the *Reactor safety study*, and one of many unearthed by the Inquiry (notably in Days 211 and 212, though the Transcripts for Days 166–170 and 334–6 are also relevant). Doubts were expressed on both sides of the Atlantic as to whether the $10^{-6}$ criteria could in practice be demonstrated (see Days 151–3, 165, 183, 187, 230). These doubts were especially pertinent with regard to PRAS of common-mode failures, a matter which was analyzed at considerable length in George (1982; see also Days 194–7) and which we take up in Chapter 8. The CEGB's response to all of this was to stress that PRAS are only part of the safety case and that design safeguards are a vital complementary element. Particularly relevant design safeguards are:

(a)   the provision of more than a minimum number of components needed to
      fulfill a particular task to ensure reliability of operation (the redundancy
      criterion) and the use of diverse features (the diversity criterion);
(b)   the specification of operating requirements, supplemented by the pro-
      vision of appropriate monitoring equipment, thereby ensuring that suffi-
      cient safeguards equipment is always available;
(c)   the specification of regular maintenance and testing of safeguards equip-
      ment to enable it to perform its required functions reliably.

In addition, the CEGB stated (CEGB/P/11/Add 5) that its aim in the treatment of
PRAS was "to bias the estimates of probability in the conservative direction to a
sufficient extent that there can be good confidence that margins exist to
accommodate any residual errors in the non-conservative direction."

In a nutshell, PRAS are designed to be pessimistic in their assumptions so that
the inevitable margins of error are still conservative, even on their worst-case
assumptions. This occurs less by statistical juggling than by actually improving
the design and the reliability of the component systems. It is this generic effort
to achieve comprehensive approach to safety management which distinguishes
the contemporary UK approach from the US counterpart in the mid-1970s.

Under cross-examination on Day 212, Dr. Gittus, head of UKAEA Safety
Research Design, noted that whereas the *Reactor safety study* had examined a
comprehensive range of hazards, the more recent PRAS had often been more
limited. This is because modern analysts strive for greater certainty and work
on subgeneric systems rather than whole clusters of events. Dr. Gittus summarized this distinction very clearly (Day 212, p. 30):

> When I look at probabilistic safety assessments that have been completed,
> then, in cases where hazards have been studied, it is, I think, comparatively
> rare to find a list as comprehensive as the one which Rasmussen used. We are
> looking at a technology which is under development, and what is happening
> is some areas have been able to carry skills forward so that they can do
> considerably better than was done in WASH 1400. So there is a tendency to
> concentrate on making studies of those hazards which can be evaluated with
> improved confidence, and, no doubt for the time being, to give little or no
> attention to some of the other hazards which were looked at by Rasmussen
> crudely in many cases and for which our capability has hardly advanced since
> WASH 1400 times.

For the Sizewell B case, the major improvements lay in internal plant fault
sequences, seismic risk, aircraft and missile impact, and internal or external
fires. A separate but even more important issue was the incorporation of
human error (see below). However, Dr. Gittus praised WASH 1400 for providing the right sort of proportionality for all the various risks. The contemporary
numbers in many cases would be different, he noted, but the relationships
between categories of hazard – the risk burden of each event – were broadly the

same. In general, the Board's view was that the bias of danger came from internally initiated events (plant design/operation failures), not from external hazards which were easier to fix. But the Board also argued that safety features aimed at internal hazard often reduced the threat posed by an external hazard – a philosophy and an approach first outlined in the *Reactor safety study*.

## Regulation, licensing, and public confidence

The CEGB approach to PRA, safety analysis, and engineered design seems comfortably acceptable. The Sizewell B Inquiry, however, was anxious that it be justifiable to a skeptical public. One problem was that some of the Westinghouse codes were classified and hence not available to independent external examination. This point was fiercely contended by Friends of the Earth (FOE), the leading objector on safety issues. Friends of the Earth argued that it could not adequately assess the safety issue because critical information was missing and because the CEGB was constantly changing its evidence. This position by FOE was partly in response to points raised at the Inquiry, partly because the safety case was always being updated, but mainly due to the fact that the Inquiry cross-examination was being shadowed by the plant licensing process.

The "official" answer to the query as to whether "true independence" could apply to the review of the safety case, where important information was missing, was that the regulatory system of separate tiered review should take this into account. This leads us to an examination of the NII's approach to plant licensing.

That process is a matter for continuous negotiation between the licensee and the NII. In the past, the process has been secretive, and the fascinating aspect of the Inquiry was that it had to be opened up to public scrutiny. This put the NII on its toes and forced it to justify its whole approach to safety assessment. That approach rests on seven elements (NII 1983b).

### DESIGN SAFETY PRINCIPLES AND CRITERIA

In 1979 the NII published its *Safety assessment principles for nuclear power reactors* (NII 1979b). These broad guidelines seek to provide a consistent and uniform approach within which the licensee is expected to prepare the safety case. The objectives aim to keep radiation exposure as low as is reasonably practicable. This is known as the ALARA or ALARP principle (the "A" stands for achievable, the "P" for practicable, and the industry prefers to think that there is no difference between the two). The definition of what is reasonably practicable is vague, but a legal judgment puts it as

> a computation . . . in which the quantum of risk is placed on one scale and the sacrifice involved in the measures necessary for averting the risk (whether in money, time or trouble) is place on the other . . . if it be shown

that there is a gross disproportion between them – the risk being insignificant in relation to the sacrifice – the defendents [*sic*] discharge the onus upon them (cited in NII 1984, p.1, A.8).

The NII's aim is to push the licensee toward an ever more stringent analysis of the "gross-disproportion" factor, notably in those aspects of risk that generate greatest controversy and public concern. The rule of thumb for the gross-disproportion test for a major hazard is a risk–benefit ratio of 1 : 10. The really contentious cases often significantly exceed this ratio.

Much depends upon calculations of both probability of death and the value of a life. The Sizewell B Inquiry heard days of evidence on this topic (notably Days 158, 159, 278) during which it became evident that the CEGB, the NRPB, the Health and Safety Executive (HSE) and the NII all differed – by up to a factor of 10 – in their assessments of the value of a life. In a nutshell, the argument hinged on the appropriate mix of "objective" and "subjective" factors. The NRPB view is that a life is worth £100,000–£200,000, with a mean around £150,000. This is not supported by Department of Environment (D.En.) and other government agencies, plus the HSE, who argue for a figure around £1–2 million with a mean around 1.5 million (see Webb 1984). It is almost certain that the Inspector will have some comments and recommendations on these important discrepancies, because they have an important bearing on the point at which a safety criterion is viewed as "acceptably safe." In addition, the Inspector is bound to look at how far the NII should depart from risk–benefit judgments regarding other (non-nuclear) hazards in determining its "acceptably safe" criterion. The issue of "risk comparability" caused much vexing cross-examination at the Inquiry (see O'Riordan *et al.* 1985).

PRELIMINARY SAFETY REPORT

The preliminary safety report outlines the reference design and provides an indication of how reactor safety parameters are designed to be in accord with the assessment principles. The preliminary safety report also provides a preliminary analysis of critical fault conditions and assessment of performance and standard of proposed protection equipment.

SAFETY CASE AND FAULT STUDIES

The safety case and fault studies supplement the preliminary safety report and form the preliminary input of PRAS and associated safety documentation.

SUPPORTING RESEARCH AND DEVELOPMENT

The supporting research and development usually involve a wide array of accredited consultants, forming an important backup to the preliminary safety report and a preparation for the main safety report, the preconstruction safety report (see below).

QUALITY ASSURANCE AND IN-SERVICE INSPECTORS' PROPOSALS

These proposals cover both the arrangements offered by the licensee and those demanded by the licensee on all contractors and subcontractors.

THE CONTRACT DESIGN

The contract design contains details of all safety-related items to an advanced level of specification.

THE PRECONSTRUCTION SAFETY REPORT

This report is the major safety case, within which all the evidence prepared above is included. This forms the basis of the case which the HSE must approve before a site (safety) license can be granted. That license is an essential prerequisite for the pouring of concrete.

The licensing conditions imposed by the NII are unfettered. They are not subject to appeal by the licensee. On Day 158 (p. 48), the Chief Nuclear Installations Inspector outlined how this power was used:

> We . . . try to approach our task in a professional and reasonable way. While it is true that the law does not permit an appeal, we do not, I hope, arbitrarily impose our requirements on the licensee. Any judgements we arrive at are based on considerable discussion and interchange . . .

The point here is that licensing is a closed and professional process that both the NII and CEGB would prefer to retain. Where there is trouble, it is resolved internally, by persuasion and technical argument, so that "common-sense solutions" are arrived at by reasonable-minded people.

## The NII approach to risk assessment

We turn now to an illustration of the NII's approach to risk assessment, notably with regard to degraded-core analysis. The relevant proof is NII (1983b) together with the cross-examination on Days 182 and 215. What emerges is the determination of the NII to conduct its own assessments of the PRAS, set in a much broader safety context. It carried out its own sensitivity studies of the Westinghouse work and asked for a much more detailed assessment because of the many differences between the containment designs of Zion and Sizewell B. The NII will expect the CEGB/NNC teams to reanalyze all the assumptions before approving the revised PRA.

Perhaps more significant is the NII caution over the importance of the PRA as a tool for safety assessment. The NII's view is that there are so many unquantifiables in the safety analysis that it would be misleading to rely too heavily on PRAS.

So the NII looks at the integration of plant-related failure with external hazard *and* human error, and, on top of that, the quality assurance procedures for equipment manufacture and maintenance during service. The maintenance scrutiny is an important aspect of the "human error" problem because the plant is designed to be "error free" if the equipment is working satisfactorily. So the NII carries out a series of precursor studies to provide a feel for the range of possible human errors, including circumstances in which operator response may be beneficial to controlling a fault condition. So design *characteristics* (including all protection systems) and *whole plant safety assessment*, not PRA or other numerically based analyses, dominate safety regulation. In the NII's words

> . . . it is not until one can perhaps freeze the design rather more than it is at the moment and have a look at the operation rules and instructions in order to see what is going to be required of the operator in terms of accident situations that one can be more confident of the numbers one has put in or perhaps has not put in . . . (Day 215, p. 41).

One must also bear in mind that the international nuclear community is continually striving to improve both PRAS and design features. International exchange of technical innovation is a vital part of both the design and the regulatory processes. The preconstruction safety report part of the licensing process for the Sizewell B plant would take four years to complete (1982–6) and cost more than £20 million. It is revealing that the CEGB has had to commit itself to £20 million of design work and £200 million of associated software contracts at least nine months ahead of the Inspector's report and any government approval, in order to be "on target" for its safety case and its construction program.

What became evident from the Sizewell B cross-examination was that pre-commission licensing procedures will have to be changed. It is impossible at the time of writing, when publication of the Inspector's report is imminent, to predict what these changes will be. The following developments appear very likely:[*]

(a)  a better justification of the consistency and predictability of the criteria underlying the safety assessment principles;

(b)  a clearer definition of what is meant by as low as reasonably practicable, its relation to ALARA and the "best practicable means" concept, and how the "gross disproportion" test should be applied;

(c)  more agreement on the criteria of what constitutes "acceptable safety" for engineered systems and for fault sequences and the relationship between the technical evidence and publicly observable mechanisms to ensure that such criteria can be achieved;

(d)  a re-examination of the membership of the Advisory Committee on the Safety of Nuclear Installations and (possibly) other key safety advisory committees with a view to widening their expertise and ensuring their genuine commitment and independence (NII 1984, pp. 49–52);

(e)    some improvement in the coordination of the NII licensing process, through a policy body within the upper echelons of the NII aimed at monitoring performance, together with a more structured set of meetings (at different levels of technical detail and complexity) between the NII and the licensees (NII 1984);

(f)    an improvement in the relationship between the CEGB Project Management Team and the safety authorizing department with the CEGB – at present that relationship looks rather shaky;

(g)    observations and recommendations as to how the NII and HSE can classify how they go about their business in a manner that the public can understand and follow.

Most of the specific proposals that are likely to arise from these points will not affect the safety case of the Sizewell B plant. But they will have a significant bearing on the safety management of any future nuclear reactor and will also influence the safety analysis of the "back end" (waste disposal and decommissioning) of the fuel cycle. It is at this final fuel cycle stage where the Sizewell B Inquiry and a recently completed review by the House of Commons Environment Committee (1986) will have important implications for future public-inquiry procedures, although government policies towards the back end of the fuel cycle are unlikely to change very much.

Once the site license is approved, construction begins. The British approach to safety management – continuous monitoring, dialogue, and upgrading – continues remorselessly. The licensee has to complete two additional reports:

(a)    *The plant commission report.* This report requires a series of specific tests, the results of which must "as far as possible" be fully documented. They are reviewed by the Plant Completion Committee, chaired by the station superintendent and serviced by the plant safety officer. The committee includes representatives of the NNC and the CEGB but not an NII inspector. (This is to preserve the independence of the NII for the actual management of safety.)

(b)    *The integrated commission report.* This follows the actual start-up of the station. It is prepared by the Station Commission Committee which must ensure that all plant personnel are suitably trained. Again, the NII is not represented. This report is essentially an operation and maintenance manual, providing a detailed case history of each item in the plant.

## Alterations in the UK PWR design

The proposed Sizewell B PWR will be an American-designed plant based upon the Westinghouse–Bechtel Standardized Nuclear Unit Power Plant System (SNUPPS), using the reference design of the Callaway Plant at Fulton, Missouri.

The actual plant will be a British version that will contain a number of safety features that are required to meet CEGB and NII criteria. These major design variations are not the result of any particular generic nuclear risk study but an outcome of the UK plant licensing process. In 1979 the NII (through the HSE) gave its blessing, in principle, to the PWR as a reactor that could be designed and operated safely in its generic risk assessment of the Trojan PWR in Oregon (NII 1979a). This "amber light" (i.e., qualified acceptance) was an important aspect in the safety case of the Sizewell B PWR and formed part of the analysis that led to the following design changes:

(a)  The acceptable dose rate to operators must not exceed ⅟₆₀ of ICRP standards. This rate is achieved by stainless-steel cladding of the fuel rods and the inside of the pressure vessel. The design dose targets for normal plant operation are 240 person-millirem (2.4 mSv) (close to the bottom of the international range for PWRS) for plant operators and 17 millirem (0.17 mSv) per year for the public (cf. 500 millirem (5 mSv) per year for the ICRP reference level).

(b)  In case of an accident, two independent reactor shutdown processes, namely fuel-rod removal and injection of fuel rods *in situ* by boronated water, are available.

(c)  The number of emergency core-cooling pumps is increased from two to four, two of which will be driven by diesel and two by electricity. These pumps will have a larger capacity than their US equivalent, and the injection mechanism will involve a lower head and will be provided by two independent systems (four not two pumps). In addition, two separate pumps for spraying cooling water onto the nuclear innards will be provided.

(d)  The temperature of the emergency core-cooling water will be increased before injection to reduce the problem of cracking. Four accumulators, compared with two in the US design, will discharge coolant.

(e)  A second outer shell, 1 m outside of the first containment shell, also made of prestressed concrete, will act as a final protection to the surrounding public. This is not regarded as an engineering necessity, but, in view of some uncertainty over that judgment and bearing in mind that the margin of error was small, the second shell was regarded as desirable.

(f)  The control room layout will be simplified, with full visual displays of all critical plant functions. This should permit operators to call in on the computer any plant function which might be suspect during ·an emergency. The plant is designed so that not only does it scram (shut down) immediately upon an emergency, *but operators need take no action for 30 minutes*. This provision is supposed to avoid the Three Mile Island problem of hasty and ill-conceived operator response (in the UK regarded as *the* major cause of the Three Mile Island problem) and to give operators every possible opportunity to understand precisely what is happening and why before any action is taken.

(g)   The pressure vessel will be constructed out of steel free of copper and cobalt (to reduce brittleness under prolonged radioactive exposure), the welds will be made of ring-forged steel (to reduce stresses), the vessel will be constantly operated at high temperatures (the so-called "upper-shelf" range of fracture toughness), and it will be tested for cracks by the latest and most sophisticated ultrasonic techniques by three independent teams. This inspection will be conducted according to standards established by the Plate Inspection Steering Committee using the focus beam and multiple (tandem) probe technique which is reputed to be 95 percent reliable (cf. 50 percent reliability for the manually operated pulse echo technique). However, cracks of less than 10 mm or group cracks may still not be detected with sufficient reliability (though improved techniques depending upon the measurement of the time of flight of the pulse are proving highly satisfactory). Hence the need to operate at high temperatures and to design the vessel so that all joins in it are located *above* the high temperature core and to ensure that all valves and pumps associated with the cooling circuits are designed to operate at higher temperatures and pressures (at least 20 percent higher) than normal operation should ever require.

The whole issue of the integrity of the pressure vessel and the possibility of stable (as opposed to inevitably unstable) crack growth under conditions of high temperature and pressure was the subject of exhaustive testimony at the Sizewell B Inquiry (see Days 190, 191, 203, 207). This attention occurred partly because the pressure vessel is the only nonredundant system in the plant, and partly because doubts had been expressed about the quality of management and inspection skills necessary to ensure a "fault free" vessel (see Fordham 1983 for a good, if biased, review).

The debate in the Inquiry followed the pattern already described in this chapter, namely a detailed justification by the CEGB designers and the contractors (Framatome), an independent judgment by various experts either invited to give evidence or whose writings were used in cross-examination, and supplementary evidence of how points of criticism were being addressed. The net result was an unrivaled compendium of information on the public record, in the face of which it is unlikely that the Inspector will do other than note his approval.

## The strengths and weaknesses of the UK approach to nuclear safety

The major strengths of the UK approach to nuclear safety can be summarized as follows:

(a)   A close consultative relationship based on a sense of mutual trust, collective self-regulation, and professional competence exists among licensee, manufacturer, and regulator.

(b) The onus of responsibility for safety rests upon the plant operator who must be totally familiar with plant design and manufacture.

(c) The emphasis upon best practicable means without recourse to externally imposed rigid standards tends to shift the burden of responsibility for safety from the regulator to the operator.

(d) There is sequential and continuous safety monitoring with everlasting review of safety standards and operational/component reliability requirements set according to international and national experience and advances in technology and inspection.

(e) Probabilistic risk analysis is used to detect key accident sequences for total plant operation, whereas specific engineered safety features and component reliability are undertaken both by the operator and by the manufacturer, and are subject to continuous inspection.

(f) Major generic risk studies only provide general guidelines and serve as a basis for more detailed work on risk probability. The major risk studies are treated as part of a general program of international collaboration on nuclear safety.

(g) Sophisticated quality assurance management systems are designed not only to ensure a reliable part or system of parts, but also to ensure that the design and execution of the manufacturing process is properly managed. Quality assurance acts as much as a management device as an engineering function and is a key element in the control over power plant manufacture.

(h) Independent lines of communication exist between the director of health and safety and the managing director/board level of management in all key organizations including the NNC, the CEGB, and, to a lesser extent, the UKAEA. This allows the director of health and safety (or project safety) to communicate directly on any matter of safety without information being channeled through middle management. If may also mean, however, that safety considerations may receive fairly narrow interpretations with relatively little internal review. This could be a dangerous arrangement but there is no evidence either way that this situation is being abused.

The weaknesses of the UK approach are:

(a) Until recently, all relevant safety documents in a formative state of preparation have not been made available for independent review. The publication of the preconstruction safety report and the reference design for the Sizewell B PWR partially overcome this limitation, but even so, arguments rage as to how much information is still to be kept confidential.

(b) Technical judgments do not appear to be transmitted faithfully through the civil service or the senior management hierarchy for a political decision. The British civil service is not always competent to review technical evidence, and too few checks see that the departmental interpretation is sound. There is also a constant danger that once the civil service and senior management are convinced of a course of action, it is almost impossible for a minister to adopt another course.

(c)   Technical assessments by specialist advisory groups are kept in confidence and neither minutes of their discussions nor internal correspondence including commentary from consulted experts are made available – even to senior management, let alone the public.

## Conclusions

British nuclear safety management is a very comprehensive process. The generic safety assessment studies of the mid-1970s, notably that carried out for the *Reactor safety study*, have but a small part to play. Nevertheless, probabilistic risk assessment, an essential feature of these generic risk studies, has advanced to a high degree of development in British safety assessment, mostly following up work done for the *Reactor safety study*. The modern breed of PRAS are truly international creatures.

One important outcome of public concern over nuclear safety has been the massive collaboration of research and technical evidence being generated and upgraded within the international nuclear community. More important is the emphasis upon specialized subgeneric risk studies (i.e., of specific hazards or classes of failure) rather than cruder but more comprehensive "whole-plant" assessments. The modern PRAS apply especially to internally initiated events, but an important development has been the improved analysis of combinations of in-plant failures occurring at the same time as external hazards (earthquake, aircraft crash and missile damage, fire). PRA now has a firm hold on UK safety assessment philosophy and practice, and its increasing sophistication suggests that the original work for the *Reactor safety study* is essentially outdated. A complete overhaul of the *Reactor safety study* is now in draft form (US Nuclear Regulatory Commission 1987), in progress.

Equally pertinent to the UK analyses, however, is that safety assessment involves tiers of independent analysis, carried out by groups of authoritative experts with international reputations. Not only PRAS are subjected to this scrutiny; all aspects of design and component manufacture are also treated in this way.

These improvements in assessment are, however, creating considerable strains on procedure and on communication among responsible individuals and organizations. It is evident that major, but progressive, reforms will have to be made to streamline communication and to simplify procedures. This will serve to assuage public opinion, especially the intervenor groups who seek a stake in both the safety assessment and licensing process. How the possibly paradoxic requirements of greater openness and more general accountability (which means clearer statements of definitions, principles, assumptions, and detailed analyses so that they are intelligible to the interested layperson) can be accommodated with the manifest need to make the whole process more reliable and efficient will prove extremely interesting to observe. This will be the greatest test facing the UK nuclear safety authorities in the years that lie in the aftermath of the report and governmental decision over the Sizewell B Inquiry.

## Acknowledgment

This chapter is based on a report specially commissioned by the Beijer Institute in 1982. The author is grateful to the Institute and the Swedish R&D Commission for funding that study. This revised version arises from research into the Sizewell B Public Inquiry. The author is grateful to the Economic and Social Research Council for funding this research.

## References

Bending, R. & R. Eden 1984. *UK energy*. Cambridge: Cambridge University Press. ·

Chicken, J. C. 1982. *Nuclear power hazard control policy*. Oxford: Pergamon Press.

DOE (Department of Energy) 1981. *Nuclear power*. Cmnd. 8317. London: HMSO.
DOE (Department of Energy) 1982. *Proof of evidence for the Sizewell B Inquiry*. London: HMSO.

Farmer, F. R. (ed.) 1977. *Nuclear reactor safety*. New York: Academic Press.
Farmer, F. R. 1982. *Code validation for loss of coolant accidents*. CEGB/P/34. London: CEGB.
Fordham, R. F. 1983. *The risk of explosion of the Sizewell B reactor pressure vessel*. TCPA/P/9. London: Town and Country Planning Association.

George, B. V. 1982. *The decision of the Sizewell B PWR*. CEGB P/10. London: CEGB.
Gittus, J. H. 1982a. *Degraded core analysis*. CEGB/P/16. London: CEGB.
Gittus, J. H. (Chmn.) 1982b. *Degraded core analysis: report of a UKAEA committee*. ND-R-619(s). London: UKAEA.
Green, A. E. & A. J. Bourne 1977. *Reliability technology*. New York: Wiley.

Harrison, J. R. 1982. *Fault and event tree analyses*. CEGB/P/11. London: CEGB.
Harrison, J. R. 1983. *Health and Safety Department assessment*. CEGB/P/45. London: CEGB.
House of Commons Environment Committee 1986. *Radioactive waste*. HC Paper 151, I–III. London: HMSO.

Ince, M. 1982. *Energy policy: society, technology and science*. London: Junction Books.

Kelly, G. N. et al. 1982. *Degraded core accidents for the Sizewell B PWR: a sensitivity analysis of the radiological consequences*. NRPB-R-412. Chilton, Oxford: NRPB.
Kemp, R. V., T. O'Riordan & H. M. Purdue 1984. Investigations as legitimacy: the maturing of the big public inquiry. *Geoforum* 15 (3), 477–88.

Matthews, R. E. 1980. Using quantitative analyses in Britain. *Nuclear Engineering International* **25**, 45–7.
Matthews, R. E. 1982. *Design safety criteria for nuclear power stations.* HS/R167/81. London: CEGB.

NII (Nuclear Installations Inspectorate) 1979a. *Generic safety issues of pressurised water reactors.* London: NII.
NII (Nuclear Installations Inspectorate) 1979b. *Safety assessment principles for nuclear reactors.* London: NII.
NII (Nuclear Installations Inspectorate) 1983a. *On the work and responsibilities of the NII.* NII/P1/Add. 2. London: NII.
NII (Nuclear Installations Inspectorate) 1983b. *Proof of evidence of the work and responsibilities of the NII.* NII/P/1. London: NII.
NII (Nuclear Installations Inspectorate) 1984. *The relationship between NII's assessment principles and levels of risk.* NII/S/83 (SAF). London: NII.
NNC (National Nuclear Corporation) 1982. *A review of the Westinghouse integrated plant and containment study for the Sizewell B reference design PWR/RX 531.* Booths Hall, Knutsford, Cheshire: NNC.
NRPB (National Radiological Protection Board) 1981. *Cost benefit analysis in optimising the radiological protection of the public: a provisional framework.* NRPB ASP4. Chilton, Oxford: NRPB.

O'Riordan, T. 1984. The Sizewell B inquiry and a national energy strategy. *The Geographical Journal* **150** (2), 171–82.
O'Riordan, T., R. V. Kemp & H. M. Purdue 1985. How the Sizewell B inquiry is grappling with the concept of acceptable risk. *Journal of Environmental Psychology* **5**, 69–85.

Patterson, W. 1985. *Going critical: an unofficial history of British nuclear power.* London: Paladin.

US Nuclear Regulatory Commission 1975. *Reactor Safety Study.* WASH-1400, NUREG-75/014, Washington, DC: The Commission.
US Nuclear Regulatory Commission 1987. *Reactor Risk reference document: draft for comment.* NUREG-1150, vols 1–3. Washington, DC; Office of Nuclear Regulatory Research, The Commission.

Watt Committee 1984. *Nuclear power: a professional assessment.* Report no. 13. London: Watt Committee on Energy.
Webb, G. A. M. 1984. *The requirement to keep radiation exposures as low as reasonably achievable (ALARA).* NRPB/P/3/Add. 1. Chilton, Oxford: NRPB.
Westinghouse Electric Corporation 1982. *Sizewell B probabilistic safety study.* WCAP 9991. Knutsford, Cheshire: Westinghouse.
Williams, R. 1980. *The nuclear power decisions.* London: Croom Helm.

# 8 Large-scale nuclear risk analysis: its impacts and future

ROGER E. KASPERSON, JAMES E. DOOLEY,
BENGT HANSSON, JEANNE X. KASPERSON,
TIMOTHY O'RIORDAN, and HERBERT PASCHEN

The foregoing country chapters make clear that the international emergence of the large-scale nuclear risk study has stimulated both common and divergent responses and societal impacts. The commonalities doubtlessly owe much to the nature of this "technique" as an innovation in technology assessment and safety assurance institutions and practices. Divergences arise from a number of sources – the emphasis placed upon nuclear power as part of a national energy strategy, the scale and political effectiveness of antinuclear sentiment, the degree to which safety regulation is a public or relatively closed exercise, the particular mix of nuclear generation systems adopted, and, above all, the configuration of the particular political culture. It is striking that the large-scale risk study emerged in those countries (the United States, West Germany, and Sweden) where public scrutiny of government is extensive, where the law and the constitutional norms encourage citizen use of the courts to test the legitimacy and administrative fairness of regulatory decisions (not applicable to Sweden), and where local government (state, land, commune) plays an important role in licensing the construction of a plant. It also emerged in countries where public (notably *informed* public) suspicion of nuclear power was growing and where new developments or an accleration in the existing nuclear program were in process or proposed.

The large-scale risk study did not, by contrast, develop in those countries (the United Kingdom and Canada) where a more consensual (internal) form of accountability prevails, where the indigenous nuclear industry was regarded as competent and able to complete its own safety analyses (drawing only when necessary for support from the major US and West German studies), and where public opposition, whether directly through political channels or indirectly through the courts, was subdued, obstructed, or simply not allowed to voice criticisms. Again, Sweden occupies a middle position in this spectrum of adoption.

Risk analysis, used broadly, refers to a broad miscellany of techniques and analytic methods. Probabilistic risk analysis is but one form of the more generic activity, and the plant-specific analysis is a recent form of this type of analysis.

The comprehensive risk study addresses an ambitious scale of broad issues, usually intended to characterize the risks of a technology or program. In this sense, it functions rather like a generic environmental impact statement. These various species of risk analysis coexist in considerable tension with one another.

The purposes of generic risk analysis are several – to increase knowledge about risk, to inform licensing and regulation, to improve plant design, construction, and management, to provide a base for energy policy decisions. The purpose of the *comprehensive risk study*, by contrast, has been largely political – it has been initiated to solve or serve as background for overtly political questions (see Ch. 2) and its emergence, therefore, shows a clear connection to the general political "style" in the countries studied. It is therefore valuable to summarize the effects of the risk studies treated in this volume on society at large and on public attitude toward nuclear power in particular. These impacts will include those that are *inward looking* or on the *private dimension* of the risk studies – effects on the nuclear industry and institutional complex – as well as those that are *outward looking* or on the *public dimension* – effects on national politicians, the scientific community, environmental groups, the media, and the general public.

## Standard-setting, safety improvements, and plant design

Large-scale risk studies have deeply and extensively influenced safety work in nuclear power. Their methods penetrate safety thinking. They have substantially affected, and improved, the design of the plants planned and built during the latter part of the 1970s and the early 1980s. In addition, extensive changes have been retrofitted to plants already in operation. One major example is the filtered vent containment (to control iodine release) to be built at the Swedish Barsebäck plant, which was a direct result of the *Swedish reactor safety study* (Ch. 3). Another is the introduction of automatic control devices for emergency cooling as a result of the *German risk study* (Ch. 4). Still another is the improvement of control room instrumentation called for in the Kemeny report (Ch. 6). More important than even such conspicuous safety improvements is the extensive penetration into safety philosophy and approach of the methodology of the probabilistic risk analysis (PRA). Thus, safety questions have for the first time come to be regarded as an integral part of nuclear engineering, with integrated assessment of system design, training of operators, and formulation of administrative rules and guidance.

The significance of risk studies for nuclear plant design is, as pointed out in Chapter 4, quite apparent in the Federal Republic of Germany. Given the finding in the *German risk study* of the important contribution of operator error to serious accidents, improvements in plants have centered upon the installation of automatic control devices for cooling down the plant at Biblis B. Similarly, results pointing to stuck-open pressurizer relief valves have led to design and monitoring improvements designed to reduce significantly the probability of this accident sequence (Ch. 4).

Common lessons from risk studies are apparent in all five countries. Safety managers are giving renewed attention to quality control, particularly with respect to pressure vessels, pipes, valves, pumps, and motors. The importance of designing control rooms and operator panels so as to aid operator understanding of what is going on inside the reactor, thereby reducing the risk of operator error and increasing the probability that the operator will be able to handle situations which have not been explicitly covered or foreseen in the instruction, is widely recognized. Whereas the need for such measures was, of course, quite obvious after the Three Mile Island accident, a subcommittee to the Swedish Energy Commission (EK-A 1978) and the Lewis Commission (US Risk Assessment Review Group 1978) in the United States had earlier emphasized these issues.

A recent review of plant safety enhancements attributable to plant-specific probabilistic risk analysis found no shortage of examples, including

(a) six design changes and one procedural change associated with the Big Rock Point risk study;
(b) modification of the design of viewing windows on containment hatches so that their ultimate strength matched those of other structures in the containment;
(c) the preferability of a diesel-driven containment spray pump modified to be independent of AC power over other proposed design changes at the Zion plant;
(d) modifications to increase the gap between the control room building and an adjoining structure and the installation of rubber bumpers to reduce the potential for loss of the control room as the result of an earthquake at Indian Point 2;
(e) procedural changes to reduce the probability of a core melt at Arkansas Nuclear 1. (Joksimovich 1984, pp. 263–4)

Perhaps most significantly, the risk studies have deeply influenced general attitudes toward safety questions. First, is the recognition, particularly in the aftermath of the 1986 disaster at Chernobyl, that the unthinkable can happen, namely that serious accidents involving releases are possible (albeit at very low probabilities). This is a healthy realization, for it directs energy to the constant need to assess and reduce further highly unlikely combinations of events and accident sequences. Second, it is now understood that the combination of several commonplace failures can be as, or even more, important than the risk of large pipe breaks or leaks. Third, whereas safety philosophy previously focused almost exclusively on the prevention of major accidents, more attention now goes to mitigating the consequences. Part of this has produced new efforts on emergency preparedness and evacuation. These efforts, in turn, have led to new arguments about public communication and evacuation procedures, to the question of siting in proximity to population centers, to consideration of secondary containment, and to the merits and demerits of providing potassium iodine tablets. All of these issues will receive heightened attention over the next several years as a result of the Chernobyl accident.

Within these commonalities lie divergences. Many industrial practitioners continue to believe that the primary stimulus for specific safety improvements comes from feedback from operational experience. Those close to policy tend to be advocates of the large-scale risk studies. Those in hands-on positions, however, like to stress the importance of assiduous work with small improvements, based on collected operational experience, and often view the comprehensive study recommendations as theoretical or somewhat out-of-touch with reality. The tension between these different viewpoints, also apparent among the regulators, appears to decrease as risk studies become more detailed and more site-specific, although even there a tension remains between the contributions of plant level versus subplant level assessments, between the engineering and the conceptual approach, and between the divergent viewpoints of licensees and regulators.

## Nuclear institutions

The most apparent outward indication of new safety emphasis in nuclear power in the five countries was the considerable internal reorganization of nuclear institutions that occurred over the past eight or so years.

In Sweden, for example, the State Radiation Protection Institute and the State Nuclear Power Inspectorate received increased funds, the State Power Board set up a permanent reactor safety section, and two new bodies – the Council for Nuclear Safety (established by industry) and the Board for the Handling of Spent Nuclear Fuels (a state organization) – were created.

In the United States, despite recommendations by the Kemeny Commission for a radical restructuring of the Nuclear Regulatory Commission (NRC) and a strengthening of the Advisory Committee on Reactor Safeguards, no major organizational changes took place in the regulatory bodies or other federal departments and agencies. The one new public institution – the Nuclear Safety Oversight Committee – lived a short life before its termination by the Reagan Administration. The NRC, to be sure, established a new Office for Analysis and Evaluation of Operational Data, aimed at learning from past reactor incidents and malfunctions. In addition, its Office of Inspection and Enforcement was reorganized and strengthened (to a staff of 1,000), with resident inspectors established at each plant site (Phung 1984, p. 10).

By contrast, the private sphere reacted much more swiftly and extensively to the Three Mile Island accident. Within a month, the US nuclear industry had established the Nuclear Safety Analysis Center to conduct technical studies of the accident, to interpret the lessons to be learned, to develop strategies to prevent future accidents of that kind, and to consider generic safety issues. The industry also established an Institute of Nuclear Power Operations (INPO) to look initially at operator training and capabilities on a plant-by-plant basis. The emergence of INPO as a major new force in American nuclear institutional structure may well alter the traditional regulator–regulatee relationship, as indicated by the role that highly critical INPO reviews placed in the closing of nuclear plants in the Tennessee Valley Authority System.

The UK, Canada, and West Germany show a slightly different picture. In the United Kingdom, the House of Commons Select Committee on Energy made a number of recommendations dealing with both the supervision of safety and the institutional organization of safety. The Committee sought a technically strengthened Nuclear Installations Inspectorate, a safety monitoring group in the Department of Energy, and a more effective organization of safety responsibility between the National Nuclear Corporation (NCC) and the Central Electricity Generating Board (CEGB), with the latter becoming less involved in the specifics of plant design. But the government reply indicated that it was broadly satisfied with existing arrangements, though it did add a specialist technical expert on nuclear matters to the staff of the Government Chief Scientist in the Department of Energy.

Subsequently, however, the government agreed to a reorganization of the project-management arrangement for the design and contraction of pressurized-water reactors (PWRS). Enter the Project Management Board, a separate organization within the CEGB but incorporating the NCC. In addition, Westinghouse and the NCC each own half of a PWR Plant Project, responsible for designing and constructing the nuclear island of all future PWRS in the United Kingdom. The project will coordinate export as well as domestic contracts. These changes strengthen the CEGB's hold on the design and construction of nuclear plants and lock in an international component for the British PWR.

In Canada, the Porter Commission in Ontario did suggest a number of organizational changes, but since the Commission was provincially created and advisory, its policy-related recommendations produced little institutional response at the federal level or by the nuclear industry generally (although the safety division at Ontario Hydro was upgraded). This lack of response probably reflects the secure position of nuclear authority as well as the distribution of political power in Canada. In the Federal Republic of Germany, although substantial societal conflict over nuclear power continues, the *German risk study* elicited little executive or parliamentary response and no major institutional initiatives.

To the extent that a generalization is possible, it is that industry has probably undergone the greatest institutional change. Beyond that, it is apparent that a constellation of political forces is required to overcome inertia, built-in basic institutional structures of management, and existing allocations of political stakes. The Three Mile Island accident in the United States and the Swedish referendum were key events, not replicated in the other three countries, that permitted the development of a momentum for change. It is too early to assess the impacts of a major event outside these countries – the Chernobyl accident – upon the array of contending forces within the five countries studied in this volume.

## Impacts on the scientific community

Since only the Swedish chapter addresses in depth the response of the scientific community to the major nuclear risk studies, the evidence on this subject draws on that case, with more limited indications and perspectives from the other four countries. Generally, the studies have not, except perhaps for the two KBS studies, contributed substantially to new scientific knowledge. In the scientific flow of information, the scientists have generally been the donors, not the recipients.

Nevertheless, the risk studies have wrought a rather profound effect on the engineering sciences. This impact manifests itself mainly through more frequent contacts, both among different research areas and in relation to other groups in society, through new ways of posing problems in the individual sciences, through the emergence of new areas of research (often on the border of two old ones). Meanwhile, there has also been a stir in the scientific community: people have been forced to reconsider their work and positions, to become more versatile and more open in their ways of thinking. These effects are most pronounced for those who have taken part in the *process* of the risk study, rather than from lessons imparted by the final product.

A notable difference between Sweden and the other countries is that a sizeable percentage of all Swedish scientists in nuclear-related disciplines has participated more or less actively in a major nuclear risk study. Considering the comparatively large number of Swedish risk studies and the small size of the Swedish scientific community, practically all scientific voices have had a chance to be heard. By and large, the studies have tapped what Swedish science has to offer on the applied side. The rub is that many scientists have been so busy that fundamental research in some areas may have suffered. In the other countries, where the scientific communities are so large that the risk studies have not to any discernible degree increased competition for the services of qualified scientists, these effects are certainly less manifest. In such settings it should be easier to find scientists for peer review who have not previously been involved in that particular study.

To be sure, such scientists are in scarce supply in Sweden. Given the vigor and high quality of Swedish science, this hegemonistic situation – which also exists in the United Kingdom – carries an alert for small countries moving to large-scale risk analysis in safety work and national policy making. Interestingly, the Swedish scientific community harbors a certain disquiet over the quality of the risk studies. The unease turns on suspicion that the competence of the scientists could have been better used, both in the assessment itself and in the dissemination of risk information to politicians and the public. At the same time, scientists are uncertain, often perplexed, about how to remedy the situation. Across countries, scientists are disenchanted over the performance of the media and the apparent inability of the public to deal with risks rationally (i.e., as scientists do!). It may well be that PRAs and major risk studies serve to increase the scope of public dissatisfaction and lack of understanding.

## Impacts on politicians and policy makers

The success of risk studies in the public arena is less apparent – and certainly much more uneven – than that within the internal nuclear complex. Yet, it is probably the politicians who have been most impressed and reassured by the risk studies. This is not to say that antinuclear politicians do not abound, only that risk studies appear to have done more to assuage or reassure than to spark official opposition. Basically, and not surprisingly, the impressive amount of work and technical resources put into the risk studies has, on balance, reached conclusions generally favorable for nuclear power. Comparable risk studies of other industries also serve the nuclear option. And nuclear fares extremely well in comparative, albeit controversial, risk analyses of competing energy technologies (see, for example, Inhaber 1982). If politicians have not been convinced that nuclear power is desirable, at least they have not concluded that reactor safety is an intractable problem.

The United States appears to be an exception to this generalization. There the risk study results appear to have disturbed politicians rather than reassure them. This is not to suggest that US politicians have a more critical attitude toward nuclear power than politicians in other countries; rather it may be that the original vision in the United States involved greater illusion, or at least commitment, than in other countries. The dismantling of the American nuclear dream owes more to the overextension of the technology, the inaccuracy of utility economic projections, and the presence of a committed and vigilant opposition than to the results of nuclear risk studies.

Indeed, it seems doubtful that the substantive work and findings of the large-scale risk studies, despite their imposing bulk and prestige, have been major political determinants anywhere. In the Federal Republic of Germany, Parliament largely ignored the *German risk study*. In Canada, the Porter Commission report met a similar fate. In the United States, political debates over the *Reactor safety study*, the Lewis report, and the Kemeny Commission report were often acrimonious and generally inconclusive. In all three countries, the summaries of studies largely dominated the general picture of their results among influential politicians.

Not so in Sweden, the smallest country, where neither the studies *nor* their written summaries were influential among national politicians. Rather, the important sources of information were verbal contacts with those who performed the studies. Many of the committees that conducted the studies in Sweden were of a parliamentary character, and those that were not had close links with leading parliamentarians. Since all the major parties have assigned the task of looking after energy questions to a trusted member of the inner circles (who then sits on the parliamentary committees and serves as the intermediary between the committees and his fellow party members), the bulk of politicians' risk information comes through a single channel. Since the "party specialist" filters out much of the information, most members of a political party tend to regard the risk studies in a uniform way, and a wealth of information in the study reports remains untapped and of little political consequence.

A party's political stance on overall energy policy is likely to color political response to particular risk studies. In the United Kingdom, for example, only the ruling Conservative administration is strongly pronuclear. Other parties are adopting a variety of pro-coal and pro-conservation positions and placing greater emphasis on renewable energy sources and cogeneration schemes, thereby distancing themselves from a nuclear commitment. In this post-Chernobyl era, nuclear power generation is a major electoral issue in the UK. This political jockeying is far more influential in political contexts than the results of particular studies or public inquiries.

## Impacts on the nuclear debate

The debate in the scientific community and within society as a whole is the implicit but pervasive issue that underlies the major nuclear risk studies. Whereas risk analysis addresses many goals, it is doubtful that the large-scale, comprehensive risk study would have arisen in the absence of the active controversy during the 1970s over nuclear power. This is perhaps most striking in the case of the US *Reactor safety study* which sought to end once and for all the debate over reactor risks. The Swedish risk studies typically aimed to shape a broader societal consensus for energy choices. The Ontario Royal Commission on Electric Power Planning came to view its role as a vehicle for public scrutiny and education.

The motivation for the risk study, in this context, is to clarify the risks, to narrow the debate to the axes of "real" disagreement, to develop, in the parlance of the expert, a more "rational" approach to risk by policy makers and publics. The results in the five countries show conclusively that the risk studies have enlarged, not narrowed, the debate. Instead of shaping an accepted discourse for the discussion of risk, they have intensified the conflict over the proper range of consequences to be treated in the assessment and whose values should prevail in their weighting. Instead of greater acceptance of the bases upon which numerical calculations rest, they have heightened suspicions over the motivations for the studies and those who conduct them.

This conflict is directly apparent in the concept of risk itself, as discussed in the Canadian context (Ch. 5). For the practitioner and the professional risk assessor in the nuclear arena, risk is typically the estimated probability of expected consequences, nearly always restricted to radiation-induced fatalities and other health effects. The means for calculating the risks are formal analytic procedures relating to events and faults that get propagated into accidents. For many outside this professional community, risk means something quite different: specifically, it refers to a broad array of technology impacts upon society as well as health, including qualitative attributes of the risks involved, and the decision processes which produced the risk in the first place. The narrower treatment of risk excludes many of the broader concerns that are crucial for the nonprofessionals. This divergence has been manifest in risk perception research, which has emphasized the differences between expert and lay assessments of risk (Slovic *et al.* 1985). So the first-order political conflict over risk assessment, characteristically fought out in debates over the study methods and results, concerns the conception of risk that should guide public policy and management efforts.

The five country chapters also demonstrate that the comprehensive risk study typically has something for everyone. Differing groups and perspectives invariably find evidence to support their claims, as was evident in the different messages drawn in the adversarial press to the Kemeny report (Ch. 6) or the contrasting interpretation of the major Swedish risk studies in the Swedish mass media (Ch. 3). Whereas individual risk areas rarely are "settled" or dropped off the public agenda by the risk study, new risk issues often appear. Thus the characteristic net effect is to broaden the arena of debate.

A second way by which risk studies spawn new issues or intensify the debate over existing questions is that they often lay bare problems in risk management which previously have been contained within the authority structure and hidden from the public view. This is particularly the case in political cultures where the public decision process is opaque. The Sizewell Inquiry has permitted a public view of the nuclear risk assessment and management process which is quite remarkable in the United Kingdom. Similarly, the Ontario Royal Commission on Electric Power Planning provided extensive information on the workings of the major governmental institutions and Ontario Hydro. But even in more open governmental systems, the revelations of management deficiencies and problems can add to the debate and revitalize dormant issues (as happened with the Kemeny report).

## Responses of the media and the general public

The response of the mass media shows considerable variation in the five countries studied. On the whole, the press appears to have treated the risk studies with reasonable accuracy. Whereas factual mistakes were not unusual (and a source of much concern to scientists), almost all were obvious misunderstandings by the journalist of complex technical matters and did not distort the overall picture. The publication of the risk studies, as opposed to risk events, were treated as ordinary news items. In Sweden, detailed studies of media response indicate that most newspapers relied on the material delivered by the national news agency, which in turn relied heavily upon summaries by the risk study committees themselves. West German newspapers relied heavily upon the press conference materials summarizing the *German risk study* and paid little attention to the report itself. In Sweden, when the newspapers used their own correspondents, their reports were nonetheless remarkably similar. The striking uniformity of news reporting in the Swedish press finds parallels in the us and West German experiences.

Despite the general factual accuracy of information, the press was not always impartial. Rather, there was often selective reference to risk reports or selective choice of risk topics to be addressed. A typical case was *Dagens Nyheter*, a major Swedish morning newspaper with an editorial policy pronouncedly antinuclear, which referred to a number of otherwise largely ignored sources, most of which were critical of nuclear power.

Several other characteristics of press coverage of the reports are notable. As was quite evident with the Kemeny report, news coverage often tended to dwell on the process that created the report, on prereport "leaks" of upcoming issues and recommendations, and on the likely political ramifications of the results. Such aspects received more attention than the substantive risk issues in the studies. Once the report appeared, there was typically little sustained attention to the results. Also, experience from Sweden, West Germany, and the United States points to the tendency to stress certain risk issues in the reports and to ignore others, even though the neglected items often appear no less, or even more, important. In the United Kingdom, a generally antinuclear and anti-industry bias in journalists has resulted in a corresponding selection bias in most media coverage.

Television shows several notable differences from the press. Typically, because of characteristics of the medium perhaps, the coverage was considerably more narrow and superficial. In Sweden, this included an emphasis on spectacular scenarios and very few references to the actual risk studies. In West Germany, television news reporting appeared to be biased against nuclear power, whereas British television viewers received most of their information from impartial documentaries rather than from news reporting.

It may be concluded, then, that media coverage was generally balanced but uneven, factually accurate, but in many cases unsophisticated and superficial in treatment. Unfortunately, the media tended to regard the risk reports as isolated news items, with little context as to how society grapples over time with the issues of nuclear safety, and with a lack of sustained follow-through on the eventual results wrought by the study findings.

As to the impact of risk studies on the general public, the general conclusion shows little evidence of any significant direct effect, either on levels of knowledge or attitudes. This is not surprising insofar as reports in the media only touch upon the detailed findings of the studies, and attitudes to nuclear power involve basic value, as well as factual, considerations. Also, since various viewpoints readily draw supporting messages from the studies, the member of the general public probably does not receive sharply delineated messages. In short, the risk study has done little to draw the public into the fray. If there are effects, they are probably primarily indirect and cumulative in nature. As suggested in the chapter on West Germany, the risk study indisputedly becomes a datum in the continuing public discussion, which has to be considered in all future deliberations of nuclear power. To the extent that the risk studies over time have a cumulative impact on the ability of the public to deal with probability and uncertainty, to place risks in broader context, or to engage in comparisons among diverse risks, then a certain shift or evolution in the center of gravity of public response may occur.

## Current developments and future prospects

Risk or reliability analysis is still very much in the heyday of its development, most notably in nuclear power risk management but present in other areas (e.g., chemical plants, oil drilling rigs, aircraft safety) as well. Considering that risk analysis techniques were only modestly employed in the 1970s following the pioneering work of Farmer in the United Kingdom, the Swedish risk assessments, and the us *Reactor safety study*, the growth since the Three Mile Island accident in 1979 has been quite remarkable. In the United States alone, where the embrace of these techniques has been greatest, some 13 "full-scope" (level 3)[1] probabilistic risk assessments (Table 8.1) and at least 9 level 1 or level 2 assessments had been completed by 1984.

The large-scale (i.e., level 3) studies have been sponsored by the utilities of the Electric Power Research Institute (EPRI), a utility research organization. The motivations for the studies have been diverse: several were initiated in response to regulatory requests (e.g., concern over proximity to metropolitan areas), one (Big Rock Point) was viewed as a means of evaluating the cost-effectiveness of risk reduction measures proposed by the us Nuclear Regulatory Commission, and most of the remaining were part of long-range utility risk management programs (us Nuclear Regulatory Commission 1984, pp. 58–9). In addition to these assessments, four other major comprehensive nuclear risk studies – the *German risk study* (Ch. 4), the us Department of Energy risk assessment for a high-temperature gas-cooled reactor, an assessment of the Clinch River Breeder Reactor in the us, and the Sizewell B study (Ch. 7) – have been completed. Other major studies are now under way, including the broad-scale assessment of Ontario Hydro in Canada (Ch. 1), as well as a host of smaller nuclear risk assessments in Italy, Japan, Spain, Switzerland, and Taiwan and the continuing subgeneric studies that characterize the risk analysis effort in the United Kingdom.

Interestingly, this growth has emphasized research in the private dimension of risk. With the exception of the Sizewell B Inquiry, the political motivations for the studies have receded into the background. The Sizewell B Inquiry was very unusual in that the Inspector took it upon himself to assess safety management by interpreting the terms of reference very broadly and by following up on specific issues raised in the proof-of-evidence of the CEGB.

The contributions of the studies treated in this volume have been recounted in the individual country chapters and summarized above. When placed in the context of the overall effort in probabilistic risk analysis over the past five years, it is evident that the many assessments have enhanced our understanding of nuclear power plant risks and are beginning to contribute to the regulatory process. Notable contributions include:

**Table 8.1** Completed full-scope (level 3) US probabilistic risk analyses (as of 1984).

| Plant | Issuance | Operating license | Rating (MWe) | NSSS/AE* | Containment | Sponsor | Report |
|---|---|---|---|---|---|---|---|
| Surry 1 | 1975 | 1972 | 788 | W/S&W | dry cylinder | NRC | NUREG-75/014 (WASH-1400) |
| Peach Bottom 2 | 1975 | 1973 | 1,065 | GE/Bechtel | mark I | NRC | NUREG-75/014 (WASH-1400) |
| Big Rock Point | 1981 | 1962 | 71 | GE/Bechtel | dry sphere | utility | USNRC docket 50-155 |
| Zion 1 & 2 | 1981 | 1973 | 1,040 | W/S&L | dry cylinder | utility | USNRC dockets 50-295 and 50-304 |
| Indian Point 2 & 3 | 1982 | 1973 | 873 | W/UE&C | dry cylinder | utility | USNRC dockets 50-247 and 50-286 |
| Yankee Rowe | 1982 | 1960 | 175 | W/S&W | dry sphere | utility | USNRC docket 50-29 |
| Limerick 1 & 2 | 1983 | — | 1,055 | GE/Bechtel | mark II | utility | USNRC dockets 50-352 and 50-353 |
| Shoreham | 1983 | — | 819 | GE/S&W | mark II | utility | USNRC docket 50-322 |
| Millstone 3 | 1983 | 1986 | 1,150 | W/S&W | dry cylinder | utility | controlled document |
| Susquehanna 1† | 1983 | 1982 | 1,050 | GE/Bechtel | mark II | utility | draft |
| Oconee 3† | 1983 | 1974 | 860 | B&W/Duke | dry cylinder | EPRI/NSAC | draft |
| Seabrook | 1984 | — | 1,150 | W/UE&C | dry cylinder | utility | draft |

\* NSSS – nuclear steam system supplier; AE – architect–engineer.
† Completed but not yet publicly available.
*Source:* US Nuclear Regulatory Commission (1984), p. 58.

**Table 8.2** P.R.A. study results: estimated core-melt frequences (per reactor year)*.

| Plant | Rating (MWe) | Type NSS supplier | Core-melt probability, $(yr)^{-1}$ |
|---|---|---|---|
| Arkansas 1 | 836 | PWR, B&W | $5 \times 10^{-5}$ |
| Biblis B | 1,240 | PWR, KWU | $4 \times 10^{-5\dagger}$ |
| Big Rock Point | 71 | BWR, GE | $1 \times 10^{-3}$ |
| Browns Ferry 1 | 1,065 | BWR, GE | $2 \times 10^{-4}$ |
| Calvert Cliffs 1 | 845 | PWR, CE | $2 \times 10^{-3}$ |
| Crystal River 3 | 797 | PWR, B&W | $4 \times 10^{-4}$ |
| Grand Gulf 1 | 1,250 | BWR, GE | $2.9 \times 10^{-5}$ |
| Indian Point 2 | 873 | PWR, W | $4 \times 10^{-4\dagger}$ |
| Indian Point 3 | 965 | PWR, W | $9 \times 10^{-5\dagger}$ |
| Limerick | 1,055 | BWR, GE | $3 \times 10^{-5\dagger}$ |
| Millstone 1 | 652 | BWR, GE | $3 \times 10^{-4}$ |
| Millstone 3 | 1,150 | PWR, W | $1 \times 10^{-4}$ |
| Oconee 3 | 860 | PWR, B&W | $8 \times 10^{-5}$ |
| Peach Bottom 2 | 1,065 | BWR, GE | $8.2 \times 10^{-6}$ |
| Ringhals 2 | 800 | PWR, W | $4 \times 10^{-6}$ |
| Seabrook | 1,150 | PWR, W | $2 \times 10^{-4}$ |
| Sequoyah 1 | 1,148 | PWR, W | $1.0 \times 10^{-4}$ |
| Shoreham | 819 | BWR, GE | $4 \times 10^{-5}$ |
| Sizewell B | 1,200 | PWR, W | $1 \times 10^{-6}$ |
| Surry 1 | 788 | PWR, W | $2.6 \times 10^{-5}$ |
| Yankee Rowe | 175 | PWR, W | $2 \times 10^{-6}$ |
| Zion | 1,040 | PWR, W | $1.5 \times 10^{-4}$ |

* Includes external event contribution where appropriate. Comparisons of values listed should be made with extreme caution. Different models, assumptions and degrees of sophistication were employed.
† Median values; otherwise point estimates are listed.
*Source*: US Nuclear Regulatory Commission (1985, 1987).

(a) the estimated frequency of core melts is generally higher and also covers a broader range of core-damage/frequency point estimates (about $10^{-6}$ to $10^{-3}$ per year) than had been previously believed possible (Table 8.2). The small fraction of accidents that might result in offsite consequences generally involves either an early failure of containment or a containment by-pass;

(b) estimated risks of early fatalities and injuries are highly sensitive to source-term magnitudes and the timing of releases and emergency responses;

(c) accidents beyond the design base (including those initiated by earthquakes) are the principal contributors to public risk;

(d) human interactions are extremely important contributors to the safety and reliability of plants;

(e) small loss-of-coolant accidents and transients are dominant contributors to core-melt frequency;

(f) the loss of offsite power is a key risk event;

(g) certain common-mode failures – such as earthquakes, internal fires, and floods – appear to play an important role in risk, but may be highly plant-specific. (US Nuclear Regulatory Commission 1984, pp. 63–5, Garrick 1984, Budnitz 1984)

Beyond these specific findings, it has become clear that probabilistic risk analysis has a number of values and uses in nuclear risk management. First, plant risk assessments can become "living" mathematical representations of the system as it evolves over time, with constant updating from operating experience and integration of modifications. Such a "living" system has potential for overcoming the traditional split between safety assurance and the operations/reliability segments in the organizational structures of utilities and reactor vendors. Second, because of its integrated nature, probabilistic risk analysis can be very helpful in assigning priorities to either generic or plant-level safety issues or in allocating resources among various safety or regulatory needs. Much the same use is possible in allocating resources for inspection and enforcement. Third, risk assessment may be used to guide decision making – where should regulations or standards be strengthened or relaxed, where is there confirmation for existing approaches, where are there gaps in the regulatory regime? Finally, the assessments at the plant level can be very helpful in identifying design or operational deficiencies.

Despite these virtues and despite the continuing evolution of risk assessment methodology, significant uncertainties and limitations remain. It is difficult to know whether a given risk assessment underestimates or overestimates risk, so that such studies need to be used with great caution and a healthy dose of skepticism. The US General Accounting Office, in a recent review of probabilistic risk assessment, concluded that these methods entail four sources of high uncertainty:

(a) *Completeness of analysis.* It is patently impossible to ensure the identification of all events and combinations of events that could initiate or direct the course of an accident. Logic diagrams or initiating-event/mitigating systems analysis may not succeed in identifying events that are outside of historical operating experience.

(b) *Sufficiency and reliability of data.* Lack of historical experience or lack of understanding usually renders scarce the data requisite to quantify the systems analysis. In the absence of historical data, subjective judgment enters into the selection of appropriate data, thereby introducing additional uncertainty.

(c) *Assumptions made by study analysts.* Inevitably the analyst must make assumptions for purposes of simplification or to fill gaps in data or understanding. One basic assumption attendant on nearly all assessments is that the nuclear plant was actually built according to the design specifications. Invalid assumptions increase uncertainties.

(d) *Relationship of computer models to reality.* Risk assessment invariably relies upon abstract models to portray plant systems, accident phenomena within the containment building, human interactions, and accident consequences. Such models cannot be subject to strict validation in real-life experience. Moreover, the extent of conservatism – which impinges on both design and theory – introduced by the analyst often defies quantification (US General Accounting Office 1985, pp. 16–17).

Research programs are under way in various countries to reduce the uncertainties in these (and other) areas. But the uncertainties cannot be completely eliminated; indeed they may remain large, because they are intrinsic to the methods themselves and to inherent limits on the data that can be made available.

Another broad limitation is that such risk studies cannot answer some of the questions of greatest concern to the policy makers and the public. Risk assessment, viewed narrowly, has little to say about the level of risk that should prevail, the so-called "acceptable risk" problem. Thus although the mobilization of various results and a comparative perspective may enhance that effort, the assessments themselves provide no intrinsic guidance. Also the assessments cannot provide assurance that safety goals are met. In the face of some temptation to judge the overall safety achieved by the results of a plant-specific risk assessment, then, it is important to remember that significant model components and the overall system model are unvalidated and that such use is sure to encourage mischief in the assessment process.

The rapid development of risk analysis over the past five years has not yet stimulated substantial discussion of the social impacts of this new technique upon the institutions and people who use it or upon the society in which it is embedded. Yet, as illustrated by the cases of program planning budget review and systems analysis during the 1960s, such methodologies can disburse far-reaching impacts. Environmental impact statements also have certainly altered the planning and decision processes of federal (and often state) agencies, as well as the roles of citizen groups and members of the public. Probabilistic risk analysis is considerably more complex and resource-demanding than other methodologies which have been introduced. Somehow (no easy feat!), it must be incorporated into the institutions responsible for managing nuclear safety. The institutional and social impacts associated with this integration need to be anticipated and, where adverse, perhaps ameliorated. Numerous significant social impacts seem likely.

Whereas risk analysis carries the potential for clarifying major tradeoffs and safety decisions as well as for placing a particular plant or risk issue in broader context, few groups or individuals outside the technical community now boast or are likely in the near future to possess the requisite expertise and resources to penetrate a large-scale nuclear risk assessment. Widespread use of such assessments in licensing and regulation could have the net effect of greatly narrowing the range of outside scrutiny, review, and public participation in a technology that has drawn fire for the centralization of its decision making and the limited opportunities for citizen participation in licensing, rulemaking, and management.

The general problem could find specific representation in several problems:

(a)  In societies with more open and participatory political cultures, large-scale probabilistic risk analyses are likely to produce increased difficulty for potential intervenors to participate in formal licensing and regulatory procedures. In addition to existing obstacles associated with the need for high technical expertise and sizeable financial resources, additional capability is required to penetrate and review the methodology, analysis, and documentation of a massive nuclear risk assessment. Such independent review is difficult even for governmental regulators who have access to extensive expertise and substantial resources. It is noteworthy, for example, that the US Nuclear Regulatory Commission had by January 1984 reviewed four major full-scope risk assessments at a per study cost of $200,000–$600,000 and a time commitment of 9–18 months (US General Accounting Office 1985, p. 74). Such review demands may exceed the resources available to regulators in small countries and are certainly beyond the capability of nearly all potential critics outside the industry and its regulators.

(b)   Members of the general public should be less directly affected, since they usually already lack the capability to understand highly technical issues. But the licensing of nuclear facilities and the management of nuclear safety will likely become even more inscrutable.

(c)   Communication of risk and safety issues to public officials, the mass media, and members of the public, already difficult, will face substantially enlarged burdens of explaining probabilistic risk analysis, its contributions to a technical understanding of risk, and why its results should provide added assurance and public confidence.

(d)   As indicated most dramatically by experience in Sweden, large-scale risk assessments consume much of the existing expertise in their creation. This leaves few highly qualified technical experts available for peer review and continuing criticism. Such hegemony could, particularly in smaller countries, contribute to a further closure of nuclear power management to diverse viewpoints and social criticism.

(e)   The long-standing debate between the hands-on school that endorses quality design and process engineering and the proponents of formal analysis (i.e., the probabilistic risk assessors) is unlikely to abate.

Paradoxically, given the means to overcome these problems, risk analyses could serve to demystify and open up the risk management process, particularly as assumptions and calculations necessarily become very precise, the importance of particular failures and accident sequences clearer, and the approaches and expertise of management more transparent. This was very apparent in the experience in Canada and the UK. What is required is that the interested party acquire enough capability, knowledge, and experience to overcome the entry prices or hurdles of involvement.

Beyond these impacts, a number of other potential broad societal and institutional implications merit continuing attention. An increase in the diffusion and use of probabilistic risk assessment carries with it the potential for undue overconfidence in the results of the particular assessment and an erosion in sensitivity to the inherent limitations of the models and techniques. As risk assessment becomes routine, so there may be a loss in quality as implementation becomes standardized and passes to those who are users rather than architects of the methodology. Also lurking is a danger that assessment results may come to exert undue influence in licensing and regulation, leading to inadequate emphasis upon more traditional (and potentially broader) means of safety assurance. This is precisely the issue that produced caution in the United Kingdom concerning the uses of probabilistic risk assessment.

The rate of transfer of these techniques to management systems may also be a concern, for incorporation in institutional processes may outstrip the relatively small accumulation of experience. Then the dominance of a small number of firms or groups conducting such assessments in any country may unduly concentrate too much authority, whether in public or private hands. Finally, in the utilities and regulatory agencies responsible for nuclear power, organizational change must be anticipated. Influence and authority are likely to pass to a small group of analysts who have had limited experience with traditional management approaches and who lack hands-on experience with the technology.

It is apparent, then, that large-scale risk analysis has made and is evolving important contributions to the understanding of nuclear risks and means for their minimization. The contributions have occurred, and will likely continue to occur, in the private dimension of nuclear power – with the utilities and with regulators charged by society with primary management responsibilities. As vehicles for formulating public policy, for resolving social conflict, and for educating the public, their role appears sharply limited. Increased use of these techniques appears to bear strong ties to political culture, so that their role in broad societal management of technology will vary from country to country. Yet in all cases it is evident that large-scale risk studies can involve broad societal impacts. Continuing vigilance is needed to ensure that such studies realize, rather than drive, societal values for responding to risk.

## Note

1   The US Nuclear Regulatory Commission distinguishes among the studies according to scope: level 1 includes systems analyses for scenarios leading to core-melt frequency; level 2 also includes containment analyses leading to assessment of releases; level 3 provides a full assessment of public risks by including offsite consequence analysis (US Nuclear Regulatory Commission 1984, p. 13)

## References

Budnitz, R. 1984. External initiators in probabilistic reactor accident analysis: earthquakes, fires, floods, winds. *Risk Analysis* **4**, 313–22.

EK-A (Energikommissionens Expertgrupp fur Säkerhat och Miljö) 1978. *Miljvesfek-*

*ter och risker vid utnyttjandet av energi* (Environmental effects and hazards of energy exploitation). Stockholm: Allmänna Fötlagg.

Garrick, B. J. 1984. Recent case studies and advancements in probabilistic risk assessment. *Risk Analysis* **4**, 267–79.

Inhaber, H. 1982. *Energy risk assessment*. New York: Gordon & Breach.

Joksimovich, V. 1984. A review of plant specific PRAS. *Risk Analysis* **4**, 255–66.

Phung, D. L. 1984. *Assessment of light water reactor safety since the Three Mile Island accident*. ORAU/IEA-84-3(M). Oak Ridge: Institute for Energy Analysis.

Slovic, P., B. Fischhoff & S. Lichtenstein 1985. Characterizing perceived risk. In *Perilous progress: managing the hazards of technology*, R. W. Kates, C. Hohenemser & J. X. Kasperson (eds.), 91–125. Boulder: Westview Press.

US General Accounting Office 1985. *Probabilistic risk assessment: an emerging aid to nuclear power plant safety regulation*. GAQ/RCED-85-11. Washington: USGPO.

US Nuclear Regulatory Commission 1984. *Probabilistic risk assessment (PRA) reference document*. Washington: The Commission.

US Nuclear Regulatory Commission 1985. *NRC policy on future reactor designs: decisions on severe accident issues in nuclear plant regulation*. NUREG-1070. Washington, DC: Office of Nuclear Reactor Regulation, The Commission.

US Nuclear Regulatory Commission 1987. *Reactor risk reference document: main report, draft for comment*. NUREG-1150, vol. 1. Washington DC: Office of Nuclear Regulatory Research: The Commission.

US Risk Assessment Review Group 1978. *Report to the US Nuclear Regulatory Commission*. NUREG/CR-0400. Washington: The Commission.

# Index

Numbers set in Roman type are page numbers.

Numbers set in italic type are figure numbers.